Ingeborg Bachmann's Telling Stories
Fairy-Tale Beginnings and Holocaust Endings

Studies in Austrian Literature, Culture and Thought

Ingeborg Bachmann's Telling Stories: Fairy-Tale Beginnings and Holocaust Endings

By

Kirsten A. Krick-Aigner

ARIADNE PRESS
Riverside, California

Library of Congress Cataloging-in-Publication Data

Krick-Aigner, Kirsten A.
    Ingeborg Bachmann's telling stories : fairy-tale beginnings and
    holocaust endings / Kirsten A. Krick-Aigner.
        p.   cm. -- (Studies in Austrian literature, culture, and
    thought.)
    Includes bibliographical references and index.
    ISBN 1-57241-096-5
    1. Bachmann, Ingeborg, 1926-1973--Technique. 2. Fairy tales--
History and criticism. 3. Holocaust, Jewish (1939-1945), in
literature. I. Title. II. Series.
PT2603.A147Z764 2002
833'.914--dc21

                                        00-055839

Cover design:
Art Director & Designer: George McGinnis

Copyright ©2002
by Ariadne Press
270 Goins Court
Riverside, CA 92507

For my grandmothers
Elisabetha Rindfuss and
Kathleen Woodbury Krick

Part of me would like to fill in the gaps of your story, to give you a well-rounded biography, as if everything would be rectified then. But I believe that would almost be as if I wanted to carefully darn the holes in a piece of lace, or weave a spiderweb into a piece of cloth. It is precisely there, in the absence, that I seem to feel your presence.

Renate Welsh, *Das Lufthaus* (334)

They did not understand why Trudi Montag wanted to dig in the dirt, as they called it, didn't understand that for her it had nothing to do with dirt but with the need to bring out the truth and never forget it. Not that she liked to remember any of it, but she understood that whatever she knew about what had happened would be with her from now on, and that no one could escape the responsibility of having lived in this time.

Ursula Hegi, *Stones from the River* (450)

Soon she could surely include fragments, fragments of occurrences and observations in the next essay. Somehow I can get rid of it in this way – everything is easier to deal with if I look at it from the beginning as if it were only material for a report, Ilse realized. Material which wants nothing from me but to be passed on.

Graziella Hlawaty, *Die Stadt der Lieder* (33)

Contents

Writing a Life
Todesarten: Conception and Context
Todesarten: Reception and Historical Context
Fairy-tale Scholarship
Bachmann's References to the Fairy Tale
Bachmann's Prose as Historical Narrative
Summary of Chapters

Malina and the Kagran Tale
Malina as Montage: Folklore and Romantic Imagery in the
Kagran Tale
Malina in the Context of the Postwar Austrian Novel
Writing to Survive: Bachmann's Experiences as a Writer
in Postwar Austria

The German-Language Tradition of the Bluebeard Tale
Defying Bluebeard: Contextualizing Bachmann's References to Bluebeard

Bluebeard Jordan
Bachmann's Personal History and the Third Reich
Bachmann's Relationship to German-Speaking Jewish
Writers and Intellectuals
Writing History: Bachmann's Relationship to the German
Language
Bachmann's Association of Women with Jews

Abbreviated Titles of Sources

References to Ingeborg Bachmann's works are cited paren-
thetically in the text and are cited from the 1993 edition of *Werke*,
eds. Christine Koschel, Inge von Weidenbaum, and Clemens
Münster. 5th ed. 4 vols.

Vol. 1: *Gedichte, Hörspiele, Libretti, Übersetzungen*

Vol. 2: *Erzählungen*

ALL	"Alles"
BLA	"Die blaue Stunde"
DREI	"Das dreißigste Jahr"
GOM	"Ein Schritt nach Gomorrha"
JUG	"Jugend in einer österreichischen Stadt"
KAR	"Die Karawane und die Auferstehung"
MEN	"Menschenlos"
UNT	"Unter Mördern und Irren"

Vol. 3: *Todesarten: Malina und unvollendete Romane*

FF	*Der Fall Franza*
MAL	*Malina*
FG	*Requiem für Fanny Goldmann*

Vol. 4: *Essays, Reden, Vermischte Schriften, Anhang*

FRA	"Fragen und Scheinfragen"
ICH	"Das schreibende Ich"
LIT	"Literatur als Utopie"
OPF	"[Auf das Opfer darf sich keiner beru-fen]" Entwurf
RED	"[Rede zur Verleihung des Anton-Wild-gans-Preises]"
SYL	"Das Tremendum-Sylvia Plath: >Die Glasglocke<"
WAH	"Die Wahrheit ist dem Menschen zumut-bar"

ROM   "Was ich in Rom sah und hörte"

Frequently cited secondary literature

BF   Ingeborg Bachmann. *Das Buch Franza: Das "Todesarten" Projekt in Einzelausgaben.* Eds. Monika Albrecht und Dirk Göttsche. 1995. Munich: Piper Verlag, 1998.

NL   *Nachlaß.* Manuscript and typescript pages of Bachmann's works at the *Handschriftensammlung* at the National Library in Vienna, Austria.

WIR   Ingeborg Bachmann. *Wir müssen wahre Sätze finden: Gespräche und Interviews.* Eds. Christine Koschel und Inge von Weidenbaum. 1983. Munich: Piper, 1991.

HIB   Hans Höller. *Ingeborg Bachmann.* Reinbek bei Hamburg: Rowohlt Taschenbuch Verlag, 1999.

LUG   Hans Höller. *Ingeborg Bachmann. Letzte unveröffentlichte Gedichte, Entwürfe und Fassungen.* Frankfurt a. M.: Suhrkamp, 1998.

WIB   Sigrid Weigel. *Ingeborg Bachmann: Hinterlassenschaften unter Wahrung des Briefgeheimnisses.* Vienna: Paul Zsolnay Verlag, 1999.

All translations of German passages into English are by the author, Kirsten A. Krick-Aigner.

Acknowledgments

I would like to express my gratitude to the Fulbright Association, the *Austrian Bundesministerium für Forschung und Wissenschaft*, DAAD, and the University of California at Santa Barbara General Affiliates for their support of this project on Ingeborg Bachmann. Two generous summer grants from Wofford College in 1998 and 1999 enabled me to focus on the editing and revising of this book. I would also like to thank Hans-Jörg Uther of the *Arbeitsstelle der Akademie der Wissenschaften zu Göttingen* for sharing his knowledge about the Bluebeard tale, the librarians at the *Staatsbibliothek zu Berlin, Preußischer Kulturbesitz* for assisting me with the Grimms' tales and legends, the staff of the *Grimm Museum Kassel* for their support with my research, Robert Pichl at the University of Vienna for sharing his catalog of Ingeborg Bachmann's private library with me, and the staff of the *Handschriftensammlung* at the Austrian National Library for enabling me to study Bachmann's unpublished work. Further thanks go to the helpful staff of the *Literaturhaus* in Vienna for providing me with material on Bachmann and other Austrian writers. Heinz Bachmann and Isolde Moser generously permitted me to quote Bachmann's unpublished work in my book. Portions of this book have appeared in the article "Ingeborg Bachmann's *Death Styles*: A Narrative Historiography of Fascism and the Holocaust" in *Thunder Rumbling at My Heels*, edited by Gudrun Brokoph-Mauch, "Representations of Gender in the Works of Ingeborg Bachmann and Sylvia Plath" in *After Postmodernism: Austrian Literature and Film in Transition*, edited by Willy Riemer, and "Staging a Legend: Claus Peymann's *Ingeborg Bachmann. Who?*" in *Postwar Austrian Theater: Text and Performance*, edited by Margarete Lamb-Faffelberger and Linda DeMeritt. My enduring gratitude goes to Hans Höller at the University of Salzburg who has generously given me his continued, enthusiastic support throughout this project. I am especially grateful to Torborg Lundell, Günther Gottschalk, and Gerhart Hoffmeister at the University of California at Santa Barbara for their most generous support of my dissertation from which this book emerged. Special thanks go to Natalie Grinnell of Wofford College for her friendship and insightful editing skills. Thanks also to Kim Henry for her computer powers and cups of tea. My admiration and heartfelt gratitude go to Jeanne Cooper, who generously took from her precious free time to edit the final draft of this book. I would also like to express my appreciation for the editing skills and guidance of the editors of Ariadne Press. Finally, I would like to recognize the unwavering support and patience of my husband, Martin Aigner, as well as my family and friends, who made the completion of this book possible.

Introduction

> *In our day there once lived a little
> girl who went in search of the fairy
> tale. Because she had heard every-
> where that the fairy tale had gotten
> lost. Yes, some even said that the
> fairy tale was long dead. It was
> probably buried somewhere, maybe
> even in a mass grave.*
>
> Ödön von Horváth, "Das Märchen
> in unserer Zeit"[1]

Ingeborg Bachmann (1926-1973), an Austrian author whose
name and work have become highly recognized in German-
speaking countries, is still relatively unknown in the United States,
even though her *oeuvre* deals with important contemporary and
universal concerns such as war, xenophobia, and gender relations.
At the close of the twentieth century, it has become especially
crucial to seek out the historical significance of Bachmann's work
and its relevance for postwar western European culture. Faced with
the resurgence of Neo-Nazi movements in western democracies
and with "ethnic cleansing" in the former Yugoslavia, scholars and
readers would be irresponsible to dismiss xenophobia, fascism, and
genocide as irrelevant in the present. Bachmann's work is
dedicated to uncovering the history and structure of xenophobic
thought and fascism within western European society throughout
history. By addressing topics such as male-female relationships,
social oppression, mental illness, and genocide, Bachmann's
fiction stands as a personal history, as well as a social history of
World War II, the Holocaust, and their consequences for postwar
Austria.

This book concentrates primarily on Bachmann's prose; the
original published version of *Malina* (1971) and the published

fragments of *Der Fall Franza* (Franza's Case/The Case of Franza, 1978) from the *Todesarten* (Death Styles/Ways of Dying) novel-cycle, and the collection of short stories *Das dreißigste Jahr* (The Thirtieth Year, 1961), in which the author employs fairy-tale elements to explore gender issues and historical events of the Holocaust as a means of coming to terms with her experiences during the Third Reich. Within the context of Bachmann's prose, I focus mainly on her literary fairy tale "The Secrets of the Princess of Kagran" in *Malina* and on references to the Bluebeard tale both in the novel fragment *Der Fall Franza* and in the short story "Ein Schritt nach Gomorrha" (A Step towards Gomorrah). Bachmann's use of fairy-tale elements in her prose reflects her conscious continuance of the German literary tradition, informed by both the literature of nineteenth-century German Romanticism, in which the fairy tale represents the pinnacle of "Poesie" (Poetry) and artistic expression, as well as the political interests of "Gruppe 47" (Group 47), who utilized fairy tales in their works as a means of criticizing post-World-War-II society.

Fairy tales assume a dual function in Bachmann's prose. First, she uses the narrative devices and structures of the fairy tale – the happy-ending, for example – both to emulate and criticize its traditional utopian function within culture, as exemplified in the Kagran tale. Second, she extricates motifs – the princess and the Bluebeard figure, for instance – from western European fairy tales and integrates them into the new context of the *Todesarten* novel cycle in order to expose social and historical issues within twentieth-century culture. The intertextual components of *Todesarten*, specifically the Kagran tale in *Malina*, provide a complex framework within which Bachmann comes to terms with the Third Reich. By alluding to the fairy-tale tradition of German Romanticism, Bachmann also explores the role of the poet in establishing a personal history. She makes reference to the Bluebeard tale in her unfinished novel *Der Fall Franza* and in the short story "Ein Schritt nach Gomorrha" to examine the social questions of gender and power relations. By drawing upon Bachmann's Kagran tale and on references to Bluebeard in *Der*

Fall Franza and "Ein Schritt nach Gomorrha," I will also explore aspects of the Holocaust, such as the treatment of women intellectuals and the mentally ill, historical events which are crucial to understanding Bachmann's work and have been underrepresented in earlier Bachmann scholarship.

Writing a Life

> *It is useless; I am unable; she will not show herself; stays hidden behind insufficient words. But I am a witness: she was there.*
>
> Hilde Spiel on Ingeborg Bachmann[2]

Bachmann's personal experiences and education during World War II and the postwar era play a critical role in her literary career. Born in Klagenfurt, Austria, in 1926, her childhood was marked by the occupation of her home town by Hitler's troops in 1938, an experience which inspired her lifelong struggle against Austro-Fascism and National Socialism. Bachmann began writing poems, stories, and dramas while attending the Ursulinen High School from 1938 to 1944, occupied thereafter by Nazis troops to house injured soldiers. She published one of her first prose works, "Die Fähre" (The Ferry), on July 31, 1946 in the weekly newspaper *Kärntner Illustrierte.*[3] After breaking off her teacher training at the Klagenfurt Teacher Training Institute (Klagenfurter Lehrerbildungsanstalt) at the end of the war, Bachmann went on to study philosophy at the University of Innsbruck during the fall semester of 1945 and continued her studies in philosophy and law at the University of Graz during the spring semester of 1946. In June 1946, an English officer stationed in Austria questioned Bachmann about her involvement in the National Socialist Girls' Club *Bund Deutscher Mädel* (BDM). She denied being a member, but wondered in a diary entry why she had blushed and trembled while telling him the truth (HIB 8-9). Bachmann enjoyed a brief yet special friendship with this officer, who, as the son of Austrian

Jews, had managed to escape on one of the last child transport ships to England. The author's neighbors, many of whom had supported the National Socialists not long before, reacted unfavorably towards the blossoming relationship between Bachmann and the Jewish officer (HIB 9). In her diary Bachmann reveals that the officer was thrilled by her familiarity with novels by Thomas Mann, Stefan Zweig, Arthur Schnitzler, and Hugo von Hofmannsthal, authors whose works had been banned by the Nazis.

The following semester Bachmann transferred to the University of Vienna, adding German literature and psychology as minors to her philosophy major. She quickly became integrated in the Viennese literary circle led by Hans Weigel and was supported by Rudolf Felmayr of RAVAG (Radio-Verkehrs-Aktiengesell-schaft), the predecessor of the Austrian National Radio station ORF, and Hermann Hakel, who was responsible for promoting young writers in the Austrian writers' P.E.N. club.[4] In 1950 Bachmann was awarded her doctoral degree for her dissertation entitled *Die kritische Aufnahme der Existentialphilosophie Martin Heideggers* (The Critical Reception of the Existential Philosophy of Martin Heidegger). During her studies, Bachmann completed an internship at the well-known mental institution *Am Steinhof* in Vienna in September of 1947, gaining firsthand experience in psychiatry and the treatment of the mentally ill, a subject she would explore in depth in her novel cycle *Todesarten*, specifically in the novel *Der Fall Franza*. From 1951 to 1953 Bachmann was employed as a scriptwriter and editor for the state-operated radio station "Rot-Weiß-Rot," the name signifying the colors red-white-red found in the Austrian national flag. It is here, in the course of working on radio editorials, that Bachmann wrote and produced her first radio play, *Ein Geschäft mit Träumen* (A Shop of Dreams), in 1952.

A child of World War II, Bachmann's literary work was first introduced to the German-speaking public in 1952 when she read from her poetry at the tenth meeting of the "Gruppe 47" (Group 47) in Niendorf, Germany. This group, founded by Hans Werner

Richter, comprised German-speaking postwar writers who wished to liberate both author and reader, as well as past and future, from the history of National Socialism by making a complete break with the Nazi past. After the publication in 1953 of her first volume of poetry, *Die gestundete Zeit* (Mortgaged Time), for which she won the *Group 47* literary prize, Bachmann became a celebrated freelance author, living and writing primarily in Vienna, Berlin, Zurich and Rome.

Bachmann's second volume of poetry, *Anrufung des großen Bären* (Invocation of the Great Bear), published in 1956, won the literary prize of the Rudolf-Alexander Schröder Foundation in 1957, for which she was awarded membership in the well-regarded German Academy for Language and Literature in Darmstadt, Germany. After writing three radio plays, Bachmann won the prestigious "Hörspielpreis der Kriegsblinden" (Radio-Play Award of Those Blinded in the War) in 1959 for the radio-play *Der gute Gott von Manhattan* (The Good God of Manhattan). Her popularity as a German-speaking author led to an invitation as the first guest lecturer on Poetics in the series of Frankfurt Lectures at the University of Frankfurt am Main from 1959 to 1960. After collaborating with the *Group 47* member Hans Werner Henze on the ballet *Der Idiot* (1960, The Idiot) and on the libretto for his opera *Der Prinz von Homburg* (1960, The Prince of Homburg), Bachmann went on to win a literary prize from the "Associates of German Critics" in 1961 for her first published volume of short stories, *Das dreißigste Jahr*. After Bachmann's four-year relationship with the Swiss author Max Frisch ended unhappily in 1962, her mental and physical health declined steadily. She lived in Berlin from 1963 to 1965, the first year of which was funded by a grant from the Ford Foundation. Her libretto for another Henze opera, *Der junge Lord* (The Young Lord), premiered in 1965 at the German Opera of Berlin.

It is during this emotionally turbulent time that Bachmann began to write a series of novels that would later be known as the novel cycle *Todesarten*. Of these, only one novel, *Malina* (1971), would be published during her lifetime. In an interview, Bachmann discussed her plans for *Todesarten*: "There will be several volumes, and first only two that will probably be published at the same time. It is called 'Todesarten' and is for me one big study of all possible ways of dying, a compendium, a manual, as one would say here, and at the same time I imagine that it could become a picture of the last twenty years, always with Vienna and Austria as its scene" (WIR 65-66). Bachmann hoped that her novels would portray Austrian society as she perceived it: "Austria – that is something that always continues for me, it is not only a strong memory. ... One cannot yet see what will become of this theme: it is a reflection. I hope that it will someday become a picture of Viennese society, a picture of the Austrian situation" (WIR 121). Two years following the publication of her novel *Malina*, Bachmann stated that although she was unsure of the content of her future novels, she was certain that *Todesarten* would be a representation of Austrian society: "On the whole it will be a story of the society from the Carinthian farmers, from the provinces to the intellectuals. The volumes will not be coherent; instead each book will stand on its own and have its very own theme. The surroundings are very different yet intersect so that the characters all come into contact with one another–everyone bumps into everyone else" (WIR 127). From 1965 to 1973 Bachmann lived in Rome where she continued to work on *Todesarten*, as well as on her second collection of short stories *Simultan* (1972, Simultaneous), for which she won the Anton Wildgans Award. After Bachmann's father died in 1973, she gave readings in Poland, where she visited the concentration and death camps of Auschwitz and Birkenau. Bachmann was never able to carry out her numerous plans for *Todesarten*, for she died on October 17, 1973, from the complications of accidental burns sustained in her apartment in Rome.[5]

Todesarten: Conception and Context

Because my book focuses primarily on the novels *Malina* and

Der Fall Franza, the following discussion provides an initial context within which to view the complex conception and reconstruction of the *Todesarten* cycle, as well as a brief summary of the novels. *Malina* and the novel fragments *Der Fall Franza* and *Requiem für Fanny Goldmann* were published posthumously as the trilogy *Todesarten* in 1978. Although *Malina* was published first, Bachmann had originally intended *Der Fall Franza* to be the introductory novel of the *Todesarten* cycle.[6] *Requiem für Fanny Goldmann* was initially written as a short story, but Bachmann later conceptualized the work as the second novel in the cycle. The order of the novels in the 1978 edition of *Todesarten* was configured by the editors according to the order of their completion. In 1995 the novel fragments were re-edited by Monika Albrecht and Dirk Göttsche and published in five volumes as *Das Buch Franza: Das "Todesarten" Projekt in Einzelausgaben.* Through careful detective work, the editors were able to reconstruct novel fragments – some dating back to the 1950s – under the headings "Eugen-Roman" (Eugen-Novel), "Goldmann/ Rottwitz Roman" (Goldmann/Rottwitz Novel), "Wüstenbuch" (Desert Book), "Das Buch Franza" (The Book of Franza), as well as a collection of novellas entitled "Wienerinnen" (Viennese Women). The 1995 edition of *Todesarten* makes evident that *Der Fall Franza* and *Requiem für Fanny Goldmann* are interpretations of the many possible versions that could be assembled from the numerous fragments the author was working on from the 1950s until her death. Aside from the aforementioned novel fragments, additional published and unpublished fragments concerning fairy tales from the posthumous collection of Bachmann's work in the *Handschriftensammlung* at the Austrian National Library reveal information pertinent to my discussion of fairy-tale elements and emphasize the historical significance of Bachmann's prose.[7]

Despite the difficulties of summarizing *Todesarten* as a body of work, the novels and novel fragments reveal common themes that emphasize their intertextuality and relationship to one another. Bachmann's narratives explore the everyday life experiences of women, more specifically of intellectual and educated middle-class

Austrian women in postwar Vienna, and relay the author's critique of gender, race, and class relations in the twentieth century as expressed through her descriptions of father-daughter and male-female relationships. The female protagonists of *Todesarten*, who waver between sanity and insanity, first- and third-person narrators, writer and the "read," become a site of destruction, oppression and subjugation. For instance, whereas the first-person narrator of *Malina* is a writer, Franza becomes a written psychiatric case history for her husband Jordan, and Fanny reads about herself in her ex-lover's novel.

Malina is set in Vienna in a continuous present – although clearly during the postwar years – and tells the story of a nameless female first-person narrator, her male *Doppelgänger* Malina, and her romantic relationship with Ivan. The novel's central dream chapter "Der dritte Mann" (The Third Man), describing the female narrator's nightmares, becomes a figurative prehistory of her destruction by a powerful father figure who represents the murderer "whom we all have" (WIR 89). While for Bachmann any one person can be this murderer, he or she will always appear "with the face of the father" (WIR 89). The ever-present father figure and the description of the father-daughter relationship in *Malina* establish a pattern for the various male-female relations of Bachmann's adult female characters in *Todesarten*. The father figure is, however, a complex, ambivalent character because he stands for both salvation and destruction throughout *Todesarten*.

Bachmann's female characters inhabit a society in which criminality and war permeate everyday life. Society is a battlefield in *Malina*, in which the female narrator addresses the presence of war and the certainty of being murdered under such conditions: "I had long since come to understand – that one does not just die here – one is murdered here. ... War always exists. There is always violence here. It is eternal war" (MAL 236). Later in the novel the female narrator concludes that society itself is the greatest murder scene of all (MAL 276), a society in which peace is a dangerous illusion, as Bachmann warns in an interview: "It is such a great mistake to believe that one is only murdered in a war or in a concentration camp – one is murdered in the midst of peacetime" (WIR 89). Bachmann's work makes evident that although the postwar era in Austria was marked by political peace, she nonetheless perceived society to be criminal and violent. Primo Levi, an author whose work Bachmann was surely familiar with, also writes that "war always exists" in his 1963 Italian novel *La tregua* (The Truce), an autobiographical novel describing his survival in Auschwitz and his difficult journey home to Italy. Levi demonstrates that war exists in everyday experiences, even after war has officially ended, as the following conversation between the narrator and his friend Mordo illustrates: "'But the war is over,' I argued – and like many in these months of breathing freely I really believed that it was over in a complete sense, more than one hopes to believe today. 'War always exists,' was Mordo Nahum's pensive answer."[8]

The powerful introduction of the novel fragment *Der Fall Franza* reiterates Bachmann's concerns about criminality during times of peace expressed in *Malina*. *Der Fall Franza*, originally entitled *Das Buch Franza,* recounts Franza's relationship to her brother Martin and her destructive marriage to the prominent psychiatrist Dr. Leopold Jordan. The novel is set in culturally and geographically diverse settings, such as postwar Vienna, the town of Galicia in Carinthia, and the Arabian, Libyan, and Sudanese deserts. In an earlier fragment of her introduction Bachmann writes that the real setting of a novel occurs in the mind: "The real scenes, those inside that are brought outside and are stronger, occur in thoughts; first of all in what leads to crime, second in that what causes dying" (BF 199). The published introduction states that the crimes of the postwar era are more subtle and therefore more destructive than the visible and "obvious" war crimes committed during World War II: "this book is not only a voyage through an illness. Ways of dying include crimes. It is a book about a crime. … Yes, I believe and will only attempt to produce a first piece of evidence: that even today many people don't die but are murdered instead. … Those crimes that demand spirit, that touch our soul and less our mind, those that touch us the most deeply – no blood flows there and the slaughter occurs within what is permitted and customary, within a society whose weak nerves tremble before its bestialities" (FF 341-42). Bachmann's introduction explains why the individual characters of her novel constantly find themselves at war within society during what appears to be a period of political peace. In an earlier version of the introduction, Bachmann claimed that literature is incapable of expressing even a small portion of the crimes that society commits on a daily basis (BF 197). She further maintained that although her novel explored the present time, she was not ignoring the past: "You should not believe that I am withdrawing from the past. I just want to know what is happening now, and this book comes afterwards. The now is hard to find, because everything is wrapped in cotton, ... " (BF 155). The most fragmented and disjointed published novel of the *Todesarten* cycle, *Requiem für Fanny Goldmann*, explores other "ways of dying" by revealing Fanny's life in terms of her relationships to men, first to her ex-husband Harry Goldmann, then to various lovers who use and then destroy her.

The novels in *Todesarten* portray women's experiences and explore the difficulty of writing a specifically female history and autobiography, as illustrated by Bachmann's use of multiple and often overlapping narrative voices. *Der Fall Franza* shifts from a third-person narrator, describing Franza's situation from her brother Martin's perspective, to Franza's fragmented first-person account of her childhood and marriage. The third-person narrator of the *Requiem für Fanny Goldmann* tells the story of Fanny, who is devastated by the fact that her lover Toni, once a struggling writer, becomes famous for publishing all the stories that Fanny has told him about her own life. Fanny's voice is thus doubly silenced in Bachmann's novel: neither Fanny's voice nor Toni's novel are revealed to the reader.

The identities of the women in *Todesarten*, as well as their histories, remain fragmented. In *Malina*, for example, the narrator is split between the male voice Malina and the female voice of an unnamed narrator who, according to a multivalent image at the conclusion of the novel, is confined to a crack in the wall. Therefore, it seems as if the male Malina is left to tell and complete the female narrator's story. However, since what occurs in the story has already been told *before* the female voice disappears at the conclusion of the novel, the first-person narrator becomes fluid and dispersed between the female first-person narrator and Malina. It is specifically this narrative fluidity that Bachmann defines as a narrator "without guarantee" (ICH 218). In *Malina,* the female narrator views herself as an inextricable part of her male double Malina, which is emphasized by the portrayal of her "fluidity" as complementary to his "solidity" (MAL 22). Whereas Malina seems to marginalize the female narrator as "other," she describes her "dark story/dark history" (dunkle Geschichte) as integral to Malina's story: "Because I am a too unimportant and too unfamiliar self to him, as if he had expelled me, trash, a superfluous human creation, as if I had been created from his rib and were since that time expendable, but also an unavoidable dark story, that accompanies his story, that wants to fulfill it, that he nonetheless separates and cuts off from his clear story" (MAL 22-23).

In order to solidify her identity, the female narrator in *Malina* attempts to recall her past and the memories that have affected not only her story, but also the larger history. The female narrator sets the stage for her memory in the introduction to *Malina,* which becomes a key for understanding her personal history. She claims here that, although her memory holds nothing out of the ordinary, she is still far from being undisturbed by it: "But if my memory only meant the typical memories, the past, the out-lived, the left-behind, then I am still far, very far from the silent memory in which nothing may disturb me anymore" (MAL 23). The narrator continues, while asking herself what should bother her about the city in which she was born, "but do I have to remember that?" (MAL 23). The narrator realizes that remembering her past history will be painful: "I do not want to tell my story, everything in my memory bothers me" (MAL 27). Malina, however, appears to make certain that she will recall her past, reminding her: "But it is another memory that disturbs you" (MAL 27). The two narrators, the female narrator and the male Malina, are both engaged in a struggle between remembering and repressing events in order to deal with the past.

Todesarten reflects Bachmann's theory of the fragmented nature of the narrative voice in contemporary literature, the progressive and inevitable destruction of the self (ICH 225), as well as her critique of postwar western European culture in which such personal voices have been previously ignored. Bachmann's montage of narrative passages from the point of view of multiple narrators seeks to uncover the individual histories of her female narrators, who are buried beneath dominating and repressive representations of history. Hans Höller describes Bachmann's prose as the archaeology of the buried and forgotten which uncovers the signs and promises of another history, the history of the "other" and "others."[9]

Todesarten: Reception and Historical Context

The *Todesarten* novel cycle has gained popularity since Bachmann's death in 1973 and has been subject to a wide variety of theoretical readings with an emphasis on psychoanalysis and feminism. *Malina* represents the most well-known portion of the novels, although it is perhaps Bachmann's most complex and controversial work. Whereas her collections of poetry *Die gestundete Zeit* and *Anrufung des großen Bären* were met with great enthusiasm by German-speaking readers and literary critics alike, her subsequent prose publications, such as the short story collections in *Das dreißigste Jahr* and *Simultan*, and the novel *Malina*, were often negatively received and misunderstood.[10] Throughout the 1970s, the majority of readers and scholars focused on Bachmann's poetry and her critique of everyday language (Sprachkritik) rather than on her prose and her essays, which illuminate historical and social issues. Perhaps because of its challenging plot structure, *Malina* received mixed reviews yet managed to be on the 1971 German-language bestseller lists. It was attacked for not being political enough,[11] which caused many literary critics to find it "a story far removed from the world," "detached from any social reference" and to claim that it "did not deal with social problems."[12] Contrary to these reviews, Bachmann's work clearly confronts both social and historical issues most other authors avoided discussing at that time in Austrian history. Bachmann's personal history colors her writings, often causing critics to use this as an excuse to disregard the broader societal implications of her work. Fortunately this changed in the 1990s thanks to more recent studies by scholars like Karen Achberger, Hans Höller, Dagmar Lorenz, Karen Remmler, and Sigrid Weigel.

By the late 1970s, feminism in German-speaking countries had reevaluated women's literary traditions, and *Malina* was read in new ways with emphasis on women's issues. Barbara Kosta's study of women's counterfictions in contemporary German literature and film, *Recasting Autobiography* (1994), views the 1970s as a period when the women's movement in Germany politicized the private sphere by emphasizing child-rearing, power relations within the family, and gender issues in literature by women.[13] Introspection and the question of national and personal identity became focal points of autobiographical writings as a new means for authors to come to terms with German history. With the dawn of what German-speaking writers in the 1970s termed "New Subjectivity" (Neue Subjektivität), the autobiographical writing style was rediscovered, leading many interpreters to view *Malina* as an autobiographical work. Scholars emphasized primarily the development and psychological condition of the female character and drew conclusions about Bachmann's personal life, rather than focusing on the novel's critical political and social implications.[14] Bachmann, however, disagreed with many scholars and readers who viewed her novel as an autobiography and argued in an interview: "And if one were to call even the whole thing an autobiography, then it is certainly not one in the traditional sense of the word because no story is told there, not by this woman, not by this man, nor by her double. If you will, a spiritual process occurs, but also a completely different one" (WIR 71). Bachmann defined "autobiography" less in terms of the outward events of a person's life, than as a process of "identity-construction." The female narrator in *Malina* is portrayed as experiencing such a process, as Bachmann explained about her novel: "I would only call it an autobiography if one views it as the first person's spiritual process, but it does not recount biographies, rumors, and similar embarrassments" (WIR 88).

In response to Bachmann's understanding of "autobiography," Kosta's definition of the term shows an appreciation of the cultural and historical importance of *Malina* for readers in the 1990s. Kosta views the autobiographical writing style as one which counters "the 'objective' capitalization of meaning by dispersing one story into a plurality of stories or voices."[15] According to Kosta, the general tendency in the 1970s was to view women's autobiographical narratives such as Bachmann's *Malina* as "self-indulgent, egocentric, and separatist."[16] Instead, she argues that placing all women's texts exploring female identity into the category of "New Subjectivity," constitutes a "gross misrepresentation."[17] She views women's autobiographical writing as an attempt to write personal histories that differ from traditional male texts: "Women's personal answer to theory was to document their experiences, thereby challenging traditional epistemologies and scripts, either by disbanding them through women's life stories, or subverting them through counterperspectives. By focusing on women's experiences and female identities, women writers hoped to diverge from male paradigms and to write themselves free."[18] For Kosta, Bachmann documents her personal experiences as a woman in *Malina* by dispersing her novel into a plurality of voices in order to create a counterfiction to the traditional, male, 'objective' narrative. At the same time, however, Bachmann also thematizes the *difficulties* of writing about women's perspectives and experiences, thereby documenting the experiences of intellectual women in the years 1950 to 1970. Bachmann's emphasis on the perspective of women has led her work to be read within the context of feminism since it was first published.

Heidi Borhau, for example, traces *Malina's* reception by feminists to Margret Eifler's appeal to readers in 1979 to read the novel as one that exposes the submissive position of women within male-female relationships.[19] In the early 1980s, the German author Christa Gürtler read *Malina* within the context of German feminism by portraying the novel as a reflection of women's personal experiences.[20] Christa Wolf formally initiated the so-called Bachmann renaissance in her fourth Frankfurt Lecture in 1982, by stating that *Malina* reflects Bachmann's own realization that she felt it impossible to give form to her experiences as both a woman and a female writer in her literary work.[21] Hans Höller emphasizes Wolf's reading by arguing that Bachmann's female voice is also present in the male characters of Malina and Martin.[22] The celebrated reception of *Malina* has led the novel to be viewed as a "cult book of feminism" in German-speaking countries,[23] as made evident by Sigrid Weigel's strong emphasis on *Malina* and *Der Fall Franza* in her 1989 study of women's writing, *Die Stimme der Medusa: Schreibweisen in der Gegenwartsliteratur von Frauen* (Medusa's Voice: Writing Techniques in Contemporary Literature of Women).

Fairy-Tale Scholarship

My study focuses less on the impact of Bachmann's work on feminism and women's writing than on the importance and value of her fiction as a historical document by demonstrating how she portrays Austrian history and women's roles within society through references to fairy tales in her prose. Despite the extensive secondary literature concerning Bachmann's work, little research has been done on the employment of fairy tales in her novel, perhaps because her use of fairy-tale motifs has been regarded as less significant than her more socially and politically relevant writings. Whereas the general reading public has long viewed the fairy tale as a genre of children's literature, scholars such as Karen Achberger and Angelika Rauch have sought to examine fairy-tale references in Bachmann's writings in a more scholarly light.

Understanding Ingeborg Bachmann, Karen Achberger's detailed 1995 study of Bachmann's life and work, introduces the Austrian author to an English-speaking audience. In a unique and interdisciplinary approach, Achberger explores the musical structure of Bachmann's work, especially evident in the *Todesarten* cycle which Bachmann "composed like an operatic score."[24] Achberger, who portrays Bachmann as an author who believed music to be a form of expression superior to language, reads *Todesarten* in the context of Richard Wagner's *Tristan and Isolde* (1858/59) and Arnold Schoenberg's *Moses and Aron* (1957). The female narrator of *Malina* communicates with Malina, her father, and her lover, Ivan, in a lyrical and poetic voice which counteracts more traditional modes of speech. Bachmann's fictional writing is portrayed as a "musical lamentation full of hope" expressed foremost in *Malina*'s fairy-tale fantasy, the Kagran tale."[25] One of the few scholars who has explored Bachmann's use of fairy tales, Achberger, in her 1985 essay "Beyond Patriarchy: Ingeborg Bachmann and Fairy-tales," locates the author's fairy-tale references in the so-called prose subtext. There, fairy tales can be read as a "corrective or utopian counterpoint to the narrative, which is set in contemporary Austrian society" and "offer glimpses of a timeless, mystical realm where real limits are suspended while fantastic possibilities are entertained."[26] Achberger reads Bachmann's numerous fairy-tale references as an attempt to salvage women's "otherness" which has resisted male domination and therefore "still provide[s] a glimpse of female authenticity and responsible selfhood."[27]

Similarly, Angelika Rauch's "Sprache, Weiblichkeit und Utopie bei Ingeborg Bachmann" (1985) views Bachmann's references to fairy tales and utopia as an attempt to use femininity as a means of counteracting materialistic perceptions and experiences resulting from a culture defined by patriarchy and "rationality."[28] Rauch suggests that Bachmann's utopian Kagran tale, in which a princess is repeatedly captured by male invaders, thwarts the silence and suppression of women's emotions and thoughts by rendering them in writing.[29] As the title of Rauch's essay implies, utopia, femininity, and the problem of language are closely linked in Bachmann's *oeuvre* as a means of illustrating the failure of existing language to express women's experiences and desires. In her conclusion, Rauch regards "fairytales, myths, dreams and concrete utopias" as feminine metaphors through which Bachmann successfully expresses female identity within artistic creation.[30]

For Achberger, the Kagran tale represents the fantasy of women's oppression as "just one passing moment" in history.[31] In other words, she reads the tale as a confirmation of a "women's golden age," a hypothesized early matriarchy that existed in the past and may possibly exist in the future. [32] Hope that such a "Golden Age" will once again be realized is, however, undermined by the novel's conclusion, in which the female narrator is denied the fulfillment of her utopian dream. Achberger's reading of Bachmann's Kagran tale as a "female counter-myth" is therefore only possible if read independently of its context within *Malina*.[33] As the following chapter shows, Bachmann recognized the destructive socializing factors of the western European fairy tale for men as well as women and attempted within her Kagran tale to show its adherence to the patriarchal power structure rather than to celebrate its potential "Golden Age" for women.

Achberger and Rauch support the common opinion among many readers that the fairy-tale genre is one dominated by women authors and as such a reflection of feminine creativity and production. In western European cultures, however, fairy tales as collected or written by the Grimm brothers, Hans Christian Andersen, and Max Bechstein – to name only a few – dominate the fairy-tale repertoire, while the names of fairy tales by German-speaking women authors, such as Bettina von Arnim and Maria von Ebner-Eschenbach, remain underrepresented. The well-known names of French women writers of fairy tales from the seventeenth and eighteenth centuries, such as Marie-Catherine d'Aulnoy or Jeanne-Marie Leprince de Beaumont, are exceptions to the rule.

Not only fairy tales, but also German fairy-tale scholarship has also been largely male-oriented in the past. Friedmar Apel, Bruno Bettelheim, Volker Klotz, Max Lüthi, Lütz Röhrich, Heinz

Rölleke, Jens Tismar, and Paul Wührl, for example, are most often referred to as scholars of German-language folkloric studies. Scholars who emphasize the history of women in fairy tales or feminist readings, such as Jeannine Blackwell, Ruth Bottigheimer, Maria Tatar, and Jack Zipes, have gained importance only since the 1980s. Donald Haase regards the fairy tale as a central experience of German-speaking culture and portrays the genre of the literary tale (Kunstmärchen) as an integral part of the intellectual life particularly of those German writers in exile who associated their childhood, mother tongue, and native culture with this particular genre.[34] Zipes, who focuses on the socio-historical aspect of German-language fairy tales, not only discusses the relevance of the feminist perspective within tales, but also views them as vital to the understanding of German-speaking cultures and literatures. In this context, one might consider Bachmann, who lived outside of Austria in Rome, Germany, and Switzerland for most of her adult life, as a writer in exile who referred to fairy tales in her prose as a means of criticizing social and political aspects of her Austrian culture.[35] Zipes considers the Grimms' fairy-tale collection a "vital and dynamic national institution" and emphasizes that in Germany the Grimms' collection has been the second most popular literary work after the Bible during the last one hundred and fifty years.[36] By viewing fairy tales as a national literary institution, Zipes shows that their historical function can be more fully appreciated by enabling readers to "grasp literature as it transforms itself historically in unique ways and to view the extra-literary forces which influence the immanent development of literature."[37]

Zipes goes on to name Bachmann one of the many German-language authors who has composed a literary tale, "The Kagran Tale," in order to express "opinions about the form itself and society."[38] He portrays literary tales as important voices of socio-cultural critique, and as examples of how the fairy tale has informed twentieth-century literature. Transformations in the literary institution of the Grimms' tales show that, beginning in the 1920s, writers used the fairy tale to criticize their social and political world, as well as to socialize individuals. Zipes points out that literary tales were also used during and after the Third Reich by schools, literary organizations, psychologists, publishers, and writers "to influence social attitudes."[39] During the Nazi period, the Grimms' tales were used in the socialization process of children and adolescents to highlight the Nordic tradition of Germany and to portray specific gender roles: for example, the diligent, docile housewife and the brave, hardworking husband. Tales written during the Weimar Period were later banned because of their political implications during the Nazi period, as Zipes' *Weimar Tales* illustrates. In turn, literary tales were also later written to counteract the socializing forces of tales popular during the Third Reich. Zipes concludes that although the Grimms' tales have been viewed as "escapist," contemporary authors renovate, revise, and reutilize the fairy tales in an attempt to create a social impact.[40] Within this context, I will show how Bachmann has "renovated" the structure of the traditional German-language fairy tale to unmask its illusory nature for women. By referring to a revised Bluebeard tale in her prose, Bachmann reinvents women's relationship to prohibition and transgression.

Fairy tales also reflect gender role designations, as well as unspoken rules about transgressions, prohibitions, and social norms of sexual behavior. Literary tales such as Peter Rühmkorf's "Blaubarts letzte Reise" (Bluebeard's Last Voyage, 1982) and Angela Carter's "The Bloody Chamber" (1981), criticize the socialization of women by creating "feminist" heroines with whom female readers can identify. The critique of gender roles as related to the socialization process in society has become especially apparent in contemporary women's literature in which fairy-tale elements are incorporated into novels or in which entire tales are rewritten to alter the traditional roles of the female figures. In Carter's "The Bloody Chamber," it is the mother who rescues her daughter from the hands of the villainous character Bluebeard.[41]

Some feminist scholars go so far as to state that fairy tales represent a genre specific to women's literature. In *Die Stimme der Medusa*, Weigel, like Achberger, makes the problematic claim that the fairy-tale genre is a fixed component of "women's literature," in which the mythological often counters the dominating logic through its utopian function.[42] Weigel, furthermore, refers to Heide Göttner-Abendroth's 1980 work *Die Göttin und ihr Heros: Die matriarchalen Religionen in Mythos, Märchen und Dichtung* (The Goddess and Her Hero: The Matriarchal Religions in Myth, Folk Tale and Poetry), which explores transformations of matriarchal mythology in fairy tales. She traces the fairy-tale genre to a matriarchal origin and a continuation of female culture.[43] But if one examines German-language literary texts from the Romantic era to the present, it becomes evident that the rewriting of fairy tales, more specifically the writing of a literary tale and the imbedding of fairy-tale elements in novels, has been a popular writing technique for male and female authors alike. Fairy-tale elements and references play an important role in countless German-language novels written by men and women during the 1960s and 1970s, when Bachmann wrote her prose. The use of the fairy tale in the novel should therefore be understood as a broader cultural phenomenon and not merely as a reflection of femininity.

The tradition of the fairy tale is especially evident in works by the members of the *Group 47*, written from the postwar era through the 1970s. This is further confirmed by Hanne Castein's 1990 essay "Grass and the Appropriation of the Fairy-tale in the Seventies," where he writes "that the fairy tale was one of the most seminal genres of postwar German literature,"[44] and lists novels in which fairy tales are incorporated, including Bachmann's *Malina*. Walter Filz's 1989 *Es war einmal? Elemente des Märchens in der deutschen Literatur der siebziger Jahre* (Once Upon A Time? Fairy-Tale Elements in German Literature of the 1970s)[45] represents a further study of the authorial strategies of referring to fairy-tale elements in German-language literature of the 1970s. Filz reads texts such as Bachmann's *Malina* as a type of "protest literature," reflecting the social and political reality of the 1970s. With the failure of an extensive cultural revolution in which literature was to alter its function within society, novels attempted to uncover social and political processes within the individual instead. Documentaries and political literature, autobiographies, and personal confessions with the intent of focusing on the individual swept the literary market. Filz emphasizes that the retreat into inner life in no way signals a withdrawal from the political and social agenda; instead, the view of the individual led to a new world view.[46] Filz recognizes the Kagran tale in Bachmann's *Malina* as depicting "the ideal and complete love" in which the "the autistic self" is identical with the female narrator in the novel and signaling that love is the female narrator's only existential safeguard.[47] He concludes his reading of the Kagran tale with the observation that the fairy tale is valued as a positive element of "escapism" in the novel, and one that reaches beyond the destruction of the individual.[48] In contrast to Filz's reading, the first chapter of my study demonstrates how the so-called utopian promise of the Kagran tale is undermined throughout *Malina*, and how the traditional utopian outlook of the Kagran tale is destroyed by the historical and social realities experienced by the female narrator.

Bachmann's References to the Fairy Tale

Bachmann refers to fairy-tale elements in her prose in order to explore the social structures and gender roles that are transmitted into culture by the socializing influences of traditional and popular literature of fairy tales and cultural mythologies. Her fairy-tale references in the Kagran tale and throughout her prose address the more traditional fairy-tale traditions of the Grimm brothers. However, she also refers to popular Austrian legends and fairy tales, crucial for a socio-historical understanding of her work. The diverse languages and cultures that Bachmann refers to (German, Hungarian, Czech, Slovak, Italian, Serbo-Croatian, and Romany) have all contributed to Austria's rich, multi-cultural collection of folk and fairy tales. In the novel *Malina*, for example, both Malina and the female narrator come from an Austrian town bordering the former Yugoslavia and speak "Slowenisch" and "Windisch" (MAL

20). Bachmann emphasizes the multi-ethnic heritage of Austria and the former Austro-Hungarian Empire by referring to the cultures' diverse legends and fairy tales, as two biographic fragments from Bachmann's posthumous collection make evident. In the first fragment she calls Austria "a world in which many languages are spoken and many borders run together," and writes that the "encoded metaphors of her homeland" still dominate her thoughts.[49] In a second passage written on the same subject, Bachmann notes that she continues to be influenced by the imaginary world of her multicultural homeland, one she defines as being "rich in mythology."[50]

Although Bachmann viewed herself as an author grounded in a culturally diverse, Austrian literary history, she distanced herself from the German literary tradition. She saw Germany linked ineluctably to its Nazi past, a problematic issue she addresses in *Todesarten*. In a 1965 interview, Bachmann spoke about her ambivalent relationship to the German language: "For a long time I have seen the difficulty in the fact that I write in German, that my relationship to Germany exists only through this language, ..." (WIR 63). It is precisely Bachmann's critical perception of language that is most evident in her collection of short stories *Das dreißigste Jahr*.

Bachmann's poetic *oeuvre* contains fairy-tale elements that signal the traditionally perceived utopian era of childhood, as do her earliest prose works, such as "Die Fähre," (The Ferry, 1945) "Das Lächeln der Sphinx" (The Smile of the Sphinx, 1949), and "Die Karawane und die Auferstehung" (The Caravan and the Resurrection, 1949). In the latter short story the power of telling fairy tales comes to represent a means of consolation, healing, and salvation, in that a grandmother wishes her grandchild had come to beg her for a fairy tale so that she would not have frozen to death in her cold and lonely home (KAR 25). Bachmann's poetry, especially the collection *Anrufung des großen Bären*, nonetheless shows her awareness of the illusory nature of the salvation and happiness in traditional fairy tales. In the poem "Menschenlos" (Without People), for instance, humanity is deceived by an illusory castle in the sky, which obscures its vision of so-called reality (MEN 19). In her earlier work, Bachmann assigns fairy tales to a mythic time untouched by the isolation and violence of modernity, as is for example illustrated in the author's reference to the classic fairy tale of "Sleeping Beauty" in the poem "Die blaue Stunde" (The Blue Hour), in which a young girl remains silent until her spinning wheel begins to spin again and time passes behind a hedge of roses (BLA 107).

For Bachmann, the binary oppositions found within German-speaking cultures are reflected in the oral and written culture of the fairy tale in which good is always pitted against evil.[51] Her prose discusses the boundaries fixed by binary thought structures in western European culture and depicts the bipolar structures of western thought, in which both men and women are portrayed as confined within rigid gender roles and binding social structures.[52] Xenophobic and misogynist thought is grounded in precisely such polar structures within culture, always causing one social group to be designated as "good" and another as "bad," in which the dominant social group is defined by the so-called negative characteristics of the minority. Bachmann's more philosophical short stories in the collection *Das dreißigste Jahr* make her critique of the polarity in fairy tales especially evident. Her narratives show that humankind would be forced to repeat history and would therefore never be able to achieve an improved and more progressive society without evolving beyond these polar structures to more complex and flexible thought structures. The narrator in the short story "Das dreißigste Jahr" wishes such progress for himself and for humankind. He tells himself: "If you could give that up, could get out of your usual fear about the good and the bad and would not keep stirring around in the porridge of old questions; if you had the courage to step into progress ..." (DREI 112). For Bachmann, the polar structure of good and bad is perceived to be the traditional, "natural" order of society that prevents humankind from achieving an alternative mode of being. For example, the narrator of "Das dreißigste Jahr" implores the reader: "If you gave up humankind, the old one, and took on a new one, then/ Then, when the world would no longer go on between man and woman ... If you no longer believed in fairy tales and were no longer afraid of the dark/ Then jump up once again and tear into the old unworthy order. Then be different, so that the world may change, that it may change its direction, finally! Then, you take it on!" (DREI 112-14). For Bachmann, fairy tales represent a cultural mythology that encourages polarities, thus hindering progress. No longer believing in fairy tales, "humankind" might initiate positive changes for the benefit of humanity. In the short story "Alles" (Everything), a father seeks a new kind of fairy tale for his son through which he may experience the world differently. The father envisions a new world with the birth of his son whom he desires to raise outside of and beyond polar structures: "I wanted completely different, pure games, fairy tales other than the familiar ones ... Everything is always divided into up and down, good and bad, light and dark, order and grace, friend and foe; and wherever other beings or animals appear in fables, they immediately take on the image of humans" (ALL 148). Although the father longs for a new language, he is ultimately unable to break away from the polar structures of fairy tales and his cultural heritage, and is therefore unable to offer his son a better life.

Despite Bachmann's critique of the fairy-tale genre in her prose, her relationship to the fairy tale is ambivalent. On the one hand, she is drawn to the traditional harmony and simplicity of its polar structure which promises resolution and victory of good over evil as seen, for instance, in the happy endings of the Grimms' well-known fairy-tale collection *Kinder- und Hausmärchen* (Nursery and Household Tales). On the other hand, Bachmann questions the fictitious harmony of the fairy tale by overturning the traditional gender roles and plots found in traditional western European fairy tales. Her critique of the presumed utopia of fairy tales – as illustrated in *Das dreißigste Jahr* and *Malina*, for instance – must, however, also be read within the larger context of her knowledge of social, political, and cultural history. Bachmann's strong interest in history, and more specifically in the Holocaust, is evident throughout *Todesarten* and many of her short stories, such as "Jugend in einer österreichischen Stadt" (Youth in an Austrian City) and "Unter Mördern und Irren" (Among Murderers and Madmen), which I discuss in the following three chapters. Up to the mid-1980s, when Kurt Waldheim's campaign spurred Austrians to confront their past under National Socialism, very few Austrian writers had come to terms with National Socialism in their works. This helps explain why it has only been in the past two decades that literary scholars and readers have been able to appreciate Bachmann's work in its historical context.

Bachmann's Prose as Historical Narrative

More recently, Bachmann's work has been read in the context of its value as a historical narrative. Marie-Luise Gättens is one scholar who has focused on writers who explore historical events in their fiction. In her essay "Die Rekonstruktion der Geschichte: Der Nationalsozialismus in drei Romanen der siebziger Jahre" (The Reconstruction of History: National Socialism in Three Novels of the 1970s, 1989), Gättens discusses Bachmann's coming to terms with National Socialism in her novel fragment *Der Fall Franza*. Gättens' critique is based on the premise that women's histories are regarded as invalid for the constitution of the "collective memory" of history. Gättens, like Sigrid Weigel, views women's thirty-year silence from 1945 to circa 1975 of women regarding fascism as the result of the fact that everyday life during the Nazi period was always retold from the memories of men, and women were portrayed primarily in the home and in private relationships with each other.[53] However, women authors of the 1970s such as Christa Wolf, Ruth Rehmann, and Bachmann reached back to the era of the Third Reich as a framework within which to discuss their personal histories, thereby reconstructing history from a female perspective and freeing historical discourse from the tradition of what has been defined as "male pre-dominance."[54]

In a discussion of one specific passage of Bachmann's novel

Der Fall Franza, Gättens illustrates Franza's observation that her personal history has been dismissed as irrelevant by traditional historical representation. During a trip to the Temple of Queen Hatshepsut in Egypt, Franza realizes that her husband Jordan and brother Martin have denied her her past. The men in Franza's life have dismissed her own accounts of her past as unimportant, even pathological. During her visit to Egypt, Franza finally comes to retrieve and value her own past, even though her realization of the importance of her early history has come too late to change her adult life. According to Egyptian history, Hatshepsut, born in 1520 B.C., ruled for twenty years before disappearing from Egyptian records. Despite her "joint rule" with Thutmose III, she declared herself "King of Egypt" and awarded herself full pharaonic powers. She was occasionally referred to in masculine terms and was often portrayed wearing the royal skirt, crown, and ceremonial beard of a male pharaoh. After her disappearance and death, Hatshepsut's statues were destroyed, and her name and figure eradicated from temples and structures throughout Egypt and Nubia, in an attempt to erase all memory of her reign. Franza, who is denied the memory of her adolescence during the war by the men in her life, relates her own existence to that of Hatshepsut. As she explains to Martin: "He (Thutmose) had not been able to destroy her (Hatshepsut). This here was neither stone nor history to her, but, as if no day had passed, something that occupied her" (FF 437). *Der Fall Franza* represents another example within the framework of the novel cycle *Todesarten* in which Bachmann voices the personal history of its female figure and explores history through legends and the fairy tale.

As stated earlier, Bachmann is one of the first of a number of German and Austrian women writers who deal with the history of World War II and the Holocaust in their fiction. Maria-Regina Kecht's essay "Resisting Silence: Brigitte Schwaiger and Elisabeth Reichart Attempt to Confront the Past" notes that few Austrian authors – in particular women authors – have discussed the history of the Third Reich in the past.[55] Kecht, however, does go on to mention several women authors, including Ilse Aichinger and

Ingeborg Bachmann, who have addressed the history of World War II and the Holocaust in their fictional writings.[56] Kecht describes the authors Schwaiger and Reichart as "young Austrian writers" who "have reacted primarily against the decades of stifling silence shrouding the events of the Nazi past and rejected the unsatisfactory answers to their questions about Austria's complicity in the Third Reich."[57]

More recently, in the 1980s and 1990s, German-speaking women authors have come to confront their childhood and youth during National Socialism by writing and rewriting the history of the war and its aftermath in Europe in the form of historical fictional narratives, for example Graziella Hlawaty's *Die Stadt der Lieder* (City of Songs, 1995), Elisabeth Reichart's *Februar-schatten* (1984. Trans. *February Shadows*, 1989), Ruth Klüger's *weiter leben Eine Jugend* (Survival, a Youth, 1992), and Elisabeth Trahan's recent novel *Geisterbeschwörung* (1997. Trans. *Walking with Ghosts*, 1998).[58] Like Bachmann, these authors present a more personal history, one that narrates the history of women during the war. Ruth Klüger describes the difficulty of finding a voice for the history of women who have experienced war: "I also tell some, stories I mean, when I am asked, but few ask. Wars belong to men, therefore also the memories about war. And even more so fascism, whether one was against it or for it: purely a man's thing. Besides: women do not have a past. Or should not have one. It is not lady-like, almost obscene."[59] While the writing of history has been traditionally male-oriented, German-speaking women authors are finding a voice to tell their personal histories.

The more one examines Austria's past general failure to acknowledge its role during the Third Reich, the more remarkable it becomes that authors such as Ilse Aichinger and Bachmann confronted the issues of anti-Semitism and the deportation and murder of Jews and other victims so early in the postwar era.[60] Austria's government had cited the Moscow Declaration of 1943, which had defined Austria as "the first victim of Hitler-Germany." This official political viewpoint helped shield Austria from accusations of wrongdoing and kept its citizens from coming to terms with their past (HIB 40). It would take almost half a century before Austria formally took responsibility for its role in the Third Reich and the Holocaust. In 1991 a government statement was issued by Austrian Chancellor Franz Vranitzky recognizing Austria's role in the crimes committed during the Third Reich. Since its acknowledgment, the Austrian government has made a concerted effort to trace the lives and histories of its Jewish-Austrian population, and to record their fate during the Holocaust. In 1938, 185,250 Jews were registered in Austria. The Nürnberg laws against Jews went into effect in Austria on May 20, 1938, and beginning on November 9 of that same year, twenty-four synagogues as well as apartments and stores owned by Jews were set on fire and destroyed by National Socialists. After the Wannsee Conference in 1942, where the Nazis declared the total annihilation of the Jews as their goal, 65,000 to 70,000 Jews were deported to concentration camps from Vienna alone. Approximately 2,000 of those survived the Holocaust, with a reported 822 male and 905 female death camp survivors returning to Vienna in 1945. By 1952, only 970 Jews were documented as living in Austria. In 1998 approximately 7,000 Jews are listed as members of the "Israelitische Kultusgemeinde" (Israelite Worship Community) and a further 5,000 Jews reportedly live in Austria.[61]

It is precisely this larger history of the Third Reich, one reflected in dates and statistics, that is composed of individual lives and experiences. Bachmann portrays the personal experiences of her characters as an integral and vital part of history by showing that an individual's experience is affected by a larger history. Jean-François Lyotard's *Instructions païennes* (1977), for example, portrays history and identity as made up of fragments of experience and narrations thereof: "History consists of wisps of narratives, stories that one tells, that one hears, that one acts out; the people do not exist as a subject but as a mass of millions of insignificant and serious little stories that sometimes let themselves be collected together to constitute big stories and sometimes disperse into digressive elements."[62] Bachmann, for whom fairy tales represent such "stories that one tells," writes the Kagran tale as one of the "wisps of narratives" that make up *Malina* and *Todesarten*. Bachmann's character Franza, for example, questions the position and validity of her own experiences and history in *Der Fall Franza*: "My story/history and everyone's stories/histories, which do make up the larger story/history; where do they come together with the larger story/history?" (FF 433). In this context, Bachmann's use of the German word *Geschichte* refers to the interrelationship of both its definitions of "history" and "story." The character Franza seems to speak for Bachmann when she questions the validity of each individual story, each personal experience, within the context of a larger, more traditional representation of history.

As each narrator in *Todesarten* voices a personal experience, the complex interplay of individual perspectives plays a significant role in Bachmann's novel cycle. The female first-person narrator in *Malina* and the characters Franza and Fanny from the trilogy tell, or attempt to tell, their personal stories. Bachmann, however, does not identify with her female narrators. Instead she describes women's situations and demonstrates what is dishonest and deceitful about her characters. She shows how the women characters are passive and collaborate in their own destruction by the male figures. In this sense, Bachmann not only views the first-person narrator as having a personal history, but also as reflecting a larger history. In Bachmann's Frankfurt Lecture "Das schreibende Ich" (The Narrator as Author, 1960), the author traces the position of the first-person narrator in literary history, concluding that such a narrator is "without guarantee" (ICH 218). The first-person narrator is illusory and elusive by Bachmann's definition because he or she is composed of a "myriad of particles," is a "dreamt-of identity" (ICH 218). For Bachmann, the only unadulterated form of expression for a truly subjective first person narrator is the diary, a genre not addressed in her prose. Instead, the novel and the poem allow for simultaneous narrators – many "I's," many "I-problems" – thereby creating a new concept of the narrative voice(s) (ICH 225). Bachmann's own view of the position of the first person narrator and his or her relation to history is crucial to her lecture in which she states that "the first transformation that the self discovered is that it does not exist *within* history, but that more recently, history exists *within* the self" (ICH 230). For Bachmann the individual is no longer a subject of history; instead, history is imbedded in the individual. Bachmann's writing reflects her belief that each individual is personally responsible for the developments of history, a concept crucial to understanding the historical significance of her work. How then does Bachmann's personal and cultural memory influence her work? Which narrative devices does she use to tell her story, depict her personal history and thus the larger history? In Bachmann's narratives, storytelling becomes an instrument used to create the narrator's life in a voice other than the traditional, "historical" one. History is thereby reflected in the telling of the personal, historical-cultural narrative, and not in the history represented and assumed to be factual in traditional historical works.

Summary of Chapters

My study explores Bachmann's prose as a personal historical-cultural narrative by reading it in light of the discourses of postwar Austrian culture, as well as the historical and political discussions of 1950 through 1970 concerning fascism and the Holocaust. The first chapter demonstrates how Bachmann composed *Malina* and its integral "Kagran tale" within the folkloric tradition of German Romanticism by uniting dream narratives and elements of German and Austrian fairy tales. Although Bachmann wrote within the folkloric tradition of German Romanticism by bringing together fairy-tale and dream narratives in her novel *Malina*, she cannot be considered a Romantic novelist. Instead, by referring to Romantic elements of salvation and ideal love, the female narrator uses the Kagran tale to come to terms with her personal history as a woman and as a writer living in the postwar era in Austria. The Kagran tale, for instance, is linked to two later dream sequences, more specifically to the dream depicting the female narrator's nightmares of the Holocaust. It is during this dream that the female narrator realizes that the historical events of the Holocaust negate any salvation or utopia that she may have hoped for in writing the Kagran tale. Bachmann comes to terms with the Holocaust by exposing the violence of specific events such as the deportation and murder of Jews and the mentally ill in gas chambers. The portrayal of the female narrator in *Malina*, her nightmares and her inability to write a "beautiful book" for her lover Ivan, also make evident the difficulties facing an intellectual, freelance female writer during the postwar in Austria. The female narrator in *Malina* struggles to voice her experiences as an author torn between writing her hopeful book for Ivan, and documenting the violence she experiences in history and everyday life in her work-in-progress, "Todesarten." The female narrator demonstrates that the act of writing functions both as a tool for coming to terms with events of her past and as a means of surviving what she describes as the murderous present. Whereas the female narrator in *Malina* portrays herself at the conclusion of the novel as a writer who fails to find a voice to relate her experiences, Bachmann herself successfully portrays the experiences of individual women in postwar Vienna in her novel cycle *Todesarten*.

The second and third chapters illustrate how and why Bachmann refers to the tale of Bluebeard in *Der Fall Franza* and "Ein Schritt nach Gomorrha," namely to raise questions about history, gender, and language. Her numerous references to the Bluebeard tale in *Todesarten* and her short stories reveal a fascination with this western European tale of domination and subjugation. Bachmann portrays Bluebeard as a figure who embodies those characteristics of power and destruction reflected in her observations of interpersonal relationships and social structures of her time. The literary history of the Bluebeard tale in German-speaking culture in the second chapter provides a context in which to read Bachmann's depictions of this figure in her prose. The clever heroine of the German Bluebeard tradition gains emotional, intellectual, financial, and sexual independence by transgressing Bluebeard's command not to enter the secret chamber, instead of being viewed as negatively curious as implied in more traditional versions of the tale. Bachmann alludes to the Bluebeard tale in her prose in order to emphasize the dangers of passivity and false hopes for women in a male-oriented society.

The third chapter illustrates how Bachmann associates the fascist figure Jordan with Bluebeard by exploring elements of power, domination, and destruction in the western-European Bluebeard tale and applying them to Jordan's "murder" of Franza. In this context I explore Bachmann's references to the Holocaust throughout *Todesarten* and in many of her short stories. By highlighting specific events in her life, this chapter makes evident that certain relationships and experiences prompted her interest in and concern for the history of the Third Reich. Bachmann deals with and exposes events of the Third Reich in her prose as a process of coming to terms with her past by alluding to the Bluebeard figure.

The fourth chapter illustrates how Bachmann casts the figure of Bluebeard in female guise as Charlotte in "Ein Schritt nach Gomorrha" in order to examine issues of gender relations, language, and power. While the protagonists Charlotte and Mara are portrayed as inevitably falling into existing gender roles of powerful dominator and passive victim, Bachmann also describes how it is precisely their passivity that confines them to this position.

Bachmann portrays the so-called insanity of her female intellectuals throughout the *Todesarten* novel-cycle. By depicting gas chambers in her dream sequences in *Malina*, she associates Jews and the mentally ill persecuted during the Third Reich with women intellectuals perceived to be insane. In *Der Fall Franza* Franza is described as "insane" and therefore an "unfit mother" by her Bluebeard-like husband Jordan, who is related to the violent, misogynistic, and sadistic father figure in *Todesarten*. Bachmann not only shows how the Bluebeard figure "murders" the female characters in *Todesarten*, but also how these female characters participate in this victimization through their own passivity.

Bachmann's *Malina* illustrates that female authors have been lonely and alienated, and have even retreated into madness in a postwar, male-oriented society that perceived women intellectuals as a danger to the existing social structure. Bachmann's *Todesarten* successfully depicts such experiences of anomie for women, although the author also treats in *Malina* the complexities and difficulties of finding a language to describe such experiences. Women's histories have often been omitted from traditional representations of history, especially in the 1940s and 1950s, when Bachmann's writing career took hold. By narrating from a female perspective, Bachmann seeks to fill precisely this void with the novel cycle *Todesarten*.

Bachmann's narration of events during the Third Reich reflects a concern for the cultural situation and social structures that led to the atrocities committed during the Holocaust, as well as her trepidation regarding the continuity of such social structures in postwar society. Bachmann's work can therefore be read as historical fiction, a transcription or transformation of the code of historical writing into a more literary code.[63] Perhaps one of the most compelling arguments for the historical relevance of Bachmann's work is Hayden White's call for the representation of human truth: "How else can any past, which by definition comprises events, processes, structures, and so forth, considered to be no longer perceivable, be represented in either consciousness or discourse except in an "imaginary" way? Is it not possible that the question of narrative in any discussion of historical theory is always finally about the function of imagination in the production of a specifically human truth?"[64] By using her imagination and her personal experiences to represent "human truth," Bachmann illustrates how coming to terms with her own experiences and knowledge of the Third Reich makes the writing of *Todesarten* possible.

Like Scheherazade from the ancient Persian fairy-tale collection *The Thousand and One Nights*, who saves herself from being murdered by telling the king one tale every night, Bachmann grasps at utopia through references to fairy tales in an attempt to save herself from what she perceives to be a "murderous" society[65]. An excerpt from a fragmented personal essay from Bachmann's unpublished work points to her affinity to Scheherazade: "One always does this, one does not tell a story because one wants to tell a story. The Thousand and One Nights. You guessed it, one tells a story to get by, to put off the deadline, to keep from being beheaded. Excuse these foreign terms, cannot write this in German ...."[66] For Bachmann, as for Scheherazade, writing and storytelling are a means of surviving the "Mordschauplatz," the murder scene of society.[67]

Chapter One

"...gazing at Utopia...": [68]
The Tradition of the Literary Tale and *Malina*

> *Sometimes I am asked how I came to liter-*
> *ature. I do not know exactly. I only know that*
> *I began to write at an age where one reads*
> *Grimms' fairy tales, that I enjoyed lying on*
> *the embankment, sent my thoughts to faraway*
> *places, to foreign cities and countries and to*
> *the unknown ocean that closes the earth with*
> *the sky. But then the war came and that*
> *dreamy, fantastic world was obscured by the*
> *real world in which we were not supposed to*
> *dream, but make decisions.*

Ingeborg Bachmann[69]

Bachmann's autobiographical statement recalls that she began writing at an early age when she and other children were reading the popular folk and fairy tales of the Grimm brothers. She recollects that the fantastic world of childhood fairy tales was shattered by the events of World War II and had to be replaced by a reality in which decision-making was more important than dreaming. It is unclear from this autobiographical fragment whether Bachmann's decisions were based on issues of survival during the war or on matters of personal responsibility, which many authors of the postwar era discuss in their writings. Throughout Bachmann's work it becomes evident that fairy tales are not referred to simply as memories of the utopian state of childhood. Instead, as in her Kagran tale in *Malina*, she writes within the German tradition of the fairy tale by bringing together elements of popular folk tales to create a literary tale of her own. Bachmann uses fairy-tale elements in her prose to illustrate historical events of the Third Reich, as well as to voice women's personal experiences.

In discussing how the female narrator in *Malina* attempts to come to terms with events of the Third Reich, I will show how the Kagran tale is linked to a later dream sequence in which the Princess of Kagran is merged with the figure of a woman waiting to be deported during the Holocaust. Both fairy-tale and dream narratives in *Malina* enable the female narrator to articulate her dreams, nightmares, wishes, and disappointments. Bachmann turns to fairy-tale and dream narratives to illustrate the possibility of a perspective other than the traditional one represented by the female narrator's male double, Malina. Although the dream narratives in *Malina* are not written in italics as in the Kagran tale, both dream and fairy tale belong to the "other" voice in the novel, the female narrator's vision of dreams where traumatic and repressed experiences are staged. The time and place of both dreams and of the Kagran tale are always "today" and "Vienna" (MAL 12), as the introductory "stage directions" to *Malina* reveal, emphasizing the correlation between all the sequences in the novel. In an interview about *Malina*, Bachmann pointed out that her narrative technique of unity of time and place was unusual for a novel (WIR 102). Even though dreams and fairy tales take place in the fictional time of "today," the narratives represent a past, mythic history of the female narrator that has been carried over into the present (WIR 103). The dreams bring to light the destruction that the female narrator has suffered as Bachmann summarizes in an interview: "The dream chapter is important to me because we don't discover anything about the life story of the first-person narrator or about that what happened to her – That is all in the dreams, some hidden, some also revealed. Every imaginable kind of torture, corruption, distress ..." (WIR 97). The dreams and italicized narratives become opportunities for the female narrator to share her history, which her double Malina will not allow. Bachmann explains this in another interview: "All those stories that are left out because the first-person narrator is not allowed to talk about herself–because her double forbids it – they all appear in the dreams, possibly the explanation for her destruction ..." (WIR 89).

The dream sequence about a Jewish stranger in *Malina* is vital for understanding the historical significance of the novel. It is therefore all the more surprising that so little has been written about this narrative. The Kagran tale has been the focus of many interpretations in Bachmann scholarship not only because of its poetic style, but also because of its curious italicized print and montage structure. Most interpretations of the Kagran tale, however, have treated the tale as a closed narrative, instead of tracing its relation to the two dreams within the novel. Earlier readings of the tale focus primarily on its visions of utopian love and language, thereby positioning the tale as a counterpart to the narratives of violence, betrayal, and destruction that make up the main body of the novel. The majority of readings also say very little about the tale's threatening, gothic landscape in which the princess travels in the swamps and marshes of the Danube region.

Karen Achberger's essay "Beyond Patriarchy: Ingeborg Bachmann and Fairy-tales" (1985), for example, defines the Kagran tale as an expression of the "Golden Age," "a state which clearly has been known in the past and is extant to this day in the fairy-tale image of golden hair, a state which will prevail one day again in the future (when women have golden eyes, shoes and clothes)."[70] For Achberger, the Kagran tale represents a utopian vision in which "patriarchal domination will soon be over," and one in which the description of the female narrator's present everyday life depicts just one passing moment of oppression for women.[71] Achberger reads the ending of the tale as hopeful and utopian, without referring to later intra-textual instances in which this hope is undermined by the imposition of history and society. In her more recent study *Understanding Bachmann* (1995), Achberger maintains that Bachmann's fairy-tale references "serve to suggest 'truths' about the characters, events and relationships in the narrative that cannot be known or that do not make sense within the system of coordinates operating on the primary fictional level."[72] In other words, Bachmann invests her Kagran tale with expressions of hope for ideal love and anxieties about separation and loss, issues her female narrator cannot express outside of the fairy-tale structure. Gudrun Kohn-Waechter views the Kagran tale as a key to Bachmann's *Todesarten* because it reflects the discourse of the victim, or "Opferdiskurs," apparent throughout the trilogy.[73] She contends furthermore that the trilogy's compositional unity of terror and utopia reflects the counter-narratives of the terror in the nightmares of the father figure and the utopia of the Kagran tale.[74] Kohn-Waechter, who does not view the Kagran tale as utopian, bases her reading on her interpretation of the princess' death at the end of the italicized tale.[75] Both Achberger and Kohn-Waechter, however, disregard the tale's relationship to a later dream sequence in *Malina*, which can be read as a sequel to the tale. Kohn-Waechter, for instance, interprets the destiny of the stranger in the tale as " puzzling," even though the second chapter of the *Malina* novel reveals that the stranger later drowns when a truck deporting Jews falls into a river.[76] Instead, Kohn-Waechter views the dream as a counter-narrative to the utopia set up in the Kagran tale, instead of discussing its historical significance.[77] Walter Filz, who draws parallels between the stranger in the Kagran tale and the protagonist Ivan, interprets the stranger and the female narrator's arrest as a reflection of their position outside of "mass society."[78] Although Filz does not specify why Ivan and the female narrator are "outsiders," the stranger, who is Jewish, and the female narrator, who is described as a writer, occupy positions within Austrian society that Bachmann viewed as problematic. Filz furthermore writes that "it is not Ivan who is responsible for the failure of love, but the outside world. The dream time protects the love ideal of the legend from the present."[79] Despite Bachmann's allusions to the Holocaust and her negative descriptions of gender relations, Filz portrays the Kagran tale as a representation of ideal love. Filz claims that this perfect love outweighs both the death and destruction within the framework of *Malina*, even though neither "legend" nor dream represent ideal love for the female narrator.

Bachmann's *Malina* illustrates how the voice of the female narrator is increasingly appropriated by the male narrator Malina throughout the novel and finally banned to the confines of a crack in the wall at the conclusion. This chapter will demonstrate that whereas *Malina* depicts the female narrator as unsuccessful in voicing her personal story, Bachmann herself succeeds in describing her own experiences as a woman in postwar Vienna and as a writer portraying the difficulties of establishing a specifically female voice. In order to illustrate how the Kagran tale can be read as an important and integral part of *Malina*, the following section will introduce the tale as the female narrator presents it to the reader, as well as comment on fairy-tale motifs and elements incorporated in the tale.

Malina and the Kagran Tale

> Heim: *"Is the role of today's women compatible with love?"*
> Bachmann: *"Evidently not; love is a work of art, and I don't believe that many people can master it."*
>
> Interview with Ingeborg Bachmann (WIR 109)

The first chapter in *Malina*, "Glücklich mit Ivan" (Happy with Ivan), into which the Kagran tale is integrated, begins with the female narrator's account of her everyday life as an author, as well as of her relationships with her lover Ivan and her male double Malina. Immediately preceding the narrative passage of the Kagran tale, the female narrator describes her ideal writing situation as a hypothetical circumstance that will never come to pass: "... but I would like to buy an old writing desk, because then I could write something on an old, lasting parchment like those that no longer exist, with a real quill like those that no longer exist, with an ink that one can no longer find ... . I would draw the blossoms of the Martagon lily with a red ink in the majuscule and I could hide myself in the legend of a woman who never existed" (MAL 62). The female narrator's wish to pen a literary tale is followed by the narrative entitled "The Secrets of the Princess of Kagran." The tale is then introduced into the novel as an italicized text passage that tells the story of a princess whose encounters with a mysterious stranger bring her temporary salvation. The legend, in which the female narrator would like to conceal herself, tells the tale of a princess, a horsewoman and leader of wild riders, whose ancient home is along the wild and unpopulated banks of the Danube. After having been captured numerous times by warring foreign horsemen, the princess is forced to be the bride of enemy kings. A mysterious stranger with a melodic voice, whom the princess calls "my savior," suddenly appears and frees her from captivity. When the princess falls in love with the stranger, he tells her that he must leave her, causing her to weep for the first time in her life.

In a later journey along the Danube, the stranger saves the princess a second time when she is caught in a flood. After spending a night together under his dark coat, the mysterious stranger leaves the princess for the second and last time. It is at this moment that the princess becomes a visionary, foreseeing a reunion with the stranger in two thousand years: "Over night the princess had a vision and therefore tearfully said: I know we will meet again ... It will be further up the river, there will be another crusade, it will be in another century, let me guess? It will be in more than twenty centuries, you will say as people do: my love..." (MAL 69). It is precisely the promise and hope of the stranger's return that constitutes the utopian element in this tale. Closing her eyes, on the threshold of a dream at the conclusion of the tale, the princess exclaims, "Let me see!" (MAL 69) and tells of a city that will exist in two thousand years, envisioning a windowsill full of flowers under which she will meet the stranger again. Such clairvoyance can also be found in the popular Austro-Hungarian legend of Libussa, who foresees the founding of Prague. The story is told in Friedrich Ruthmaner's *Österreichische Volkssagen* (Austrian Folk Tales) and Franz Grillparzer's popular Austrian drama *Libussa*, written between 1822 and 1848. In this legend, princess Libussa tells her husband that she envisions the existence of a city "whose fame will one day be great ...."[80] much in the same way that the princess in Bachmann's tale tells the stranger of a futuristic city: "It will be in a city" (MAL 69). Although Libussa refers to Prague, and Bachmann's princess most likely refers to Vienna, both female characters are visionaries of a positive future situated in a city representing urban life and modernity. Despite the princess' hope for salvation, Bachmann's *Malina* illustrates that as long as a woman waits for salvation – waits for a stranger or prince to "save" her – her hopes will be dashed.

Earlier drafts of Bachmann's Kagran tale, currently in the collection of Bachmann's posthumous works at the Austrian National Library in Vienna, reveal a more independent heroine and one who chooses the stranger herself. The character of the Kagran princess develops from an independent and free heroine in Bachmann's earlier versions to a captured princess, dependent on a stranger for salvation in the final draft of *Malina*. One fragment, for instance, reveals that the princess will choose someone who is "her equal."[81] The stranger, instead of leaving the heroine as he does in the published version of *Malina*, reportedly has gone insane. When the princess asks one of her entourage what has become of the beautiful stranger with whom she had shared a cup, the captain tells her that he has gone mad.[82] From the existing two typed sheets of this earlier version of the tale, the fate of the stranger and the princess remain unclear. It is certain only that the princess has a strong bond with her horse, with which she can communicate in her human language. The stranger's insanity in the tale, which is not an issue in the final published version, seems to reflect the mental state of the female narrator in the published *Malina* novel when she dreams of the Jewish stranger's death in the first dream sequence. After awaking from her nightmare, in which her "only love" drowns, she tells Malina: "... I am losing my mind, I am inconsolable, I am going crazy, ... " (MAL 196). In an earlier draft of the Kagran tale, the princess is a young and brave warrior who does not get captured as she does in the published version of *Malina*. On one of her many journeys, the princess from the earlier version meets a dark and handsome stranger whom she does not invite to stay with her, despite his sadness. She tells him:

"We will meet again. I am tired now. I have a long journey ahead of me and you will not forget me."[83] The fragment ends with the death of the princess, and it never again mentions the mysterious stranger. The situation of the princess lost and alone in the swampy Danube region in the Kagran tale reflects the dreary and difficult situation of the female narrator's everyday life in the rest of *Malina*. Bachmann's criticism of traditional fairy tales in which the man takes on the role of the savior in a male-female relationship, as exemplified in the Kagran tale, was insightful and bold in the Austrian era of "pre-feminism." Even though the female protagonists in *Todesarten* are destroyed by their purported saviors, Bachmann shows both how and why they nevertheless do "wait for the prince."

The conclusion of the Kagran tale in *Malina* is followed by the female narrator's summary of the reasons why she did not buy the desk after all. She claims the desk was too expensive and that she was disturbed by the fact that it came from a cloister, and finally she hides the written pages in a folder from her secretary Fräulein Jellinek. Originally she had hoped to buy the desk in order to "be able to write something permanent on parchment" (MAL 62). She explains, however, that because parchment and ink do not exist anymore, the possibility of permanence for her utopian legend is thereby eliminated. Following this explanation, the female narrator never mentions the Kagran tale again. Instead, the utopian tale returns throughout the novel in the form of fragmented excerpts and dreams which interrupt the main body of text. The fragments become increasingly pessimistic throughout the novel and join the non-italicized text at the conclusion. Whereas the Kagran tale seems to provide at least some hope of salvation for the female narrator, the conclusion of the novel makes clear that this is a utopian illusion. Even though it is set apart from the main body of the text, the Kagran tale is integral to the novel. The tale relates to two later dream sequences, as well as to italicized and non-italicized excerpts and references from the Kagran tale throughout *Malina*. From an examination of the various contexts in which the Kagran tale appears throughout the novel, it becomes apparent that the utopia, which the original italicized tale sets up, is undermined by the history of a woman's experience during the Third Reich, as well as by the difficulties of being a woman and author during the postwar era in Austria. By the close of the novel the resurgent memories of historical and social atrocities have destroyed the utopia longed for in the Kagran tale.

The Kagran tale is alluded to in a later dream sequence in the second chapter entitled "Der dritte Mann," in which the reality of history destroys the once utopian aspirations of true love and salvation for the female narrator. The dream illustrates the relationship between the female narrator in *Malina*, the princess in the Kagran tale and the woman in the dream. In this first particular dream, the female narrator finds herself part of a group of Jews waiting to be deported, wearing a "Judenmantel," a Jewish coat (MAL 192) that is described as "Siberian," and is thus suggestive of isolation and imprisonment.[84] The protagonist clearly views herself as independent of her father in this dream, portraying him as a destructive power and stating that he is not part of the group of Jews to which she belongs: "I would like to speak with him again, make it clear to him that he does not belong to us, that he has no right, ... " (MAL 193). The problematic parallel that Bachmann draws between the female narrator as a victim of her father and Jewish victims of the Third Reich will be more closely examined in the second and third chapters of this book. In the dream, the narrator searches for and finally finds the Jewish man whom she met two thousand years ago: "I find him in the many barracks, in the farthest room. He is waiting for me there, tired. A bouquet of Martagon lilies stands next to him in the empty room, where he lies on the floor in his blacker than black sidereal coat, in which I saw him some thousand years ago" (MAL 194). References to Martagon lilies and the stranger's coat in the dream mark the relationship between the dream and the Kagran tale.[85] The stranger from the Kagran tale, like the man in the dream, is Jewish, as he tells the princess: "My people are older than all the people of the world and scattered to the wind" (MAL 69).

The flower motif of the Martagon lily bouquet also refers to the red flower in the Kagran tale with which the princess touches the stranger the second time they meet. Before the stranger leaves her in the Kagran tale, the princess envisions their meeting place under a window filled with flowers: "... and for each century a flower will be kept behind it; more than twenty flowers; then we will know that we are in the right place and all the flowers will be like this flower here" (MAL 70). The flower-filled window also represents the location where the female narrator meets Ivan in the beginning of the novel: "... because a bouquet of Martagon lilies stood at the window, red and seven times redder than red, never before seen, and in front of the window stood Ivan, I don't remember anymore, because then I left immediately with Ivan, ..." (MAL 28). This encounter with Ivan signals the possibility of the fulfillment of a love-utopia for the female narrator, of which she dreams and writes. The female narrator's belief that her meeting with Ivan was predestined makes her oblivious to the unreciprocal and uncommunicative relationship she truly has with him, as she explains:

> I could have looked at the street, distracted by the siren of an ambulance instead of by the bouquet of Martagon lilies in the window, or Ivan should have asked someone for a cigarette light, and then I wouldn't have been seen by him. Because we were in so much danger, because three sentences would already have been too much at this spot in front of the shop window, we quickly left the hot, dangerous spot together and let many things take their natural course ... I don't even know if today one would even be able to say that we speak to one another and are able to communicate like other people do. (MAL 37-38)

The description of the lack of communication between the female narrator and Ivan suggests that they have anything but an ideal relationship. In the dream, the female narrator is certain that the man who might bring her salvation and ideal love a third time, expecting her near the bouquet of flowers, is the one described in the Kagran tale. The female narrator and stranger from the dream lie down together, although his wife and children who are present do not seem to mind. In the Kagran tale, the stranger and princess also lie down together shortly before he leaves her for the second time: "He was blacker than the earlier black around her, and in his arms she sank to him onto the sand; he placed the flowers on her chest as if she were dead and spread his coat over her and himself" (MAL 68). In the dream the Jewish stranger is then deported on a truck that must cross the Danube, although the narrator is not sure whether it is the Danube from her previously written Kagran tale or another river: "The truck has to go through a river; it is the Danube; then again it is another river; I try to stay very calm, because it is here, on the meadows along the Danube, where we met for the first time" (MAL 195). Although she is not sure of the name of the river, she assumes it to be the Danube because she wants to believe in her salvation by the stranger. However, in the dream, as in the Kagran tale, the female narrator loses the man she loves. The correlation between the female narrator's Kagran tale and her dream about the stranger becomes evident when the female narrator receives a message from a man in her dream specifically for the Princess of Kagran: "I ask: To whom, to whom do you have to give a message? He says: Only to the Princess of Kagran. I tell him abruptly: Never speak this name aloud, never" (MAL 195). After the messenger tells her that the Jewish stranger has drowned in the river during deportation, the narrator laments that her life is now over, since she had loved the stranger more than life.

The utopian desire to be reunited with the stranger in the tale is undermined by the dream, in which the repressed historical event of the Holocaust resurfaces and destroys any possibility of salvation and happiness for the female narrator. After awaking from the nightmare, the female narrator is comforted by Malina, who prevents her from remembering Siberia or the river: "then we are no longer in Siberia, no longer in the river, no longer in the meadows, the meadows along the Danube, then we are here again, in the Ungar Alley, ..." (MAL 196). The narrator's "rational" double, Malina, once again wants to "protect" the female narrator from her disturbing personal history.[86] Fragments of the Kagran tale also resurface in *Malina* in a second dream, where the female narrator demonstrates her passivity when faced with the destructive father figure.[87]

At the beginning of the second dream, the narrator attempts to grow flowers, although she is discouraged by the fact that they always come up the "wrong flowers" in the "wrong color." The flower motif signals the possibility of salvation for the female narrator as in the previous dream and the Kagran tale, in which the "right flowers" are the Martagon lilies and the "right color" is red. Yet salvation is once again denied to the female narrator throughout the dream. The narrator's father destroys her utopian fantasy of being a princess who is saved by a stranger, taunting her: "You seem to think you're a princess, eh! You'll soon want to forget it, it will be beaten out of you, and this and that–he points to my plants–that will soon come to an end, what a ridiculous waste of time this is, this green stuff!" (MAL 203). The hope of salvation and ideal love that the female narrator places in her plants is shattered by her father's argument that this hope is a deceptive waste of time. After the father injures his daughter and destroys her flower pots, the narrator and her double Malina tell the police, who have come to stop the destruction, that the father is innocent. The narrator, whose father denies her salvation by throwing flower pots at her potential saviors, is complicit in the father's destruction and violence by covering up his crimes, as she admits: "I have to wipe away the evidence ... I will keep denying it ... everything is destroyed, ruined; I lie down next to my father in the ruins, because this is my place, next to him" (MAL 206). For Bachmann, the father figure in the dream sequences represents the murderer of all people and is specifically associated with the events of National Socialism in Austria. It is precisely the memories of fascism during the Third Reich that resurface repeatedly in the nightmares of the female narrator and destroy any happiness and salvation that she may have hoped for in writing her Kagran tale.

Aside from the two longer sequences related to the Kagran tale, both italicized and non-italicized excerpts from the Kagran tale interrupt the main body of *Malina* by illustrating utopian dreams and desires of the female narrator. Such excerpts from the Kagran tale throughout *Malina* represent just one type of montage that Bachmann applies to her novel. *Malina* is in itself a montage of various forms of stunted communication, as exemplified by the fragmented letters and uncommunicative telephone conversations. The female narrator's letters, for example, are not sent but rather shoved into a desk drawer or discarded. The phone conversations, spliced into the main body of *Malina,* reveal only misunderstandings between two people and reflect frustrated monologues rather than dialogues. Passages conveying a utopian vision from the Kagran tale as well as passages portraying the distressing daily life and dreams of the female narrator become intertwined in the novel. The italicized narratives, however, call attention to their function as being "other," of a different perspective from that of the non-italicized text. Thus the Kagran tale becomes a central, propelling force within the novel, describing the hopes and fears of the female narrator in a tone and poetic language other than the non-italicized narrative frame of the novel.

Italicized passages referring to the Kagran tale appear at those points where the female narrator's everyday reality overwhelms her. During a visit with her friends the Altenwyls, for instance, the female narrator contemplates her "dark" identity while sailing on a lake: " ... I think about Vienna, I look across the water and look into the water, into the dark stories in which I drift. Are Ivan and I a dark story? No, not him, I alone am a dark story. One can only hear the motor; it is beautiful on the lake; I stand up and hold onto the windowsill; on the other shore I already see a shabby string of lights, lost and worn-out, and my hair blows in the wind" (MAL 166). Directly following this paragraph is an italicized passage with fragmented excerpts from the Kagran tale, in which the female narrator is lost in a swampy wilderness with a heavy heart, a scene very similar to that of the female narrator visiting the Altenwyls: "*...and no person besides her was alive, and she had* *lost her way...it seemed as if everything was in motion, waves of reeds, the tides had taken their own course...an unknown restlessness befell her and weighed on her heart"* (MAL 166). The emphasis on both the first and third person to illustrate the different perspectives of the same female narrator highlights that the female narrator in *Malina* and the female protagonist of the Kagran tale are related throughout the novel, which in turn shows the tale to be essential and integral to *Malina*.

At the conclusion of the novel, the first line of the legend, "Once upon a time there was a princess," is repeated. However, because it is neither italicized nor set apart from the text, the once magical story is brought into the everyday life of the female narrator. The phrase "Once upon a time" is repeated throughout the paragraph as if to negate the implication of its fairy-tale promise and instead refer to the legend as a closed event in the past. The other shorter italicized passages throughout the novel beginning with "Some day" or "A day will come" envision a utopian freedom from dominating ideologies or slavery and provide the possibility of poetic expression for the narrator. What seems to be the female narrator's "true" mode of expression, illustrated by the language, style, and subject matter of the Kagran tale, is constantly undermined by the language and style of the main text. One italicized excerpt from the Kagran tale, for example, cites the figurative sentence: "... *the reeds hissed more and more, they laughed, they screamed out and moaned"* followed by the non-italicized and less descriptive and poetic sentence: "Antoinette Altenwyl is standing at the train station in Salzburg and is saying farewell to a couple of people who are driving back to Munich" (MAL 151-152). At the conclusion of the novel, the introductory phrase "A day will come" enters the main text and is followed by the female narrator's realization that her voice will be taken over by that of Malina instead: "A day will come. A day will come and there will only be Malina's dry, cheerful, good voice, but no more kind word from me, spoken passionately" (MAL 326). The concluding sentence of the novel, "It was murder," emphasizes the brutality with which the female voice is undermined by the male voice of Malina, all of which is symbolized by the complex image of the female narrator's disappearance into a crack in the wall: "But the wall opens up, I am inside the wall, and only the crack can be seen by Malina, the one we have seen for so long ... It is a very old, a very strong wall, out of which no one can fall, that no one can break open, from which no sound can emanate anymore" (MAL 336-337). The elusive description by the first person narrator leaves the reader to wonder whether the voice belongs to Malina or to the female narrator.

Bachmann remained ambiguous about the utopian vision she sets up with her Kagran tale in *Malina*: "I really believe in something, and I call that 'a day will come.' And one day it will come. Yes, most likely it will not come since it has always been destroyed for us, it has been destroyed for thousands of years. It will not come and yet I still believe in it. Because if I cannot believe in it anymore, I will no longer be able to write" (WIR 145). Bachmann reflects upon her critical relation to utopian thought in much of her prose. It is no coincidence that the statues, surrounded by the reconstruction efforts of a bombed city, in her short story "Jugend in einer österreichischen Stadt" (Youth in an Austrian City), are facing utopia: "If only the tree in front of the theater would create a miracle, if the torch would burn, I would be able to see everything come together like the waters of the ocean: the early darkness with its flight over ember clouds, the new town square and its foolish monuments, gazing at utopia; ..." (JUG 93). Believing in a better world inspires the female narrator in *Malina,* as well as Bachmann, to write.

The relationship between the princess of Kagran and the female narrator in *Malina* positions the Kagran tale as an integral and essential narrative of the novel. The utopia set up in the Kagran tale written by the female narrator slowly dissolves as the female narrator experiences violent dreams and everyday destruction. Although the hope of establishing a utopia persists throughout the novel, the conclusion illustrates that the fairy-tale ideals of the female narrator are obliterated by the violence and destruction of the everyday world and the horrors of the Third Reich.

Malina as Montage: Folklore and Romantic Imagery in the Kagran Tale

> *There are moments when I can barely keep up with my writing. Much more effort goes into the problem of composition: that no thread is lost, that each sentence that comes up in the first chapter relates again to something else that, for instance, comes up in the third part. Such a story is indeed a web.*
>
> Ingeborg Bachmann (WIR 114)

> *There are no quotes for me; but instead, the few places in literature that have excited me; they are my life. And they are not sentences that I quote because I liked them so much, because they are beautiful or meaningful, but instead because they really excited me. Just like life.*
>
> Ingeborg Bachmann (WIR 69)

In addition to traditional German-language fairy tales by the Grimm brothers, Bachmann refers to many tales and legends found in Austrian folklore. *Malina*'s female narrator stages her Kagran tale in the region of Kagran, surrounding lower Austria and Vienna, by referring to its former historical names "Chagre" and "Chageran," a geographic location referred to in many Austrian fairy tales. Bachmann's personal library includes a copy of Felix Czeike's *Groners Wienlexikon*, an encyclopedia about the city of Vienna, in which she had placed a bookmark under the heading "Kagran," where the names of "Chagre" and "Chageran" are both mentioned. Also in her library is a catalog of the military history museum (Das Heeresgeschichtliche Museum) of Vienna, in which a section about the dragon-slayer Saint George is marked in pencil.[88]

Other historical references throughout the Kagran tale detail the fluctuation of national borders, the migration of nations, and the invasion of the Danube region by Hungarian Hussars and other warriors. Tales of pagan warrior riders can be found in many collections of Austrian folklore, such as the tale "Die nächtlichen Heidenreiter" (The Nightly Pagan Horsemen) transcribed in 1880.[89] The description of the Danube region, an area repeatedly invaded, conquered, and besieged, "always in danger" (MAL 63), reflects Bachmann's coming to terms with the German annexation of Austria in 1938, which was considered an "invasion" by the majority of the Austrian populace at the time she was writing *Todesarten*.

Fog and isolation are also common motifs in Austrian fairy tales and legends as, for instance, in the Kagran tale's descriptions of ghostly islands and swampy regions along the Danube: "As a child the princess had been told about this most serious country along the Danube, about its magical islands" (MAL 67). Gustav Gugitz's Viennese legends and Leander Petzoldt's Styrian legends are compilations and transcriptions of Austrian tales in which descriptions of fog, isolation, and swampy terrain abound.[90] Barbara Kunze found evidence that Bachmann also borrowed many phrases and images describing fog and swampy regions directly from Algernon Blackwood's neo-gothic tale "The Willows" from 1907, translated into German in 1969.[91] Although Bachmann was aware of her frequent references to literary works in her Kagran tale, she considered them a reflection of what she would have written herself (WIR 69). Bachmann also creates her own Viennese legend in the tale by describing the princess' tears as river pearls, that are later said to be mounted into the jeweled crown of Saint Stephen.[92]

Bachmann also refers to the legends and lives of saints who are popular in the traditional Roman Catholic culture of Austria. In the Kagran tale, the figure of Saint George is mentioned in connection with the Danube region as the savior of Klagenfurt and the saint in whose honor a memorial church graces the flooded region. He is the patron saint of both Klagenfurt, Bachmann's birthplace, and of Vienna, where she studied, lived, and wrote from 1946 to 1953.

Saint George is said to have slain the "Lindwurm"–a dragon-like creature found in many Austrian tales and legends, but also in the folklore of other European and Scandinavian countries–in order to save Klagenfurt.[93] The legend of Saint George is said to have come to western Europe by way of Greece and Egypt, and it gained popularity through Jacobus de Voraigne's *Legenda aurea* in the mid-thirteenth century, a copy of which Bachmann owned in her personal library.[94] Earlier in the *Malina* novel, the female narrator associates Malina with Saint George, later weaving this legend into her own fairy tale of the princess of Kagran: " ... when I was in a better mood I let him [Malina] disappear from reality and placed him in some fairy tales and legends, called him Florizel, Thrushbeard; most of all I loved to let him be St. George who slew the dragon so that Klagenfurt could arise from the big swamp in which nothing flourished, so that my first city could be born ..." (MAL 21).[95] In the role of Saint George, Malina is said to rescue Klagenfurt, Bachmann's birthplace. However, Malina's role as the female narrator's potential savior continues throughout *Malina*, both within the Kagran tale in reference to the figure of Saint George and the mysterious stranger, as well as in the dream chapter in which he becomes the narrator's savior and protector from her nightmares. In the female narrator's dreams, Malina is there to calm her: "Malina picks me up and lays me back on the bed. 'Breathe more deeply, come on. It's all right, you see, it's OK, I'm holding you, come to the window, breathe more slowly and more deeply, take a break, don't talk now'" (MAL 179, 185). Malina's role as savior is ambiguous in the novel. Not only does his rationality counteract the female narrator's so-called madness, but he also represses her memories of the atrocities that have befallen her in order to protect her from these nightmares. After telling him one of her nightmares, he retorts: "You should sleep, it is useless to speak with you as long as you hold back the truth" (MAL 209). After relating her many nightmares to Malina, the female narrator tells him that it has become easier for her to talk about them. Nonetheless, he counters: "One shouldn't speak about these things, one just lives with them" (MAL 233). At the conclusion of the dream sequence, he tells her that she may never speak of war and peace again, thereby devaluing the importance of her dreams and memories. The ambiguity of Malina's role as savior directly correlates with the stranger's role in the Kagran tale–and in turn the stranger's relation to the figure of the legendary Saint George–in which the stranger both saves the princess, and yet injures her with his departure.

Aside from fairy tales, Bachmann also alludes to diverse literary works and genres in her Kagran tale. Instead of focusing on what this technique of montage signifies for *Malina*, research has largely focused on identifying literary references found in Bachmann's tale. This results predominantly in what has been called a "Spurensuche," a search for traces, that has either treated the tale as an narrative independent from *Malina*, or, in most cases, as a dream-like, surreal countertext or mirroring of the novel itself. Literary echoes in the Kagran tale are drawn from works such as Novalis' novel *Heinrich von Ofterdingen*, Karoline von Günderode's prose work *Timur*, Georg Trakl's prose work "Offenbarung und Untergang" (Revelation and Ruin), the aforementioned tale "The Willows," and Paul Celan's collections of poetry "Mohn und Gedächtnis" (Poppy and Memory) and "Corona."[96] Kohn-Waechter contends that Bachmann's montage of literary references in the Kagran tale is purposely presented in chronological order. The literary references, which are grounded in legends of saints, myths, and fairy tales blend into various literary fairy tales from the German age of Romanticism and move from Blackwood's "The Willows" to the poetic dialogue between Bachmann and Celan.[97] Kohn-Waechter traces the conclusion of the Kagran tale, in which the princess is wounded by a thorn in her heart, to the legends of the Christian martyrs Saint George and Saint Ursula and grounds these images of martyrdom in the western-European tradition of the victim (Opfertradition).[98] In this tradition, a fatal wound becomes a necessary step towards the resurrection and return of the savior. According to Kohn-Waechter, however, the structure of the traditional Christian legend breaks down in Bachmann's tale since the mysterious stranger *saves* the princess twice before *killing* her with thorns.[99] Referring to this "Opfer-tradition" theory, she claims that both the princess and the stranger can be declared saviors, since both participate in acts of salvation. Furthermore, by examining the structures, themes, and motifs within fairy tales from German Romanticism, she attempts to attribute importance to the death of the princess of Kagran by uncovering similarities in the ways Bachmann and Novalis portray the role of the poet.[100] According to Kohn-Waechter, just as in Novalis' *Heinrich von Ofterdingen*, the poet discovers his calling through a lover's death, the death of Bachmann's princess is an initiation into poetry, "Dichtung" or "Poesie."[101] Within this paradigm of initiation into poetry through sacrifice borrowed from German Romanticism, the princess takes on *both* the role of the poet who must survive in order to create poetry and the role of the lover, who can only make poetry possible through her own death. Both the princess and the stranger become poets because they carry "the feminine traits within them which need to be sacrificed."[102] Kohn-Waechter concludes her intertextual reading by stating that Bachmann's Kagran tale effectively "breaks down" the Romantic paradigm of Novalis' poetic program.

It is my contention, however, that if one reads the Kagran tale within the context of the entire novel *Malina*, the princess, who represents another voice of the female narrator, does not die, and can therefore not inspire or create poetry in the traditional sense of German Romanticism. Instead, Bachmann refers to the structures and themes of Novalis' *Heinrich von Ofterdingen* in order to emphasize the contrast between Heinrich's successful initiation into poetry and the princess' and female narrator's unsuccessful attempt to write "the beautiful book" as well as the narrator's failure to find her own voice independently of her male double Malina.

The relationship of dream and fairy tale in Bachmann's novel reveals her familiarity with the literary structures of German Romanticism. As in Bachmann's *Malina*, the narratives in Novalis' *Heinrich von Ofterdingen* are constructed as a montage in which the plot progresses on planes representing alternative realities or events outside of the portrayed reality. By locating poetry (Poesie) in the unconscious inner world of the poet, Novalis equates dream with fairy tale: "All fairy tales are only dreams of that world we call home"[103] and "a fairy tale is actually like a dream image – without association – a coming together of wondrous elements and occurrences."[104] For Novalis, the dream has the same function as the fairy tale within poetry; it reveals "truths" about the world through poetry. Fairy-tale world and dream world overlap in *Heinrich von Ofterdingen*, bringing together similar elements and motifs within different sub-genres throughout the novel. Novalis had planned to emphasize the importance of the fairy tale in the sequels of his novel *Heinrich von Ofterdingen* and hoped that his readers would come to understand his efforts to meld novel and fairy tale. Whereas the first part of the novel was to blend the two genres, the second part would slowly be transformed into a fairy tale.[105] As in Novalis' novel, the utopian narratives and dreams of Bachmann's *Malina* are woven into the general plot of the female narrator's life. Like many of her contemporaries, such as Marlen Haushofer and Ilse Aichinger, Bachmann employs fairy-tale elements in her prose to signal utopia, longing, wonder, and salvation. Bachmann's novel, however, also relies on certain structures and narrative techniques found in Novalis' *Heinrich von Ofterdingen* to comment on the identity of the female narrator and her role as a writer.

Decades before Reinhold Grimm used the term "Neuromantik" (Neo-Romanticism) in 1969 to describe works of contemporary literature which draw upon themes of nineteenth-century German Romanticism, it had become clear that twentieth-century literature was firmly grounded in the literary traditions of Romanticism. As early as 1945, Georg Lukács' essay "Die Romantik als Wendung in der deutschen Literatur" (Romanticism as a Turning Point in German Literature) pointed out the trend towards Romanticism in postwar German-language literature.[106] In the context of contemporary Austrian literature, Adolf Haslinger speaks of "Neuromantik" in reference not only to earlier works by Rilke, Hofmannsthal, Kafka, Broch, and Musil, but also to works written after

1970 by authors such as H. C. Artmann, Peter Handke, Barbara Frischmuth, and Peter Rosei.[107] Bachmann's *Malina* joins the ranks of these Austrian postwar novels considered "Neoromantic," but it refers to Romantic literature without emulating its notion of the unity of humankind and nature. In the Kagran tale, for instance, nature is described as unrelenting and overwhelming for the female narrator, a "strange landscape" (MAL 66) in which "she [the princess] came to a total morass, overgrown with crippled reed bushes," and further, "the princess had lost all sense of direction. It was as if everything was moving, waves of willow branches, waves of grasses, the plain was alive, and nobody but her lived there" (MAL 65). As the princess comes close to drowning in a flood along the Danube, the stranger appears a second time and saves her by neutralizing and taming the dangers of nature: "The wind and the laughter of the willows grew silent, and in the rising moon that shone white and strange on the still water of the Danube, she recognized the stranger in the black coat before her ..." (MAL 68). The stranger also silences nature in order to communicate with the princess: "he had silenced the truly immortal elements" (MAL 68). It is precisely at this moment that the princess is able to communicate with the stranger who previously had not spoken her language: "The princess and the stranger began to speak as if they had always done so, and when one spoke the other smiled" (MAL 68). The stranger restores the Romantic harmony of man and nature, man and language. He re-creates the once harmonic state of nature and the bond between the princess and the natural elements of the Danube region, as well as between the princess and himself. This harmony between man and language, however, is presented as a transitory stage in the life of the princess. Bachmann reverses the typical Romantic motif of harmony between man and nature by eliminating nature in order to allow for a moment of ideal human communication. Bachmann consciously applies Romantic tropes, such as the unity of nature and man, to emphasize the utopian role that the stranger represents in the tale for the female narrator. The stranger suspends the rift between the uncanny Danube landscape and the princess, as well as the rift between human language and communication, albeit briefly. Concerning her concept of nature within literature, Bachmann once remarked in an interview that nature "plays into the hands of the lyrical first person narrator" (WIR 32). Bachmann borrows elements from Romantic literature by using a technique of montage to create a new context for the Romantic fragments and motifs within her work.[108]

Bartsch's essay "Affinität und Distanz. Bachmann und die Romantik" (Affinity and Distance. Bachmann and Romanticism, 1991) cites numerous scholars who have written about Bachmann's affinity with German Romanticism, but criticizes those who portray her as a blind follower of Romanticism.[109] He also rejects Hans-Joachim Beck's intertextual analysis of Bachmann's *Malina*, in which Beck identifies Novalis' *Heinrich von Ofterdingen* as a "pre-text" of *Malina* and attempts to show that a chronology of other textual references employed in Bachmann's trilogy reflects one hundred and fifty years of decomposition and destruction within history.[110] Beck furthermore cites Heinrich von Kleist's drama *Prinz Friedrich von Homburg,* which Bachmann reworked as a libretto for Hans Werner Henze's opera, as a third subtext in which a prince, like many of Bachmann's protagonists, is portrayed as a dreamer.[111] In response to Beck, Bartsch demonstrates that Bachmann alludes to Romantic elements with the intention of integrating the rational realm with the emotional.[112] Bartsch also views the Kagran tale as a utopian myth that draws on elements from *Heinrich von Ofterdingen*: first, in that love is valued as the highest achievable goal, and second, in that, like the dream of the blue flower in Novalis' novel, a literary fragment within the text determines the protagonist's fate.[113]

Kohn-Waechter also explores the various Romantic motifs of *Heinrich von Ofterdingen* in the Kagran tale by examining the figure of the stranger, death, the blue or red flower, and the return of the "Golden Age." The stranger in the Kagran tale, who sings in a magical and seductive voice, recalls a figure, commonly found in German Romanticism, representing both alienation and reunification.[114] In Novalis' *Heinrich von Ofterdingen*, many strangers appear whose stories have a magical attraction for the young poet Heinrich. These strangers lead Heinrich closer to the mysteries of Romantic poetry, which becomes the propelling force throughout Novalis' novel. Bachmann's princess is attracted in much the same way to the stranger in the Kagran tale.[115] In *Heinrich von Ofterdingen*, the effects of poetry are described as "foreign words, whose meaning one nonetheless understands," and "the poet's words exert magical powers; even common words sound enchanting and their spell captivates the listeners." [116] When the princess in the Kagran tale meets the stranger for the first time, she too can understand the meaning of his voice without knowing his language:

> Deep in the night she thought she had heard a voice; one that sang and did not speak, it whispered and rocked her to sleep; then it stopped singing about strangers; instead it rang only for her and in a language that captivated her and of which she could not understand one word. Nevertheless she knew that the voice was meant for her alone and called to her. The princess did not need to understand the words. ... The voice that penetrated her told her that she could make a wish and she wished it with all her heart. ... however, although she could not see him, she knew that he had lamented because of her and had sung for her full of hope, with an unheard voice, and that he had come to save her (MAL 64).

Although the stranger's voice saves the princess from enemy kings, it captivates her so that she must obey his song: "but she obeyed him, because she had to obey him" (MAL 65). The second time the stranger saves her from the flood in the Danube region, he appears with the request that she not ask about his origin: "he covered his mouth with two fingers of the other hand so that she would not ask again who he was" (MAL 68). The princess is finally able to communicate with the stranger after spending the night with him under his coat: "They told each other of darkness and light" (MAL 68). The union with the stranger finally gives the princess the ability to communicate with him in his poetic language, if only for a short time. This ideal communication, which never comes to pass between the female narrator and Ivan, remains integral to the utopian aspect of the Kagran tale.

The significance of the Kagran tale within *Malina*, especially for the authorial position of the female narrator, becomes more apparent when the structures and themes of the tale are viewed as grounded in the nineteenth-century tradition of German Romanticism. The open-endedness and multi-layered structures of the Romantic novel, *Heinrich von Ofterdingen*, are also characteristic of a twentieth-century novel such as *Malina*, in which diverse narratives are intricately woven into the fabric of the novel. In Novalis' *Heinrich von Ofterdingen*, a treatise on philosophy, religion, love, and art, the open-endedness creates a cyclical and spiraling effect that takes the reader from the world of reality to that of a mythical and folkloric realm to an inner dream world, finally propelling the hero Heinrich into inner transcendence. The dream of the blue flower at the introduction of Novalis' novel has become paradigmatic for the Romantic era, representing longing or "Sehnsucht." Because the dream narrative is a prophetic tale for Novalis' protagonist, the dream also represents an allegory of the novel. The dream narrative is telescopically presented so that each following dream phase is more detailed yet closely linked to the previous phase. Heinrich's dream of the blue flower is related to other fragments within Novalis' novel in which dream, fairy tale, and song form a totality that subverts the author's Romantic concept of the endless novel. Therefore, even though the occurrence of the fantastic dream is framed within a more realistic, familial setting, it is never clear whether or not the entire novel is in fact the protagonist's dream. In his writings concerning his philosophy of literature, Novalis asserted that each song, fairy tale, and dream reflected the whole novel, while at the same time retaining their independence.[117] The introductory dream of the blue flower can therefore be read as an encipherment of the novel, as a prophecy and vision of Heinrich's future, in which his personal experiences are inextricably linked to his fulfillment as poet. Bachmann's Kagran tale can also be read as an encipherment of *Malina*, in which the female narrator's experiences influence her role as a poet.

In contrast to Heinrich, the female narrator of *Malina* attempts to bring the fantastic fairy tale into the reality of the narrative, although the Kagran tale and her utopian fantasies are undermined by the realities of the narrator's personal history. The fact that Heinrich has the prophetic dream of the blue flower at the beginning of the novel predestines him to be a poet, for not only does he have such a dream, but he also pursues it, seeking its deeper meaning. For Novalis, both fairy tale and dream have prophetic qualities in which "the true teller is a visionary."[118] In the Kagran tale, the princess also has a vision in which she foresees her meeting with the stranger in two thousand years in a city, most likely postwar Vienna. Although this vision does not prophesy her success as an author, it does fill the female narrator with hope that a savior exists who will rescue her from the realities she is faced with. While Bachmann describes the female narrator in *Malina* as a writer, she also illustrates how the narrator's passivity towards Malina and Ivan keeps her from writing.

Kohn-Waechter points to similarities between Novalis' and Bachmann's concept of the "Golden Age" by noting that the "end and return of the Golden Age makes itself evident in the Kagran tale and in the prophetic fragments which are fundamental for Novalis' Romantic poetics."[119] By dreaming the initial dream at the beginning of the novel, Heinrich tells of his own longing for a synthesis between his world of dreams and the world of 'fictional reality.' The blue flower becomes a trope for the "Golden Age," which in turn becomes a journey into both memory and the inner self.[120] Just as the protagonist Heinrich longs for transcendence, so does Bachmann's female narrator hope for salvation in her Kagran tale.

Despite the many references to Novalis' *Heinrich von*

Ofterdingen in Bachmann's novel *Malina*, differences exist in the way both novels handle the role of the poet. Whereas Heinrich's prophetic dream of the blue flower and the "Golden Age" is fulfilled during his travels, the female narrator in *Malina* becomes ever more disillusioned with her utopian dream to write "the beautiful book" at the close of the novel. She does not find salvation and love, but rather disappears into a wall where she is silenced and remains nameless. In contrast to the female narrator, Heinrich's eventful journey leads to his *fulfillment* as a poet.[121] In referring to the Romantic motifs of poetry and salvation, Bachmann makes evident that she is not simply a disciple of German Romanticism. Instead, she demonstrates how women can be misled by the Romantic ideals of love, unity of nature, and salvation, which prevent the female narrator from becoming a successful and independent woman and author.

Malina in the Context of the Postwar Austrian Novel

> *Music and paper, that was a kind of medicine;*
> *even during the war year 1945 it seemed*
> *conciliatory and healing.*
> Graziella Hlawaty, *Die Stadt der Lieder*[122]

Bachmann's *Malina* alludes to German Romanticism's "Golden Age" and its fairy-tale tradition in order to illustrate how the female narrator is drawn to the utopian illusion of salvation and ideal love through the writing of her Kagran tale and her desire to write a "beautiful book" for Ivan. References to fairy tales in *Malina* can also be read in the context of the postwar literary tradition in which a utopian fantasy is created in order to palliate the suffering sustained during and following the war. For authors, Bachmann and others, fairy tales counter the realities of war and postwar despair and allow writers to come to terms with their experiences of World War II. Bachmann's Kagran tale, however, represents the female narrator's attempt to create a utopian existence that never becomes reality.

Like Bachmann, authors like Ilse Aichinger and Ernst Bloch speak of utopia in their works by referring to traditional fairy tales and elements from these tales. For many authors writing during the postwar era, the act of hoping became a challenging, even provocative topic to write about in face of–and in spite of–despair and destruction. Aichinger's first and only novel, *Die größere Hoffnung* (*Herod's Children*, 1948), tells the story of Ellen, an Austrian-Jewish girl in hiding during the Third Reich, who prays to the image of a saint: "I beg of you: whatever may happen, help me to believe that somewhere everything will be blue."[123] Aichinger, like Bachmann, refers to German Romanticism by recalling the metaphoric color blue, which signals longing and homecoming. *Die größere Hoffnung* makes numerous references to traditional German fairy tales, by playing out the realities of the deportation of Jews against the background of a utopian childhood world of fairy tales. Fairy tales signal the vision of hope that Aichinger refers to throughout her novel. The novel, however, concludes ironically: while Ellen dreams of building a bridge called "die größere Hoffnung" (a greater hope), which would replace the bombed bridges she has witnessed, she is killed by an exploding grenade. In another declaration of the importance of hope, Aichinger's essay "Nach der weißen Rose" (After the White Rose, 1977/78) describes her reaction to Nazi pamphlets distributed throughout Vienna announcing the execution of the members of the German resistance movement "The White Rose": "I didn't know any of these names, but I know that an unsurpassed hope came over me. This didn't happen only to me. This hope–although it made it possible to continue living during this time–had nothing to do with the hope of surviving."[124] Hope–or the faith in hope–became a means of survival in a time of danger and death. Also, Ernst Bloch, the philosopher who viewed the ideology of the fairy tale as the "principle of hope" in his Marxist-messianic work *Das Prinzip Hoffnung* (The Principle of Hope, 1938-47), regarded hope as a "utopian function."[125] For many authors of the immediate postwar era, the act of writing and recalling fairy tales became a tool for invoking a utopian future, where the realities of the past war and immediate postwar despair could be overcome.

Despite its less hopeful title, Bachmann's *Todesarten* is propelled by an unsettling tug-of-war between hope and despair. The utopian vision of love and salvation in her trilogy is constantly undermined by the realities of the everyday experiences of its female narrators. The female narrator in *Malina*, for instance, hopes that her relationship with Ivan might be loving even though he constantly degrades and belittles her. The scenes between the female narrator and Ivan which take place before she writes the Kagran tale illustrate, on one hand, how Ivan mistreats her and, on the other hand, how she allows him to do so. During a chess game, for example, he insults her as "the headless, brainless miss," after which she insists that he plays better than she does (MAL 46-47). As in Aichinger's novel, Bachmann's utopian vision is one of ironic hope. Both the hopeful and the tragic story of the female narrator are told in *Malina*; her disappearance into the wall and silencing at the conclusion of the novel is not the last word.

The desire to write a hopeful and "beautiful book" and the impossibility of doing so become a central concern for the female narrator in Bachmann's novel *Malina*.[126] In a curious allegory, in which Bachmann's *Todesarten* is referred to by name in *Malina,* the female narrator's plan to write a book called "Todesarten" is contrasted to the joyous book Ivan would rather have her write called "Exsultate Jubilate." As if to defend the validity of her own work by acknowledging criticism about the focus on death and destruction in *Todesarten*, Bachmann's character Ivan criticizes the female narrator's title suggestions "Drei Mörder" (Three Murderers), "Todesarten," "Die ägyptische Finsternis" (The Egyptian Darkness), and "Aus einem Totenhaus" (Out of a Mortuary): "all these books, lying around here in your tomb, nobody wants them, why do such books even exist, there must be others, they should be like "Exsultate Jubilate," so that one can jump for joy, you also often jump for joy, why don't you write like that then" (MAL 54).[127] In an attempt to appease Ivan, the female narrator day-dreams of the positive effects such a "beautiful book"

would have on the world, although Bachmann sarcastically
narrates: "This is what brings happiness, because finally there is a
wonderful book on earth" (MAL 56). The narrator's desire to write
for Ivan becomes a futile attempt to communicate her love to him,
as Bachmann explains in an interview about her novel: "The first-
person narrator attempts in the novel to write a 'beautiful book' for
Ivan, but she knows from a dream that it will become a book about
hell. Why? Because the first person narrator's love for Ivan
becomes so exclusive that it is no longer understood by the other
and can no longer be reciprocated. It is not livable for Ivan" (WIR
75). At the conclusion of the novel, the female narrator has given
up all hope of ever finding the words to write such a "beautiful
book" for Ivan: "I think about my book ... I have lost it, there is no
beautiful book, I cannot write the beautiful book anymore, I
stopped thinking about the book long ago, for no reason, I can't
think of another sentence. I was so sure that the beautiful book
exists and that I would find it for Ivan"(MAL 303). Bachmann
shows how the female narrator allows herself to be destroyed by
Ivan and remains unaware of her self-destructive passivity.
Whereas Franza comes to realize that Jordan has destroyed her in
Der Fall Franza, the female narrator in *Malina* is oblivious of
Ivan's annihilation of her. Instead of writing "a beautiful book,"
the narrator acts on her memories of World War II by describing
the realities of the "murder scene" (Mordschauplatz), just as
Bachmann describes postwar society in *Malina* (MAL 276).
Although the female narrator hopes to counteract her memories by
establishing a "Golden Age" through her Kagran tale, her destructive past and the realities of history make salvation impossible.

Writing to Survive: Bachmann's Experiences as a Writer in Postwar Austria

> *My existence is different, I only exist when I write, I am nothing when I don't write; I am a stranger to myself, fallen out of myself, when I don't write. ... When I do write, then you can't see me, nobody can watch me ... but nobody can see what writing is. It is a strange, peculiar way of existing; asocial, lonely, damned, ...*
>
> Ingeborg Bachmann (RED 294)

Bachmann's descriptions of her own experiences as a freelance writer during the postwar era are reflected in *Malina,* whose female narrator is a writer. Bachmann illustrates how the act of writing functions both to establish one's identity, and to help one come to terms with one's past history. Although the female narrator in *Malina* never specifies or defines her vocation at the beginning of the novel, as she does the professions of Ivan and Malina, her existence as writer is made evident throughout the novel. In *Malina,* the female narrator describes an antique desk she wishes to purchase and on which she will be able to write the "legend of a woman who never existed" (MAL 62). After writing "The Secrets of the Princess of Kagran," she hides the written sheets from her secretary, Fräulein Jellinek, in a folder so she "won't see what I wrote" (MAL 70). The narrator then states that she did not buy the desk after all, "because it would have cost five thousand Schillings and comes from a convent," a fact that "bothers" her (MAL 70). Bachmann described her own relationship to her "hated" desk as "a compulsion, an obsession, a damnation, a punishment" (RED 295). At the beginning of *Malina*, the female narrator describes the initial inspiration necessary for writing "the beautiful book," "Exsultate Jubilate," for Ivan: "A rush of words originates in my head and then an illumination, some syllables already begin to glimmer, and colorful commas fly from all the sentence-boxes, and the periods that once were black, drift, inflated, up to the roof of my brain, ..." (MAL 55). The female narrator is, however, torn between writing "the beautiful book" for Ivan, and the "Todesarten" book she wants and needs to write for herself.[128] Although the female narrator in *Malina* is unable to complete her "Todesarten" book, Bachmann herself was able to publish *Malina* from her *Todesarten* novel cycle, a novel "she always knew she had to write" (WIR 99).

Throughout *Malina,* Bachmann describes with candor, frustration, and even humor the many tasks demanded of a writer that hinder him or her from completing any actual piece of writing. The female narrator in *Malina*, for instance, describes throughout the novel how she is bombarded with letters that require an immediate reply. The letters, which largely remain unanswered, divert from their actual purpose as communicative writings.[129] Bachmann's acceptance speech for the Anton-Wildgans award refers to the mass of letters authors receive every week, as well as to her own utter frustration at dealing with so many letters (RED 296). Bachmann's unfinished sentences in her speech describing the questions asked by the authors of these letters are similar to the types of questions the female narrator is asked by the persistent interviewer Mr. Mühlbauer, in one of the few humorous passages of *Malina* (MAL 88-101). The scenes in which the female narrator cannot bring herself to answer, finish or mail her letters reflect how Bachmann may have perceived these chores to be a hindrance to her endeavors as a writer. At the close of the novel, when the female narrator is already confined to the crack in the wall, Malina destroys some of her letters that she had previously carefully hidden in her desk. The female narrator calls these hidden letters "her only letters," and states that she must write something in them in case they were ever found by strangers and her desk sold at auction (MAL 333, 336). The letters become testimonies of a writer whose identity is bound up with what she writes. The narrator's identity in *Malina* is therefore as fragmented as the letters she attempts to write.

The Kagran tale itself functions as a narrative written by the female narrator in her role as author, a tale in which her voice is independent from Malina's. This can be compared to Bachmann's short story "Das dreißigste Jahr," where the male narrator views his identity as formed by experiences, history, and the cultural mythologies he has read: "Had I not dived into the books, into stories and legends, into newspapers, the news, nothing communicable would have grown in me, I would be nothing, a collection of misunderstood occurrences" (DRE 103). The male narrator defines experiences that are not communicated to others as incomprehensible occurrences. Like the female narrator in *Malina,* he also views his identity as formed by experiences and by the act of writing about these experiences. He "dives" into legends in the way that the female narrator "dives" into her own legend, the Kagran tale. Just as the female narrator wishes to write the Kagran tale on "old, durable parchment," and wants to "hide herself in the legend of a woman who never existed," the male narrator of "Das dreißigste Jahr" wants to leave a trace with his handwriting: "... that I am an abandoned instrument on which, a long time ago, someone has played a couple of notes which I help alter, out of which I angrily attempt to create a tone that has my handwriting. My handwriting! As if it depended on whether something has my handwriting!" (DRE 103). The male narrator wishes to leave a trace of himself through writing but realizes that only nature is able to leave a mark on earth in disasters like flooding and earthquakes: "They represent handwriting, they alone" (DRE 103). He further summarizes the elements which make up his identity: "I, this bundle of reflexes and a well-bred will, a *self,* fed on the refuse of history, the garbage of lust and instinct, a *self* with one foot in the wilderness and the other on the main road to eternal civilization. *I, impenetrable,* constituted from a mixture of all materials, matted, insoluble and yet apt to be extinguished by a blow to the back of the head. A silenced *self, created from silence*" (DRE 102). The male narrator views himself as created by the "refuse of history" and defines history as something which adds dimension to his identity.

Bachmann, however, also describes how a person can easily be extinguished from this larger history by a violent act or by being silenced. Silence (Schweigen) plays an important role in Bachmann's prose, most notably in the *Todesarten* novels. Whereas the female character in *Malina* is silenced by being confined to a crack in the wall, Franza is silenced by years of mistreatment by Jordan and by being raped and "murdered" by a stranger during her trip to Egypt. The male narrator of "Das dreißigste Jahr" describes how easy it is to extinguish a person with a blow to the head and Franza's death is brought on by just such a blow to the head by the rapist. Having been so violently attacked, Franza then kills herself by smashing her head on a wall in Gizeh (FF 466-467). In *Requiem für Fanny Goldmann* Fanny is silenced because her lover Toni Marek uses her in order to achieve his own success as a writer. Fanny's description of Toni as a "butcher" (FF 517) becomes a foreshadowing of her death following a bout of pneumonia she contracts after he ends their relationship.

Being or growing silent (Schweigen) is also a very important element of the Kagran tale, one which points to the female narrator's silence or silencing – the "silenced self" – at the conclusion of *Malina*. Communication occurs between the princess and the stranger for only a brief moment once he has silenced the natural elements. This instance of successful and ideal communication represents the only moment of mutual understanding between a man and a woman in *Malina*, and in Bachmann's entire work. The ability to communicate successfully, whether in her Kagran tale with the stranger or with Malina, Ivan or her father, is an unattainable ideal for the female narrator. In the Kagran tale, during her vision of the future, the princess tells the stranger that he will speak like other humans. She emphasizes, however, that he will tell her what she wants to hear about ideal love and call her "my love" (MAL 69). The stranger's silence at the end of the tale signals his departure and their separation. In the "awful silence" (MAL 70) of the stranger's departure, the princess envisions her first death, which foreshadows the figurative death of the female narrator at the end of the novel.

The female narrator in *Malina* aspires to find her own voice in an attempt to combat this silencing that signals her demise. By voicing her experiences and defining her person, Bachmann's female narrator hopes for a specifically female poetic voice, a "Poesie." In one of the italicized fragments related to the Kagran tale, the female narrator hopes: *"A day will come when women will have red golden eyes, auburn hair, and the poetry of their gender will prevail again..."* (MAL 136). However, in the following italicized excerpt, the hope for a new poetry is instilled in all people, both men and women: *"A day will come when people will have red golden eyes and sidereal voices, when their hands will be talented for love, and the poetry of their gender will prevail again..."* (MAL 138). This vision of a new poetry reflects a kinder and better humanity, which contrasts with the violent interpersonal relationships portrayed in *Todesarten*. By writing about her hopes and fears in the Kagran tale, and by dreaming the causes of her present disturbed mental state, the female narrator aspires to come to terms with her personal history. Like the female narrator in *Malina*, the female protagonists Franza and Fanny of the *Todesarten* novel cycle voice their personal histories in an attempt to evade the threatening process of silencing.

When Bachmann wrote *Todesarten* in the 1960s and early 1970s, she, along with Marlen Haushofer, was one of the first German-speaking authors to describe the personal and everyday experiences of women in Austria during the postwar period. In contrast, in the 1980s and 1990s, German-speaking women authors and academics Ursula Hegi and Ruth Klüger have written about women's personal histories at a time when issues of female auto-biography and identity were being discussed both in and outside of literary and academic circles.[130] Hegi, a German author and scholar residing in the United States, discusses the need to write in order to come to terms with personal history in her novel *Stones from the River* (1994). The main character, Trudi Montag, finds that she must write down her personal history in order to survive the emotional burden of her memories of World War II at the close of the war: "They did not understand why Trudi Montag wanted to dig in the dirt, as they called it, didn't understand that for her it had nothing to do with dirt but with the need to bring out the truth and never forget it. Not that she liked remembering any of it, but she understood that – whatever she knew about what had happened – it would be with her from now on, and that no one could escape the responsibility of having lived in this time."[131] Klüger, an author and scholar residing in the United States and Germany, writes about her personal history as a child in her autobiographical novel *weiter leben Eine Jugend*. Klüger describes the difficulty of writing, but also observes the unconscious work of finding words to describe the repressed and "dark memories" of her own experiences as a Holocaust survivor: "I write a couple of unrelated lines, roughly about that which has come to me at dusk, graffiti, cave paintings (which the cave visitor wants to overlook in the artificial light as scribbling, until the more observant eye notices awkward figures and deciphers their intention to exorcise), write them again, ... So, sorting out, erasing, tedious seeking day-words for unspoken half-dark-thoughts."[132] The books by Klüger and Hegi portray women's experiences as personal histories that stand apart from and complement traditional representations of history.[133]

Bachmann's fiction portrays women with experiences different from those of men. Such differences were certainly more pronounced in the 1950s when Bachmann established her career as a freelance author. These experiences are not merely described in a different voice, but rather they reflect a different perspective on history and human experience. It is precisely this different perspective, however, that Bachmann's female protagonists cannot communicate to the men they relate to, as *Malina*'s female narrator demonstrates. *Malina*, for example, shows the difficulty of writing a specifically female autobiography by letting the female narrator's description of utopia be repeatedly undermined by Malina's male voice. Bachmann seems to fall into an "early feminist" trap when she describes the female narrator in *Malina*. Whereas the female narrator defines her existence as "unsolid" (unfest), her male double Malina's existence is described as "solid" (MAL 22). Sigrid Weigel's study about women's literary history since the 1970s,

Topographien der Geschlechter (Topographies of Gender) warns that the early feminist definition of women as "undetermined, undefinable and fluid," as Bachmann describes her female narrator in *Malina*, has merely been a continuation of the older, traditional metaphor of women as allegories of art, or as bearers of the mysterious truth.[134]

Bachmann depicts the experiences of a female author in postwar Austrian society in her novel *Malina* by portraying the female narrator as a writer unable to find her own voice. *Malina* demonstrates the difficulty – but not the impossibility – of women writing in a society in which perspectives are often male-oriented. For Bachmann, it was a *male* character Malina who was able to tell the story of the female narrator. In a 1971 interview about her novel *Malina,* giving her personal opinion about the act of writing, Bachmann claimed that she could only envision a male point of view when writing. In writing, her own female voice was not to be denied, yet was to be subordinate to the male voice: "I have always searched for this main character. That much I knew: it will be male. That I can only narrate from a male point of view. But I have often asked myself: but why? I have not understood it, not in the short stories either, why I had to use a male first person narrator. It was as if I had found myself; in other words, not to deny this female self and yet still emphasize the male self" (WIR 99-100). Although Bachmann perceives herself as writing from a male point of view in her work, her observations about historical events and society are based on her experiences as a girl and young woman during World War II and as a woman in postwar Austria.

Bachmann's Kagran tale and its relation to other narrative passages throughout *Malina* are an integral part of the novel and a key to understanding the significance of the female narrator's role as writer. Instead of reading the tale as a utopian fantasy of salvation, the tale – and its related dream narrative describing events of the Holocaust – becomes a vehicle for coming to terms with the female narrator's personal history and her role within the larger representation of history. Bachmann's novel describes how the historical events of the Third Reich make it impossible for the female narrator to find salvation and happiness. Her references to German Romanticism and more specifically to Novalis' *Heinrich von Ofterdingen*, show how, unlike Heinrich, the female narrator does not reach poetic transcendence. Despite the female narrator's hope for salvation and her attempt to write "the beautiful book" for Ivan, the destructive events of history and society prevent her from establishing her voice at the close of *Malina*. It is precisely Bachmann's insistent discussion in her writings about the consequences of war on society that allow for a novel such as *Malina* to be read as a significant historical work.

Chapter Two

Into the Bloody Chamber:
Rewriting the Bluebeard Tale

> *Turn back, Turn back, you young bride, you*
> *are in a murderer's house.*
> The Grimm brothers, "The Robber
> Bridegroom"[135]

> *One can only tell about the Holocaust as a*
> *fairy tale. Both touch on the unspeakable. ...*
> *Fairy tales are appropriate, they scare us:*
> *"Snow White" or "Pinocchio" are terrifying*
> *tales, and every time we believe that we have*
> *understood them they offer us new riddles.*
> *The death camps are outside of reality. They*
> *are indescribable, inconceivable. One can*
> *only describe them through the 'Majesty of*
> *Truth,' as Edgar Allen Poe called it. My film*
> *is based on this thought: it is not realistic, but*
> *a fairy tale, invented out of the truth.*
> Roberto Benigni, speaking of his
> film "Life is Beautiful" [136]

While the previous chapter illustrates how Bachmann refers to various fairy tales in general, and their tradition within German Romanticism, this chapter provides a context for Bachmann's references to the specific fairy tale of Bluebeard by exploring its tradition in German-language literature. Chapter Three follows suit by exploring how Bachmann refers to the Bluebeard tale in her *Der Fall Franza* in connection with the historical events of the Holocaust and Third Reich. Bachmann refers to the figure of Bluebeard throughout *Todesarten* and associates him with the dominant father figure who represents patriarchal society and, more specifically, fascist suppression. The fourth chapter continues the exploration of the Bluebeard tale by showing how and why Bachmann portrays her female character Charlotte as Bluebeard in the short story "Ein Schritt nach Gomorrha." Although this short story has more often been read as Bachmann's daring portrayal of a homosexual relationship – especially since it was written in 1961 when issues of homosexuality were not openly addressed in Austrian literature – I will show how Bachmann projects the traditional male-female gender polarity onto two female characters. By exposing the elements of power, victimization, and destruction in the Bluebeard tale, Bachmann is able to discuss and come to terms with the history of the Third Reich and the Holocaust. The figure of Bluebeard symbolizes the destructive element that prevents the female character from succeeding as an individual in society. For Bachmann, the tale reveals how women are victims of a patriarchal society, but also how, at the same time, they contribute to their own victimization. The heroine's role in the Bluebeard tale provides a means for understanding the tension in the tale between Bluebeard's deception of leading the heroine to enter the secret chamber and the heroine's own curiosity and desire for knowledge and independence. Variants of the Bluebeard tale in the Grimms' collection can be read and interpreted in many ways. My own reading of the Bluebeard story, however, concentrates mainly on the socio-historical issues raised in Bachmann's prose.[137]

The Bluebeard tale is well known throughout Europe and especially popular in German-speaking countries including Austria where Bachmann first might have read or heard it as a child. The tale "Ritter Blaubart" (Knight Bluebeard) from an Austrian collection of folk tales is a combination of "Der Räuberbräutigam" (The Robber Bridegroom) and "Fitchers Vogel" (Fitcher's Bird) from the Grimms' popular fairy-tale collection, the *Kinder- und Hausmärchen* of 1857. In the Austrian version Bluebeard is a thief who gives each of his wives a key and an egg (as in "Fitchers Vogel") and dismembers them for having entered the forbidden chamber (as in "Der Räuberbräutigam"). In the Austrian tale and in the Grimm brothers' tale only the third sister is clever enough not to fall into Bluebeard's trap. The heroine is able to bring Bluebeard and his band of thieves to justice by telling the tale of her husband's crimes, as in the conclusion of "Der Räuberbräutigam." Whereas the heroine in Charles Perrault's French version is saved by her brothers, the heroine in "Der Räuberbräutigam" exposes the villain's murderous deeds through the power of storytelling.[138] The following discussion of Bachmann's references to the Bluebeard tale will focus mainly on the German-language version of the tale, in which the heroine gains independence and maturity through her intelligence and exposure of Bluebeard's crimes.

The German-Language Tradition of the Bluebeard Tale

> *Elisabeth (as if bewitched):*
> *It glows—could it be a golden one?*
> *What will it open for me?*
> *Don't you wear a tiny key around your neck?*
> *Bluebeard:*
> *It opens the door to the bridal chamber!*
> *Its secret is decay and death,*
> *born out of the body's desperate need.*
>   Georg Trakl, *Bluebeard:*
>   *A Puppet Show*[139]

The Bluebeard tale plays a culturally significant role in the Austro-German literary tradition from Romanticism through the twentieth century. The universality and popularity of the tale is reflected in Emil Heckmann's 1930 dissertation, which documents hundreds of Bluebeard tales throughout Europe, Africa, India, Jamaica, and North America.[140] Ulrike Blaschek's collection *Märchen vom Blaubart* (Fairy Tales about Bluebeard, 1989) traces the motif of forbidden knowledge in the Bluebeard tale to that of the forbidden chamber of *The Thousand and One Nights*, as well as to the Old Testament story, in which the fall of humankind is brought about by Eve's biting into the forbidden fruit in Paradise.[141] Hartwig Suhrbier's *Blaubarts Geheimnis* (Bluebeard's Secret, 1984) defines the Bluebeard tale, from Perrault to contemporary rewritings, as a reflection, criticism, and parody of western culture and describes Bluebeard as "a patriach," "a type of man, who at least up until today is very common in Western bourgeois societies." Not only is Bluebeard the "older man" who "fascinates" a "young, inexperienced woman," but "the patriarchal man who would like to make women subject to him – be it ever so subtly."[142] This chapter will explore how Bachmann – a decade before Suhrbier made this observation – views the Bluebeard tale as a narrative marker of male domination and female subordination. The following paragraphs will provide a summary of the tales I refer to most frequently and will give a picture of the Bluebeard tradition.

In western Europe the Bluebeard figure was popularized by Charles Perrault's widely known fairy tale "Barbe bleue" (Bluebeard) in his 1697 fairy-tale collection *Histoires ou Contes du temps passé* (Tales of Mother Goose). His tale of the blue-bearded villain intrigued German Romantic poets, and they immortalized the Bluebeard figure in fairy tales as well as in dramas and ballads. Perrault's popular "Barbe bleue" greatly influenced the Grimms' version of "Blaubart" published in the first edition volume of the *Kinder- und Hausmärchen* (*KHM*) in 1812 and which, because of its similarity to the French version rather than the Germanic one, was only included in the appendix of later editions. In "Barbe bleue," the French version of the tale, a wealthy landowner entices one of his neighbor's daughters into marriage, even though her sisters fear him because of the mysterious disappearance of his previous wives. Barbe bleue soon takes a trip and entrusts his young bride Marie with the keys to his household. He warns her that she will be punished by death if she enters the forbidden room, whose door can be opened only by the smallest key. The tale reports that it is not only curiosity that compels her to open the forbidden door, but also temptation. Having entered the chamber despite the warning, Marie drops the key on the floor covered with clotted blood upon seeing her husband's former wives hanging on the walls. The key is permanently stained, giving Barbe bleue proof of her transgression when he returns from his trip. He announces that she will join his former wives, but grants her fifteen minutes for prayer after Marie convinces him that she wishes to repent for her disobedience. She then cleverly calls to her sister Anne and implores her to climb the tower to see if her brothers, who have promised to visit her that day, are coming. (To question the reason for Anne's presence at the castle seems irrelevant in the magical realm of Perrault's fairy tales.) After Marie calls up to Anne a third time to ask about the arrival of her brothers, Barbe bleue threatens to behead his wife. Perrault's happy end finds the brothers storming the castle to kill Barbe bleue and save their sister. Marie inherits Barbe bleue's entire wealth and marries her brothers' friend in an attempt to forget her first marriage. Marie, in a traditional male role, uses a large part of her wealth to arrange the marriage of her sister Anne to a man she had long been in love with and to furnish her brothers with commissions. At the conclusion the two sisters gain financial independence and are able to improve the course of their future because of the heroine's resourcefulness.

The Grimm brothers greatly influenced, perhaps even initiated, the German-language Bluebeard tradition by publishing various versions of the Bluebeard tale, at least one of which was fashioned after Perrault's tale, in their succession of *KHM* editions.[143] In 1812 the Grimms published the first edition of their *KHM* collection, which included "Blaubart," claiming it was of German origin in order to celebrate German nationalism. This tale, along with "Das Mordschloß" (The Murder Castle), was omitted from the 1815 edition because of its similarity with the French tale, and was instead replaced by "Fitchers Vogel" and "Der Räuberbräutigam" in later *KHM* editions, including the last one edited by the Grimms in 1857. "Der Räuberbräutigam," part of the original 1810 manuscript, was referred to as a basis for the revised 1812 publication. Many of the Grimms' informants were French-speaking Huguenots and therefore influenced by the French tradition of the Perrault tales.[144] In the Grimms' German version of Perrault's tale "Blaubart" the heroine's family includes a father and three brothers. A wealthy king woos the daughter, although it is her father who insists upon the marriage. The heroine feels uneasy about the blue-bearded man and asks her brothers to save her if she should ever call on them for help. Once again Bluebeard goes on a journey and gives his young bride the keys to his palace. Despite his threat to kill her should she ignore his command not to enter the secret chamber, the bride's curiosity grows so powerful that she enters the forbidden room anyway, dropping the key into a pool of blood.[145] Despite her attempts to rid the key of its tell-tale bloodstains by leaving it to dry in hay overnight, Bluebeard discovers her secret and informs her that she must be killed for her transgression. The heroine, however, manages to escape him by climbing a tower to summon her brothers, just as the sister in the Perrault tale had done. The brothers, hearing her cries, rescue their sister moments before she is to be murdered. Bluebeard is punished by being hanged next to his dead wives in the bloody chamber, whereas the heroine returns home with her inheritance to live happily ever after with her father and brothers. In this tale there is no resurrection of Bluebeard's victims and no second marriage for the heroine. Although the heroine in the tale is rescued from the hands of Bluebeard, her curiosity is nonetheless portrayed as a negative female trait and the ultimate cause of her misfortune.

In contrast to Perrault's Bluebeard tale, the German versions "Fitchers Vogel," "Das Mordschloß" and "Der Räuberbräutigam" portray heroines who use their intelligence and creativity to survive Bluebeard's sadistic violence. In "Fitchers Vogel" each of the three sisters is kidnapped by a sinister and seductive sorcerer and given an egg, a key, and the instruction not to enter the forbidden chamber while he is away. After the first two sisters give in to their curiosity and are consequently murdered by their captor, the youngest is able to deftly reassemble her sisters' dismembered bodies and escape dressed as a bird. The young heroine is described as intelligent and is able to use her cunning to escape her terrible fate, unlike the heroine in "Barbe bleue" who barely escapes death by being rescued. In "Das Mordschloß" and "Der Räuberbräutigam," Bluebeard's brides use the power of story-telling to punish him justly and to assert their independence.

"Das Mordschloß" differs from the other tales because Blue-beard does not forbid the heroine to enter the secret chamber, although he intends to punish her for it nonetheless. In this tale a wealthy gentleman comes to call on a shoemaker's daughters, charms the youngest, and takes her to his castle in the woods. The heroine is frightened of him at first, but his wealth and power titillate her and outweigh her fear. While her husband is away on a trip, having left his keys with her, she meets an old woman in the cellar, who warns her that her spouse plans to kill and eat her. Startled, the heroine drops the key into a vat of blood. Because the key cannot be cleaned, the old woman tells the heroine that her death is now certain. (At this point in the Grimm tale – as in my retelling of it – a note in parentheses says that the two older sisters perished in this way although this is inconsistent with the beginning of the tale.) As a haywagon pulls up in front of the castle, the heroine escapes by hiding under the hay. When the gentleman returns from his trip and calls for his bride, the old woman appeases him by lying that she has already killed her and the dogs have devoured her remains. As proof of the bride's death, the old woman presents him with the heart, blood, and a lock of hair from an animal. Upon seeing these objects as proof of his bride's death, the villain is satisfied. At this point in the tale it is perplexing for the reader that the heroine's entrance into the forbidden cellar and her death are unrelated. The husband is merely relieved that she is dead and not that she has been punished for her transgression. The heroine of "Das Mordschloß" escapes to a nearby castle and tells her story to its owner. He in turn plans a feast, to which the villain of the "Murderer's Castle" is invited. At the feast each guest is asked to tell a story, and the heroine is given the opportunity to recount her tale. The murderer, after realizing that he has stumbled into a trap himself, attempts to flee but is captured, judged, and imprisoned. The murderer's possessions are transferred to the bride who then marries the "good" castle-owner's son. In the tale "Das Mordschloß," the act of storytelling, as for Scheherazade, becomes a life-saving device and leads to a happy ending for the heroine.

"Der Räuberbräutigam," a variant of the Bluebeard tale, tells the story of a miller's daughter who is forced to take a trip through the woods to visit her wealthy fiancé. The heroine must be forced to visit her groom because she has reservations about him from the very beginning: "The girl did not really care for him, as a bride should love the groom, and did not trust him: she felt dread in her heart whenever she looked at him or thought about him."[146] An old woman in the groom's house warns the heroine that he plans to kill and eat his bride. While hiding behind a barrel in the basement, the heroine witnesses the groom returning home with his band of thieves and murdering a virgin. In an attempt to steal the virgin's gold ring, the thieves chop off her finger, which falls behind the barrel and into the lap of the heroine. The young woman manages to escape and returns to her father for protection. When the groom comes to her house to question her about her refusal to meet him, she retells her experience in the guise of a dream. As testimony to her tale, she pulls out the finger, whereupon the "Robber-groom" is captured, along with his band of thieves, and all are sentenced to death for their crime. A theme common to all Bluebeard tales is that the prohibition, spoken or unspoken, does not prevent the heroine from falling into Bluebeard's trap and facing punishment and possibly death. The heroine's life, in other words, is at stake once she receives the keys to her husband's secret chamber. Bachmann refers to this motif of the Bluebeard tale in her prose to illustrate how her female characters are trapped in their situation because of their passivity, and are therefore neither saved in the end, nor do they live happily ever after.

After having become popular in both France and Italy, the Bluebeard tale spread throughout German-speaking countries in the late eighteenth century and was retold by the authors Christoph Martin Wieland, Johann Karl August Musäus, Benedikte Naubert, and Christoph Wilhelm Günther.[147] "Blaubart" reached a wide audience with the publication of the familiar fairy-tale collection "Blaue Bibliothek aller Nationen" (Blue Library of all Nations) in 1790. Ludwig Tieck's dramatic version"Ritter Blaubart" (Sir Bluebeard, 1797) and his story "Die sieben Weiber des Blaubart" (The Seven Wives of Bluebeard) were also quite popular during this time. The Bluebeard figure was further popularized by Ludwig Bechstein's "Das Märchen von Ritter Blaubart" (The Fairy Tale of Sir Bluebeard) in his *Deutsches Märchenbuch* (German Fairy-Tale Book, 1845), influenced in turn by the Perrault, Grimm, and Tieck versions.[148] Since the height of its popularity during the German Romantic period, the Bluebeard tale has figured in many tales, plays, operas, and films up through the twentieth century.[149] The tale of Bluebeard has captivated readers throughout the centuries with its themes of violence, horror, sexuality, and serial killing.

Although Bluebeard is the one punished in the above tales, most interpreters nonetheless focus on the heroine's curiosity, temptation, and punishment by Bluebeard. Whereas the heroines' sisters are murdered by the villain for their transgression, the tale focuses on the heroine who exposes and punishes Bluebeard for his crimes. Bluebeard tales and their interpreters most often criticize the female characters for surrendering to temptation and cognitive and sexual curiosity. Perrault's moral warns: "Curiosity, in spite of its many charms,/Can bring with it serious regrets;/ You can see a thousand examples of it every day./ Women succumb, but it's a fleeting pleasure;/ As soon as you satisfy it, it ceases to be./ And it always proves very, very costly."[150] Bruno Bettelheim's psychoanalytical reading of Bluebeard, which takes Perrault's "moral" message to heart, describes the tale as a "cautionary tale" of "marital infidelity," which warns: "Women, don't give in to your sexual curiosity; men, don't permit yourself to be carried away by your anger at being sexually betrayed."[151] In her analysis of the Bluebeard tale, Maria Tatar concludes that "nearly every nineteenth-century printed version of 'Bluebeard' singles out the heroine's curiosity as an especially undesirable trait." [152] Curiosity in turn leads to what Tatar considers to be the fundamental plot sequence of the Bluebeard tale, the paired functions of "prohibi-tion/violation."[153] Ruth Bottigheimer notes that in nineteenth-century children's literature only the Grimms' tales are gender-specific in the consequences of transgressing prohibitions. She summarizes the role of women in the Grimms' tales as "clear and unambiguous" and asserts that "norms buttressed by society and religion bind women of all degrees from poverty to majesty, and a woman's transgression of these norms results in profound deprivation of selfhood, that is, muteness or the possibility of death itself."[154] Bottigheimer states that punishment is gender-specific in the Grimm tales, and that girls, having usually only committed petty transgressions, are always punished more harshly than boys. She states that the heroines of the Bluebeard tale in the Grimm tales always face punishment because "obedience is necessary for females but not males."[155] Bottigheimer, who finds that a female protagonist's punishment takes precedence over her transgression in the Grimms' tales, views this as the product of a tendency to incriminate females and, at the same time, exonerate males from guilt.[156] Though Bottigheimer believes that the biblical story of Eve accounts for the gender-specific paradigm of the tempted and transgressing heroine, she grounds the Grimms' tales in the social and moral values of nineteenth-century Germany. Although the Bluebeard character is punished by death at the conclusion of the tales, nothing further is mentioned about the horrendous crime that was committed, thus relieving the male character of any guilt. The heroine is most often expected to return to her accepted role as a daughter, sister, and wife.[157]

Within this context I will show how Bachmann's references to the Bluebeard tale demonstrate that her perceptions of male-female relations in the mid-twentieth century are rooted in the gender structures typical of nineteenth-century literature, especially popular fairy tales. I will also demonstrate how Bachmann uses the Bluebeard tale in *Der Fall Franza* and "Ein Schritt nach Gomor-rha" to look at marriage as a testing ground for women. In most Bluebeard variants, the husband tests his wife by giving her the key to his secret chamber, at the same time prohibiting her ever to enter it. When Bluebeard of both the Perrault tale and the Grimms' variants of the French tale returns to claim his keys, the heroine realizes that her husband will punish and murder her because the key is stained with blood from her entry into the forbidden chamber. In the German-language tradition, however, the third and younger sister outsmarts Bluebeard by concealing the key (or egg) in a safe place before entering the bloody chamber. In this case, Bluebeard returns to tell his bride that she has passed her test and that he will reward her with marriage. In "Fitchers Vogel," for example, the youngest sister's cleverness is portrayed as proof of her intelligence and as a benefit to her future husband: "Upon his arrival, the man immediately demanded the key and the egg, and when he did not detect any trace of blood on it, he spoke: 'You have passed the test, you will be my bride.' He now had no more power over her and had to do what she demanded."[158] Bluebeard no longer has power over his wife once she has exposed his evil deeds. In much the same way, Bachmann's protagonist Franza in *Der Fall Franza* renders the Bluebeard character, Dr. Körner, powerless by exposing the truth about his murderous past, as I will later explain.

The Jungian folklorist, J. Cooper, sees the Bluebeard tale as a "legacy from the ritual testing of the wife,"[159] in which "the custom of ritual testing and ritual riddle-solving appears to go back to the maturity and marriage tests of early cultures. In the male, intelligence as well as strength was tried; for the female intelligence and ingenuity were tested."[160] The heroine manages to survive by her ingenuity and is rewarded by material wealth and independence. Not only does the heroine's relationship with Bluebeard cause her to exercise her ingenuity, but it also allows her to transgress his prohibition, which is necessary for her personal development. Transgression and defiance of set norms and laws are ultimately beneficial to the heroine as an individual and as a woman in a patriarchal society such as Bluebeard's. Bachmann's references to the Bluebeard tale in *Todesarten* address the motif of marriage as a testing ground for women, although this institution is often also portrayed as a mental institution and a torture chamber. In a 1973 interview Bachmann claimed that marriage was an "impossible institution" for a woman and that it was a hindrance to her personal success: " It is impossible for a woman who works and thinks and wants to achieve something herself. ... I have known from the start that I am against marriage, against any legal relationship" (WIR 144). Bachmann described marriage as a "disgraceful story" in *Der Fall Franza* (FF 402) and as a "rigid," "unalterable state," and "trap" in "Ein Schritt nach Gomorrha" (GOM 202-207).

This criticism of marriage is also discussed in Marcia Lieberman's essay "Some Day My Prince Will Come: Female Acculturation Through the Fairy Tale," in which she interprets fairy tales like Bluebeard as portrayals of sexual roles in marriage.[161] She views marriage as both punishment and reward in tales such as Bluebeard: "The stories can be described as being preoccupied with marriage and male-female relationships without portraying it; as a real condition, it's nearly always off-stage."[162] In another essay dealing with women's roles in marriage in fairy tales, "Feminism and Fairy Tales," Karen Rowe views traditional fairy tales as "powerful transmitters of romantic myths which encourage women to internalize only aspirations deemed appropriate to our 'real' sexual functions within a patriarchy."[163] A heroine's so-called virtues of passivity, dependency, and self-sacrifice suggest to readers "that the culture's very survival depends upon a woman's acceptance of roles which relegate her to motherhood and domesticity."[164] Bachmann takes the theme of marriage as a testing ground from the Bluebeard tale and uses it as a means of characterizing Jordan's marriage to Franza in *Der Fall Franza* as well as Charlotte's relationship to Mara in "Ein Schritt nach Gomorrha."

Similar references to women's roles in marriage can also be found in Angela Carter's short story "The Bloody Chamber" (1981), in which the Bluebeard tale is retold from the point of view of the heroine who comes to terms with the murderous secrets of her husband. In fact, Carter's Bluebeard tale is one of the few versions told from the point of view of the young bride who is lured into the bloody chamber by her own sexual curiosity and desire for sexual knowledge. As in Franza's case in *Der Fall Franza*, Carter's female narrator is able to trace her own steps leading to this sadistic, "unguessable country of marriage,"[165] and becomes aware of her impending doom when she discovers the secret that her husband has laid out for her:

> I knew I had behaved exactly according to his desires; had he not brought me so that I should do so? I had been tricked into my own betrayal to that illimitable darkness whose source I had been compelled to seek in his absence, and now that I had met that shadowed reality of his that came to life only in the presence of its own atrocities, I must pay the price of my new knowledge. The secret of Pandora's box; but he had given me the box himself, knowing I must learn the secret. I had played a game in which every move was governed by a destiny as oppressive and omnipotent as himself, since that destiny was himself; and I had lost.[166]

I will later discuss how Franza is also "tricked into her own betrayal" in *Der Fall Franza* and demonstrates a self-awareness like that of Carter's heroine. Unlike Franza, however, whose brother Martin takes on the role of her unsuccessful savior, Carter's heroine is saved from Bluebeard's murderous intentions by her mother.

Traditional readings of the Bluebeard tale, so influential to the German-speaking literary tradition, focus on Bluebeard's murdered wives, who have been unjustly punished as if they had no choice but to transgress. Having received a key to the secret chamber and been told of its location, the heroine's curiosity pulls her towards the horrifying site of the bloody chamber.[167] There is, however, another possible reading of the Bluebeard tale. Instead of focusing on the heroine's lack of choice and freedom in entering the secret chamber, it becomes evident that she also gains independence by satisfying her curiosity and desire for knowledge. The female narrators in Bachmann's prose come to expose the murderous deeds of their own Bluebeard figures, but they are nonetheless destroyed by their passivity.

Defying Bluebeard: Contextualizing Bachmann's References to Bluebeard

> *He had no more power over her and had to do what she demanded.*
>
> Grimm, "Fitchers Vogel"[168]

> *She ... made her demands and became his wife.*
>
> Grimm, "Breiselbart, verführt alle Mädchen."[169]

In the following passages I will show how the German-language Bluebeard tale can be read from the heroine's perspective in which her curiosity leads to a positive and empowering act that exposes Bluebeard's crimes and brings justice to an otherwise unjust and violent world. Although the heroine's curiosity is most often portrayed as a negative quality, it secures her emotional, sexual, and financial independence. Grimm's heroine in "Blaubart," for example, is described as driven by curiosity: "Her curiosity began to plague her."[170] In "Fitchers Vogel," the heroine is also swayed by curiosity to open the forbidden door: "She finally arrived at the forbidden door; she wanted to pass by it but her curiosity plagued her."[171] J. Cooper classifies the Bluebeard tale as a "taboo tale," one that warns of the difficulty at resisting temptation, and an admonition against seeking premature knowledge. Cooper views the temptation motif as a cautionary element warning against foolish wishing, over-intellectualism, knowledge for knowledge's sake, and entering a spiritual or meditative state before one has the strength do to so.[172] In Bachmann's tale, the female characters are educatcd, intellectual women who are "murdered" by their society and male partners precisely because they represent a threat to the existing male-oriented societal power structure. Bachmann refers to the heroine in the Bluebeard tale to illustrate the position of intellectual women in postwar Austrian society. I argue that the heroine of the Bluebeard tale needs to be curious in order to develop the courage to go against societal laws that stand in the way of her personal development. In the Grimms' "Fitchers Vogel," for example, the heroine pieces her murdered and slaughtered sisters back together and returns them home safely using a clever plan. Most traditional Bluebeard tales, as well as Bachmann's *Todesarten*, are set in a world that does not encourage women to seek out knowledge, although it is ultimately the heroine's intelligence that saves her and brings the murderer to justice within this same society. It becomes evident that the attainment of the heroine's social, sexual, and emotional autonomy in the Bluebeard tale is only made possible by her transgression and by exposing Bluebeard's murderous deeds.

The two possible versions of the Bluebeard tale, one stressing Bluebeard's evil character and his prohibition, and the other focusing on the heroine's transgression and her desire for knowledge and independence, co-exist in tension in Bachmann's narratives. In this sense, the heroine's journey takes her both out of and into the secret chamber. If one applies this reading of the Bluebeard tale to Bachmann's *Der Fall Franza*, then Franza has ventured into the bloody chamber of Jordan's murderous intentions, as well as striven for the truth and justice in the secret chamber – without, however, experiencing the traditional happy end. Though Franza is able to break free from her marriage with Jordan during her trip to Egypt, salvation comes too late when she is brutally raped and attacked at the conclusion of the novel fragment. What does the secret chamber then come to signify in Bachmann's prose? If it is knowledge, then is it cognitive, sexual, or both? Bachmann takes apart elements of the German-language Bluebeard tale in order to illustrate the heroine's desire to gain knowledge and indepcndence, while at the same time exposing the injustices she experiences.

In this context, Bachmann's references to the Bluebeard tale both revise and interpret the Bluebeard tale. Although references to Bluebeard appear only in *Der Fall Franza* and in the story "Ein Schritt nach Gomorrha," the destructive father figure and husband whom Bluebeard represents can be found throughout *Todesarten* and other prose works. But unlike the youngest sister from the Grimms' "Blaubart" tale, who arranges to be saved by a male figure, the female characters in *Todesarten* are not saved from their involvement with Bluebeard. In *Der Fall Franza,* in which the Bluebeard Jordan "murders" his wife, Franza's brother Martin unwillingly acts the role of the savior although it becomes evident that Franza can no longer be saved. Martin is described as a "protector made powerless" (FF 429). The female first-person narrator in *Malina*, who is "murdered" by the father figure, views Malina as her savior after each nightmare. Nonetheless, her (self-) destruction culminates in her disappearance into a crack in the wall, an act she defines as "murder" (MAL 337). In "Ein Schritt nach Gomorrha," the female narrator compares herself to Blue-beard and finally contributes to Mara's and her own figurative death: "They were both dead and had killed something" (GOM 213). Although the female characters of all the aforementioned narratives have been lured into the bloody chamber by a Bluebeard figure, Bachmann also shows how they contribute to their own victimization.

Just as the fairy-tale figure of Bluebeard is always described as wealthy and successful, the careers of the male characters in *Todesarten* are portrayed as respectable and acceptable to society. Whereas the female figures of *Todesarten* are submissive and lack self-respect, the male characters are portrayed as socially success-ful and powerful. In *Malina*, for instance, Ivan has a job at an unnamed financial institution while the male narrator Malina is an anonymous state functionary at the Austrian Military Museum (MAL 11). The female first-person narrator by contrast, who is a writer and an intellectual, describes her career(s) as "a career, twice crossed out and written over" (MAL 12). In *Der Fall Franza,*

Franza's brother Martin, described as a researcher and geologist, illustrates his disrespect for the career of a writer by calling one author a "clown" (FF 351). Franza's husband Jordan is portrayed as a well-known and highly respected psychiatrist, whereas her own career as a doctor or nurse is said to have ended when she married him. In the introduction to *Der Fall Franza*, it is written that Martin later becomes a historian. His career choices are not surprising, since he is always curious about his past: as a geologist he digs in the past, and as a historian he traces his past through his sister, who is responsible for retrieving the memory of his childhood (FF 341). In *Requiem für Fanny Goldmann*, Fanny is portrayed as a struggling actress who has relationships with men who are highly respected for their talents. Charlotte, a pianist like her husband, places his career before her own in "Ein Schritt nach Gomorrha" by stating that she had practiced submission more than he had (GOM 202). Whereas Charlotte wishes to respect her husband's career more than she actually does, she demands that Mara take over this traditional role of the admiring wife. Mara becomes her "creature" (Geschöpf), promising Charlotte that she will support her career as a pianist by giving up her own identity. Mara vows to Charlotte that she will do *everything* for her: "will wake you up in the morning, bring you tea, the mail, get the phone, I can cook for you,..." (GOM 211).

The female characters in *Todesarten* desire knowledge in order to gain respect and recognition in their relationship with other individuals who make up society, although these women are portrayed as passive and self-destructive. While Bachmann's characters struggle for cognitive and sexual knowledge, they are ridiculed and therefore "murdered" by their male partners and society. Just as the heroine in the Bluebeard tale defies Bluebeard to gain independence and expose his evil deeds, Bachmann's female characters in *Todesarten* demonstrate that rebellion against the father figure is a necessary step towards maturity and independence. At the same time, however, Bachmann also shows how her female characters fail to gain this desired independence because they are not willing or able to disobey the Bluebeard and father figure.

Chapter Three

Bluebeard, Fascism, and Power:
References to the Holocaust in Bachmann's Prose

> *Last question: why did Jordan select Franza?
> ... am dealing with an unsolved case about
> Bluebeard, about a man, about a fascist,
> about who can understand it, who will ever
> understand it?*
>
> Ingeborg Bachmann, fragment [173]

Bluebeard Jordan

The repetitive cycle of domination and subjugation in the power structure is played out on the terrain of political paradigms such as fascism and colonialism in Bachmann's work. They illustrate the relationships between the individual and society and, more specifically, between men and women. The hegemonic structure is grounded in the Bluebeard-like father figure, one of the three central figures in *Malina*, who is a marginal character yet a powerful and destructive force in *Der Fall Franza* and *Requiem für Fanny Goldmann*. For Bachmann, the destruction of the female characters by the father figure precludes any possibility of a future harmonious relationship between a man and a woman, as well as between the individual and society. In an interview about her prose, Bachmann stated that the father figure represents just one type of the "murderer" who "wears many costumes," like that of Bluebeard, and "who commits those crimes society itself commits" (WIR 97). The figure Jordan illustrates how Bachmann relates the *story* (Geschichte) of the Bluebeard tale to the *history* (Geschichte) of the Third Reich in *Todesarten*. In *Der Fall Franza* the motif of fascism is carried over to the relationship between Franza and her dominating and destructive husband Jordan, as Franza tells her husband: "You say fascism, that is odd, I've never heard that used as a word for private conduct, no, pardon me, I have to laugh, no, really, I'm not crying. But that's good, because it has to begin somewhere, why does one only speak about it when dealing with opinions and public deeds" (FF 403). In an interview regarding her novel *Malina,* Bachmann stated that fascism is the first element in a relationship between a man and a woman (WIR 144). Jordan, portrayed as a fascist who uses psychological terror to destroy his wife Franza, is the one male character in Bachmann's *Todesarten* who is referred to as "Bluebeard" by name. Jordan is a domineering figure who must extinguish what he perceives to be the "other" in order to maintain his power. As mentioned earlier, the heroine in the Grimms' "Fitchers Vogel" and "Das Mordschloß" takes away Bluebeard's power by exposing him. The negative characteristics of Bluebeard in Jordan are identical to those qualities attributed to all male figures in *Todesarten.* It is in exploring the relationship between perpetrator and victim (Täter/Opfer) through this tale that Bachmann attempts to come to terms with the history of the destruction of the "other": the murder of Jews and countless other victims, such as female intellectuals and the mentally ill during the Holocaust.

The figure of Bluebeard is first introduced in the second edited chapter of *Der Fall Franza*, "Jordanische Zeit" (Jordan Time), in which Franza compares herself to Bluebeard's murdered wives. Franza is, in other words, not the clever heroine of the Bluebeard tale who exposes Bluebeard's evil in time to save herself, but one of the murdered sisters who is destroyed because of her passivity. Bachmann refers to the Bluebeard tale precisely to show how the female character plays a significant role in her own victimization and destruction.

Whereas Franza's brother Martin and a third-person narrator recount her history in the first chapter, the narrator shifts to the first person in the second chapter. There Franza narrates her own story, after finally discovering her voice.[174] It is only after a conversation with Martin that Franza realizes what role she has played in her husband's life. She observes that she has become part of a pattern in which the Blubeard figure Jordan has destroyed her emotionally and psychologically as he did his past two wives: "I have just now begun to ask myself about the other women and why they all disappeared silently, why one of them never leaves her house anymore, why the other one turned on the gas pipe, and how I am the third with this name, was the third, she corrected herself, was" (FF 400). The past tense of "was" illustrates that Franza has already been "murdered" and that it is too late to reverse the damage done to her by Jordan. At first, Franza had believed herself to be different from Jordan's ex-wives, describing them as "stupid, imbecilic," "defective," and "worthless" because of their failed relationship with him (FF 400). Jordan's villainous ploy becomes brutally apparent, as Franza explains: "It is as if a spotlight had been turned on to shine on this whole time which lay in darkness; everything is exposed, naked, horrendous, vast, evidence that cannot be overlooked" (FF 400). Franza associates herself with Jordan's past wives as a victim, and exposes the crimes found in her husband's bloody chamber at the end of her voyage. Franza's discovery of her husband's crimes becomes the spotlight to expose his evil deeds. Although she feels victimized in her relationship, Franza is nonetheless aware of her role as the passive victim in her relationship with Jordan. She realizes that her willingness to play the role of the victim has perpetuated her complicity in the destructive relationship with Jordan: "Whatever other girls want, I must have been driven to look into the last room, the drive of the bored, the boring marriage, curious about the last room, murdered mysteriously and murdered for mysterious reasons and guessing myself to death about the only figure whom I could not figure out" (FF 400).[175] Franza describes how she is drawn to "the last room" in which she is to be murdered. In *Malina*, the female narrator also describes a "last room" as belonging to Malina, her male double: "because the last room is his room" (FF 23). The female narrator, who is also drawn to Malina's "space," is silenced and "murdered" at the close of the novel. For the female characters in *Todesarten*, Bluebeard's "last room" is a forbidden place. By entering the secret chamber, they uncover the murderous and destructive qualities of their own personal history and the events of a larger history—the Holocaust.

According to Bachmann's plans for her novel cycle, the character Malina, who was originally to have been the narrator for the unfinished *Todesarten*, plays an ambiguous and complex role in her work. In fragments concerning the figure of Malina, the character is portrayed as either female or male. In this context, Malina does not necessarily represent a purely *male* figure for Bachmann, as does Jordan. However, if Bluebeard's bloody chamber indeed represents knowledge, then Malina, unlike the female narrator, nonetheless holds the key to this knowledge. Jordan is a powerful character portrayed as a father, fascist, and colonizer, figures that intersect in the character of Bluebeard. Jordan, like Bluebeard, is portrayed as "evil" and "sick," so that Franza even describes the real-life serial killer Landru as a "lovable" criminal: "Yes, I believe that Bluebeard exists, and Landru must have been a klutz, a small, lovable criminal" (FF 409).[176]

In Bachmann's *Todesarten* and "Ein Schritt nach Gomorrah," the woman's dismemberment within the bloody chamber is not physical as in the traditional Bluebeard tale, but rather psychological. The female character finds herself caught in a trap in which Bluebeard leads her to the secret chamber by giving her the key, yet punishes her for entering the same. Bachmann's female characters always fail and lose in this situation. In *Der Fall Franza*, Jordan wants Franza to find the papers from her psychiatric case history in order to destroy her mentally and emotionally. Like the heroines of the Bluebeard tale, Franza finally comes to realize her husband's true plans: "I don't know if he already wanted it back then, that I should find the stuff, certainly later he wanted it. Also maybe only because I had already begun to find it" (FF 405). By making his wife into one of his psychiatric cases, Jordan invalidates, weakens, and subsequently destroys her. Franza's goal then becomes to overcome this invalidation, to get *out* of the bloody chamber and to get *into* the secret chamber of knowledge although she is destined to fail. Like the heroine in the German-language Bluebeard tale, Bachmann's female characters set out to expose the destructive and murderous relationships in which they are trapped, in other words, to open the door to the bloody chamber. However, because Bachmann's female characters are destroyed by the Bluebeard-like figures they associate with and are unable to save themselves from destruction, they have more in common with the murdered sisters in the Bluebeard tale. Just as the bride in Grimms' "Räuberbräutigam" reveals Bluebeard's crimes through the power of storytelling, Bachmann exposes the injustices and destructive patterns in personal relationships, society, and the Third Reich in her writing.

Bachmann's Personal History and the Third Reich

> *I want to tell the story, I will tell the story,*
> *nothing bothers me anymore in my memory.*
> Friedrich Hölderlin[177]

> *We must find true sentences.*
> Ingeborg Bachmann (WIR 19)

In her prose writings Bachmann exposes the crimes of the Holocaust such as the murder of the mentally ill in gas chambers by basing her accounts on her personal experiences as a child growing up in the Third Reich and as a young woman during the postwar years. When Hitler spoke from the balcony of the Hotel Sandwirt in Klagenfurt on April 5, 1938, Bachmann was in the hospital suffering from diphtheria.[178] Bachmann, who was twelve years old at the time, describes Hitler's troops marching into Carinthia on March 12 as the first traumatic experience of her childhood and, more importantly, as the "origin of her memory": "There was one particular moment that destroyed my childhood. When Hitler's troops marched into Klagenfurt. It was something so awful that my memory begins with this day: because of a premature suffering, such as I would never again experience so strongly. ... But this monstrous brutality that was felt, this shouting, singing and marching, the advent of my first mortal terror" (WIR 111).[179] Documents reveal that Hitler's troops were not the only individuals screaming and displaying brutality in the streets of Klagenfurt that day; thousands of Carinthian Nazis also greeted the tide of German troops.[180] It is the brutality, the roar of the crowds, the troops marching into her "peaceful Carinthia," as she calls this intrusion, that brings on Bachmann's first feelings of mortal fear.[181] In fact, it is precisely this moment in her experience of history that becomes a focal point in *Todesarten* and, more specifically, in *Der Fall Franza*. In her short story "Jugend in einer österreichischen Stadt," Bachmann describes the children's reaction to the entry of Hitler's troops as she experienced it as a child: "They cannot guess that their country is in the process of selling itself, and with it the skies above at which everyone is pulling until they tear apart and become a black hole" (JUG 88-89). In referring to experiences of her childhood, Bachmann once stated that a writer's youth is the most important chapter in her life, but that one only later realizes what one actually first observed (HIB 20).

The act of remembering and writing intersects with the memory of the historic events surrounding the Austro-fascist interregnum from 1934-1938 and the Nazi regime from 1938-1945 in Austria, becoming a process of "Vergangenheitsbewältigung." Coming to terms with the Nazi past was an important part of the literary program of writers born between 1920 and 1930 in Austria and Germany who were committed to creating a democratic and non-fascist future through their writings. The intellectual literary *Group 47*, of which Bachmann was a member, was composed mostly of writers painfully aware of the events of 1933-1945 and focused on many of the same anti-fascist programs of the Federal Republic of Germany, which included compensatory payments to victims of National Socialism and summary reparations to the State of Israel. Bachmann's prose explores National Socialism in fictional form both in terms of the personal relationships of her female narrators and in historical details such as gas chambers and the deportation of Jews. Her work should therefore be understood in the wider context of her participation in the politically active *Group 47*, bearing in mind that when asked about her involvement with this group, she was careful to emphasize her independence from this particular literary scene, calling their political involvement *less* than adequate.[182] In a 1964 interview Bachmann stated that "German writers, suspected of harboring radical, dangerous views, think, with few exceptions, so moderately that they would be considered thinking too little in any other country, like Italy or France" (WIR 50).

Bachmann's writings reflect popular public discussions concerning the Third Reich during the postwar era in Austria; however, she was one of the first authors to write about the Holocaust from the perspective of its victims. Judith Ryan's introduction to her essay collection *The Uncompleted Past. Feminism and Postwar German Novels and the Third Reich* (1983) points out the ambivalent anxiety in Germany and Austria during the 1950s concerning political continuity and an apathetic generation that threatened to blot out the past. It is during this time that the complex nature of individual responsibility came to be explored in West German literature as seen in the works of the *Group 47*, as well as in Austrian literature, where Bachmann was among the first to raise these issues. According to Ryan's summary of the evolution of postwar novels written in Germany and dealing with the Third Reich, the novel as a genre went through many stages in its reflection of National Socialism, as well as in its attempt to deal with this past.[183] Ryan writes that whereas earlier novels such as Thomas Mann's 1947 novel *Doktor Faustus* (Doctor Faustus) focused on Germany's mass guilt, later novels found a more critical approach in their reconstruction of the past. The misconception of a totally passive society overrun by oppressive Nazis was corrected by more accurate information. The 1950s and 1960s marked an ambivalent anxiety about inherent fascism in an apathetic generation that wished to forget the German past. For the most part, the position of the Nazis was explored and not that of the victims, such as Jews and the mentally ill, as Bachmann discusses in her novels. Ryan observes that German novels from the 1980s and 1990s deal with events of the Third Reich, without focusing on the fate of its victims. Ryan's exploration of the German novel, however, excludes other literary genres that do focus on the lives of Germans and Austrians who were victims of the Third Reich: autobiographies and biographies, which tend to be less popular with publishers and are not included in the traditional literary canon. [184]

When Bachmann's *Malina* was first published in 1971, critics complained that the novel did not depict historical reality and that it lacked any reference to historical problems. Bachmann, however, was well aware of the impact of history on literature, being well-read in many fields including, but certainly not exclusively, German literature, philosophy, psychology, and history. When asked in 1963 what she was reading at the time, Bachmann replied: "Many factual books, documentaries which deal with the last war and recent history; in general everything tends to deal with the understanding of history, the philosophy of history, and the writing of history" (WIR 42). Ten years later Bachmann would state that a writer could in fact not afford to write in a vacuum: "History is essential for a writer. One cannot write when one does not see the entire socio-historical relationship that has led to our present time" (WIR 133). The public which had first embraced Bachmann as a poet was highly critical of her new style and content in *Malina*, perhaps feeling somewhat uncomfortable about the way it dealt with the violent father-daughter relationship, mental illness, and the references to gas chambers. In fact, much of what Bachmann wrote concerning the Holocaust was never published during her lifetime. Bachmann discusses the Holocaust primarily in her unfinished work *Todesarten*, but also touches upon the question of victimization during the Holocaust in the short stories "Drei Wege zum See" (Three Paths to the Lake, 1972) and "Unter Mördern und Irren" (Among Murderers and Madmen, 1961). In *Malina*, the Bluebeard-like father figure takes on the role of a Nazi and murders his daughter in a gas chamber. In *Der Fall Franza*, in which Franza's husband Leo Jordan is repeatedly referred to as a fascist, Franza pays a visit to a Nazi doctor by whom she wants to be murdered in the same brutal manner as he had executed his victims in a euthanasia project during the Third Reich. In *Requiem für Fanny Goldmann*, Fanny's ex-husband, Harry Goldmann, is briefly described as a man who in his later years deals with his Jewish background by occasionally traveling to Israel and by studying Jewish history. The third person narrator describes how Fanny finds her ex-husband's recent interest in his Jewish heritage peculiar: "... that she was not accustomed to his preoccupation with Judaism and she had not known an Ernst [= Harry] Goldmann who was occupied with the history of Jews, actually nobody who had felt obliged or driven by their Jewishness, and that he wanted to go to the Eichmann trial ..." (FG 494). Bachmann incorporated many of the political discussions of her time concerning the Holocaust and events like the Eichmann trial in her works and was coming to terms with the historical events of the 1940s and 1950s in Austria by writing about them in her fiction. Although the last few decades have seen much published literature about the Holocaust and the Third Reich so that one has a frame of reference – if only partial – for these events, it is important to note that Bachmann herself did not have a popular discourse with which to discuss the Holocaust at the time she began writing *Todesarten* in the early 1960s. Bachmann's prose works are historical narratives in which "history" and "story" come together in the double meaning of the German term *Geschichte*. In her Frankfurter Vorlesung "Fragen und Scheinfragen" (Questions and Apparent Questions, 1960), Bachmann speaks, for instance, of the inseparable nature of literary creation and political awareness: "That poetry written outside of the historical situation exists is something most people will hardly believe anymore – that there is even one poet whose initial point of departure is not influenced by the times. In the best case, he can achieve two things: he can represent, represent his time, and represent something for which the time has not yet come" (FRA 196). Bachmann does the latter; she writes about topics "for which time had not come yet." She was ahead of her time in discussing the Holocaust through her narratives when Austrian society was not receptive to such discussions. Added to the absence of public discourse about the Holocaust was Bachmann's awareness of the difficulties of writing of a past so loaded with meaning and yet devoid of words with which to describe it. In her Frankfurt Lecture "Über Gedichte" (About Poems, 1959), Bachmann calls on Brecht's words to describe the timidity, uneasiness, and concern about form and expression in the poetry of postwar writers: "What times are these in which a discussion about trees is almost a crime because it includes a silence about so many crimes" (FRA 215).

A brief review of Hayden White's *The Content of the Form* (1987) shows how it is possible to read Bachmann's work in light of present perceptions of historical representations and documents of the Third Reich. In addressing both narratology and historiography, White raises valuable questions concerning the relation between narrative discourse and historical representation. He contests the view that narratives only become problematic when the author wishes to give real events the form of a story because the author's desire for "the imaginary, the possible, must contest with the imperatives of the real, the actual."[185] The important question becomes whether historical events can even be truthfully represented. Like Roland Barthes, White questions the "vaunted objectivity of traditional historiography."[186] White views historical narrative as testing the "capacity of a culture's fictions to endow real events with the kinds of meaning that literature displays to consciousness through its fashioning of patterns of 'imaginary' events."[187] Although narrative historiography may "novelize" historical processes, White contends that this is only an indicator that the truths represented by narrative history are of an order different from those of its social scientific counterpart."[188] Literary fiction becomes an allegory; in other words, a "transcodation," a transcription of the code of historical writing into a more literary code.[189] In this light, Bachmann's prose, especially *Todesarten* and her references to fairy tales, can be understood as works of literary fiction dedicated to coming to terms with the Third Reich. Her writing can therefore be read as literary history that seeks to uncover the role of National Socialism in Bachmann's personal life and voices her interest in and knowledge of the Holocaust. Bachmann's personal reference library of books and documents concerning Poland during World War II is just one indication of her profound concern for and knowledge of the horrors suffered by the victims of this country.[190]

Throughout her literary career Bachmann was politically involved and acted on her desire for world peace. She also participated in the *Group 47*, although she was not uncritical of some of their views. In a 1963 interview, Kuno Raeber asked Bachmann: "You have always been interested in politics. Is that still so?" She replied: "More than ever. And I believe that this interest must be noticeable in much of what I write and say, and in my actions" (WIR 43). Such "actions" are indeed evident throughout Bachmann's writing and speaking. In September 1965, Bachmann supported the Socialist Party in Germany (SPD) by attending their convention in Bayreuth together with Günter Grass and Hans Werner Henze. That same year, Bachmann wrote a letter to Simon Wiesenthal in Vienna, demonstrating her support for an extension of the statute of limitations for crimes under the Nazi regime, stating: "I believe it will suffice to mention my name."[191] In his 1989 memoir *Justice Not Vengeance*, Simon Wiesenthal remembers sending letters to 369 public figures in West Germany and Austria requesting reactions to the limitation law. Of the ninety percent who replied, all were against this law. Wiesenthal recalls that the public figures with whom he corresponded included Ingeborg Bachmann, Fritz Hochwälder, Erich Kästner, and Golo Mann. Wiesenthal collected their comments in his book *Term Expiry? 200 Public Figures Say No*, published by the Europäische Verlagsanstalt in 1965. Wiesenthal prefaced his book with a motto Robert Kennedy had sent him via telegram earlier that year: "moral duties have no terms." Wiesenthal believes that actions taken by individual authors and intellectuals like Bachmann "did something to help change the climate." He reports that "the Austrian government decided to abolish the limitation on the prosecution of murder, and Germany resolved to extend the term until 1979."[192] Taking a further political stand in December 1965,

Bachmann signed a declaration against the Vietnam War, of which act Heinrich Böll wrote: "One should not attempt to separate this type of courage and commitment from the great poet [Bachmann], because the one goes hand in hand with the other."[193] In the early 1970s, Bachmann turned her back on the Piper publishing house where her first works had been published, in protest over its attempt to include the poetic work "Requiem" by one of her favorite poets, Anna Achmatova, in the translations of the former Nazi author Hans Baumann. Bachmann had come to know Achmatova personally in the summer of 1964 and had dedicated the poem "Wahrlich" (Truly) to her later that year (HIB 141). In her poem "Wahrlich," Bachmann writes "To make just one sentence lasting/to persevere in the ding-dong of words.// Nobody writes this sentence/who doesn't sign it."[194] Bachmann believed very strongly that her writing should – as it did – reflect her introspective and empathetic concerns about the political situation of her times. In a 1963 interview with Kuno Raeber, Bachmann stated that "writing without risks" "is to have an insurance contract with a literature that doesn't pay" (WIR 40). In her Anton-Wildgans-award speech, Bachmann reminded readers that it was not an author's task to change the world, but to not let oneself become corrupted by empty clichés and phrases. She felt that a writer's duty was to "destroy the clichés" in order to create a literature that was able to "stand on its own" (RED 297). Bachmann wrote that it was impossible for her not to have a heart and not to feel: "If that doesn't belong together, then there can be no more literature" (HIB 155). It was Bachmann's insistence in writing "true sentences" (wahre Sätze) "with heart" that led Thomas Bernhard to cast Bachmann as the protagonist Maria in his 1986 novel *Auslöschung*. The first-person narrator proclaims Maria/Bachmann "my even then greatest poet"[195] and writes: "in her poems she is one hundred percent. … In each line she writes, she is whole, everything comes from her."[196]

It was, however, Bachmann's visit to Poland in May 1973 that changed the way she wrote and spoke about the past. In interviews Bachmann expressed interest in and showed that she was informed about the extermination of Jews in Poland under the Nazi regime. In a 1973 Warsaw radio interview, Bachmann spoke to Alicja Walcka-Kowalska about her large collection of data concerning events in Poland from 1939 to 1945. *Malina* had been published in 1971 two years earlier, and a large part of *Todesarten* had been written in which she had referred to the Holocaust. However, according to Bachmann, her visits to Auschwitz and Birkenau had rendered her speechless: "And I visited Auschwitz and Birkenau. One can't be helped when one knows, because in that instant when one is standing there everything is so very different. I can't speak about it because it is really ... there is really nothing to say. Earlier it would have been possible to speak about it, but since I have seen it, I think, I can't anymore ..." (WIR 131). The pauses and loss of words in Bachmann's statement reflect the difficulty she experienced in describing her visit to Auschwitz. Bachmann was, however, able to talk about the Holocaust in interviews while at the same time stating that she could not. In a later interview in Warsaw with Karol Sauerland in May, 1973, Bachmann describes the horror and speechlessness she experienced during her reading trip to Poland:

> I have read documents ... and here, where I am in Poland for the first time, I have fitful dreams and nightmares. Because it is something different from when one reads documents about Auschwitz or Birkenau ... I have requested to drive there. To be there is something other than to read about it. I have a large library with documentaries, and also about Warsaw. I don't even know how one can live with that. Because the other countries, which certainly experienced many hardships, like Italy, Yugoslavia, Greece, or France, which I have seen, can't even be compared to Poland. There is nothing to say about it. It is truly, it renders one speechless. (WIR 142)

At the time of her trip, Bachmann was mourning both the death of her close friend and Holocaust survivor Paul Celan, who had taken his life in 1970, as well as the death of her father, who had died in March 1973. Her attempts to come to terms with the events and consequences of National Socialism were marked by the inner destruction that had already taken its toll on her physical and mental health.[197] As if the deaths of her female protagonists in *Todesarten* foreshadowed her own fate, Bachmann's life ended tragically in October 1973.

Bachmann's Relationship to German-speaking Jewish Writers and Intellectuals

> *Bronnen: "Ingeborg Bachmann, how do you, as a writer, arrive at your experiences?"*
> *Bachmann: "One has them, without wanting them, through observations, through relationships with people, through oneself."*
> Ingeborg Bachmann (WIR 120)

Many Holocaust survivors, historians, and scholars are critical of individuals who write of the Holocaust without having experienced such suffering firsthand. Although Bachmann herself was not a victim of the Holocaust, she maintained close relationships with people whose lives and literary work reflected their experiences in the Holocaust. Bachmann cultivated friendships and literary and epistolary dialogues with several German-speaking Jewish writers and intellectuals including Theodor Adorno, Jean Améry, Hannah Arendt, Paul Celan, Wolfgang Hildesheimer, Milo Dor, Gerschom Scholem, and Nelly Sachs throughout her writing career and lifetime.[198] The following documents Bachmann's relationship with some of those authors with whom she was intellectually and emotionally bound. These exchanges demonstrate why she was inquisitive and well-informed about the Holocaust, and, more importantly, why she addressed this subject in her fiction before other authors of her time.

Although the details of Bachmann and Paul Celan's relationship may never be made public, the impact of his works and the
influence of his friendship on her writings can be traced throughout
her narratives.[199] The numerous letters exchanged between Bachmann and Celan are inaccessible to the public: eighty-six letters
from Bachmann to Celan, written between 1949 and 1962, are kept
at the German Literature Archive in Marbach, Germany, and
letters from Celan to Bachmann are held in the *Handschriftenab-
teilung* of the Austrian National Library in Vienna, Austria (HIB
61). Nevertheless, the poetic dialogue between Celan and Bachmann pervades much of her prose and is most evident in *Malina*.
The italicized Kagran tale in *Malina* clearly pays homage to
Celan's poetry and prose, as well as to his friendship. Bachmann
engages in a poetic dialogue throughout the tale by citing directly
from Celan's poetic works *Der Sand aus den Urnen* (Sand from
the Urns, 1948) and *Mohn und Gedächtnis* (Poppy and Memory,
1952). Literary references to that part of Celan's work, in which he
attempts to come to terms with his experiences during the Holocaust, are woven into Bachmann's Kagran tale and dream narratives referring to the Holocaust throughout *Malina*. Bachmann's
line "They told each other of darkness and light" in *Malina*, for
instance, refers to Celan's line "we tell each other of darkness"
from his poem "Corona" (1952), which in turn makes allusions to
Bachmann's poem "Dunkles zu sagen" (Telling of Darkness) from
1952.[200]

The Bukovinian Jew Paul Antschel, who later changed his
family name to Celan, grew up in a German-Jewish family in
Czernowitz, formerly part of the Austro-Hungarian empire, now
Romania. His double allegiance to the German language and to his
Jewish identity was problematic for him throughout his lifetime.
In 1941 Celan pleaded with his parents to go into hiding with him
when it became clear that Jews were being deported from
Czernowitz. When he went ahead without them, expecting them to
follow, Celan learned the next morning that his family had been
deported. He would later make the gruesome discovery that they
had been forcefully taken to death camps, where his father died of

typhoid fever and his mother was shot to death. In 1942 Celan was sent to a forced labor camp along with 30,000 other Jews; however, because he was young and able to work, he was later sent to one of the Romanian labor detachments. When the Soviets reconquered his city in 1944, Celan was able to escape and make his way across the border through Budapest to Vienna, where he lived from 1947-1948. It is during this time that Celan began his friendship with Viennese writers and artisans such as Bachmann, Otto Basil, Edgar Jené, and Milo Dor. Dor described Celan's arrival in Vienna and wrote of his need to write about his experiences during the Holocaust: "While German intellectuals discussed whether or not it was even possible to write poetry after Auschwitz, this young man, who had only escaped Auschwitz by chance, wrote poems full of dark tones and an incredible strength, which can only emanate from someone who has lived on the brink of death."[201] Bachmann met Celan on May 16, 1948, in the apartment of the Surrealist painter and *Plan* editor, Edgar Jené. She wrote to her parents that her room had been "filled with poppies" the next day (HIB 57). Celan's first volume of poetry, *Der Sand aus den Urnen* (Sand from the Urns), was published in Vienna in 1948, after he had already moved to Paris. Because this edition was riddled with errors, Celan republished half of the poems along with more recent ones in his second volume of poetry, *Mohn und Gedächtnis* (Poppy and Memory), published in Germany in 1952 (HIB 57-58). Celan's personal copy of *Mohn und Gedächtnis* makes evident through hand-written notations by the author that approximately twenty poems were addressed to Bachmann (HIB 59).[202]

In 1948 Celan moved to Paris where he became world-renowned for his poetry and prose. From October of 1950 to February of 1951 Bachmann visited Paris to be with Celan. Höller states that she must have realized the hopelessness of their relationship, for she wrote to Hans Weigel that she and Celan "did not leave one another room to breathe," "for unknown demonic reasons" (HIB 65). After their final meeting in Zurich in 1960, Celan wrote in a letter to Max Frisch that there was something "inexpressible" and "intangible" between them. Celan wrote, "We probably touch upon this when we write" (HIB 64). After suffering from severe depressions that worsened over the years, Celan took his life by drowning himself in the Seine in April of 1970. In reaction to his death, Günter Grass wrote about the effect the Holocaust had on Celan's life and work: "Why Paul Celan's words grew more sparse and his language and existence amounted to narrowness? I don't know why. Today I seem to believe that he, the survivor, could no longer deal with his survival after Auschwitz and finally could no longer tolerate it. I am indebted to Paul Celan for so much: impulse, contradiction, the notion of loneliness, but also the realization that Auschwitz has no end."[203] Both Dor and Grass came to realize that Celan lived and wrote in the memory of Auschwitz. Bachmann's relationship with Celan, who had physically survived and yet not *survived* Auschwitz, added to her need to address the Holocaust after 1945.

Another friend and poet who played a vital role in Bachmann's confrontation with the history of the Holocaust was Nelly Sachs. Bachmann's understanding and concern for the persecuted Jew during the Third Reich was greatly influenced by her friendship with Sachs, whom she met in person together with Paul Celan during a reading trip to Zurich and Meersburg in 1960. Sachs, a German-Jewish writer born in Berlin in 1891, began writing as a child. With the help of friends, she and her mother were able to flee Germany to Stockholm in 1940, where Sachs remained in exile until her death on May 12, 1970. Although Sachs, like Bachmann, did not experience the Holocaust personally, she was affected by this tragedy emotionally and incorporated her anguished reactions to these events in her literary work, which deals primarily with the Holocaust. Celan and Sachs were mutual admirers of each others' poetic works and maintained a strong friendship for over sixteen years until her death. Bachmann first read of Sachs' work sometime before 1957, when Celan selected a few of Sachs' poems to be published in Princess Marguerita Caetani's literary magazine *Botteghe Oscure* in Rome, for which Bachmann and Celan were both guest editors. A letter from the spring of 1960 from Celan to Sachs was destroyed by Sachs at Celan's request. One can only speculate that Celan wanted Sachs to keep his relationship with Bachmann from becoming public knowledge. All letters and telegrams from May through the summer of 1960 were also not made available for the published collection of letters between Celan and Sachs.[204] Bachmann's friendship with Celan and Sachs gave her personal insight and understanding of the Holocaust, which she transformed into a literary history of the Third Reich woven into her novel cycle *Todesarten*.

The Holocaust survivor and poet Jean Améry also influenced Bachmann's work immensely. His work affected the way in which Bachmann dealt with the concept of victimization in her writings. Both authors questioned and probed the situation of the victim in their writings. Améry, who had never met Bachmann personally, felt a certain kinship (Schicksalsgemeinschaft) with the Austrian author after reading about himself in Bachmann's short story "Drei Wege zum See," upon which he composed two essays concerning the short story and later, her early death. In an essay about Bachmann, Améry wrote: "It was no mistake: because shortly thereafter I discovered the part in which she spoke about an 'Austrian with a French name living in Belgium' who had written something about torture. At first she had wanted to write to the man, but she had let it be because she asked herself: 'What should I have written him?'"[205] According to the sparse biographical information available, Bachmann was mourning Celan when she wrote "Drei Wege zum See," published in the collection *Simultan* in 1972. In this short story, the Jewish-Austrian character Trotta – whom the main character Elisabeth describes as her first and only true love – unexpectedly kills himself after their separation. The narrative revolves around Elisabeth's coming to terms with her lover's unexpected suicide. Elisabeth comes to better understand Trotta's role as victim when she discovers Jean Améry's essay "Die Tortur" (The Torture), in which Améry discusses the survival of his spirit despite torture by the Nazis. Irene Heidelberger-Leonard asserts that Bachmann based the character Trotta on Améry's life and wrote "Drei Wege zum See" in response to his essay.[206] She nonetheless cautions readers that creating a parallel between a person forced to go into exile because otherwise he will be murdered by Nazis (Améry) and another who chooses exile because of random circumstances (the character Trotta) is highly problematic.[207] Perhaps it is not necessary to say that Trotta is modeled on one or the other real-life poet, Améry or Celan, or even on Joseph Roth's character Trotta from *Kapuzinergruft* (The Capuchin Tomb). Instead, it should be acknowledged that Bachmann understood the ambivalence and crisis experienced by people like Sachs, Celan, and Améry who struggled with their Jewish-European identities. In Bachmann's "Drei Wege zum See," the protagonist Elisabeth views Améry's essay as expressing a truth journalists and Holocaust victims had not been able to discuss. Elisabeth does not state precisely to what truth she is referring. However, from the conversations between Trotta and Elisabeth, it becomes clear that the situation of the postwar victim is being discussed. Améry's essay "Die Tortur" precisely describes the situation of the victim, which is then brought up in Bachmann's "Drei Wege zum See." After being silent about the Holocaust for over twenty years, Améry explored the fate of intellectuals in Auschwitz in "Über den Geist in einer Grenzsituation" (About the Soul in an Extreme Situation). Améry, who had been arrested for his involvement in the Belgian resistance movement, was tortured by the Nazis at Fort Breendonk in Belgium, a treatment he viewed as the "essence" of the Third Reich, calling the pain of torture "the existential shock of the first blow."[208] In 1977, however, eleven years after having written "Die Tortur," Améry began to perceive his situation as a victim of the Holocaust and as a Jew in a markedly different way. It is only after realizing that his situation could not simply be summarized by the description "Naziopfer" (Nazi victim) that he came to understand the ambivalence of being Jewish and of having been a victim of the Holocaust: "... only when I reached the end, and thought about the compulsion and impossibility of being Jewish, did I find myself in the image of the *Jewish* victim."[209] The terms "compulsion" and "impossibility" of being Jewish also capture Bachmann's perception and description of the ambiguous position women hold in society as depicted in *Todesarten*, for instance. Once again, fiction and history collided in the double meaning of the term *Geschichte:* Améry took his own life in Salzburg on October 17, 1978, six years after Bachmann wrote "Drei Wege zum See," and, as Höller observed, on the fifth anniversary of her death (HIB 161).

Bachmann also corresponded with the philosopher Gerschom Scholem (1897-1982), who in 1967 dedicated a poem to Bachmann, "An Ingeborg Bachmann nach ihrem Besuch im Ghetto von Rom" (To Ingeborg Bachmann Following Her Visit to the Ghetto of Rome). Scholem had responded to Bachmann twelve years after her essay "Was ich in Rom sah und hörte" (What I Saw and Heard in Rome) was published in the literary magazine *Akzente* in 1955. Sigrid Weigel traced Scholem's poem to the collection of his posthumous works at the Jewish National and University Library in Jerusalem after discovering a reference to it in a letter Scholem sent to Siegfried Unseld. This discovery confirmed Weigel's suspicion that "Bachmann's relationship to Scholem was more personal" than was previously thought (WIB 5-6). In a brief passage about the ghetto in Rome, Bachmann observes: "In Rome I saw, in the ghetto, that nothing is definite yet," (ROM 30) to which Scholem responds in a poem: "In the ghetto you saw, what not everyone sees/and what is easily forgotten out there:/that nothing that happens has been fulfilled completely/nothing is definate yet//" (WIB 9-10). Bachmann describes a festival near the synagogue, a feast of food and music. She writes that the elderly remember their friends who were saved only to be murdered: "when they were bought free, the trucks drove up anyway, and they never came back" (ROM 30). When the "grandchildren," whom Bachmann thereby defines as the future generation of surviving Jews, dance among the tables in front of the musicians, one child calls out "Keep playing!" In describing the violinist who pales and stops playing for a measure (ROM 30) Bachmann employs a much-repeated phrase, used to admonish musicians in death camps. The fact that the musician returns to his playing after a measure and that the children continue to dance illustrates a more optimistic perception of the aftermath of the Holocaust; a position she would be more critical of in her later work. Scholem's poem reflects a loss of hope for his Jewish community: "we lived in the cracks of history: that which never completely comes to a close, has protected us." He concludes his poem by asserting that the messianic message of Judaism is no longer valid after the Shoah; that the message "arrived at the ghetto too late," that the "hour of redemption has past" (WIB 10). A decade after formulating her thoughts about the effects of the atrocities committed during the Holocaust on the lives of the survivors, Bachmann would write in greater detail about the Holocaust, the concept of the "victim," forgiveness, and redemption in her *Todesarten* novel cycle and her short story "Unter Mördern und Irren." Günter Grass' statement "We cannot get past Auschwitz"[210] holds true for Celan, Sachs, Améry, Scholem, as well as for each reader of Bachmann's work.

Writing History: Bachmann's Relationship to the German Language

> *Germany is Hitler and Hitler is Germany!*
> Rudolf Hess, Nuremberg
> Rally, 1934.[211]

> *I am a corpse who wanders ...//I with the*
> *German language/this cloud around me/that*
> *I keep as a house/I drift through all*
> *languages//oh how it grows dark/the dark-*
> *ness, the sound of rain/only a few fall//*
> Ingeborg Bachmann, "Exil"[212]

Throughout her career as a writer, Bachmann struggled with the fact that the language in which she wrote against fascism belonged to the same Germany she saw intimately connected with Hitler. Bachmann's ambivalence towards the German language can be traced to her aversion to Germany and its Nazi past: the

Germany that had "invaded" her supposed peaceful Carinthia. Interviews with Bachmann in the 1970s illustrate her idyllic view of Austria and her naive belief in its status as a victim of German National Socialism. Even after having written *Malina* and much of *Der Fall Franza*, Bachmann retained her belief in Austria's innocence during the war. The belief that Austria was a victim of Hitler's aggression was called a "Geschichtslüge" (historical lie) by German-speaking historians in the 1980s.[213] For Bachmann, the difference between Austria and Germany was not so much a matter of physical borders but rather a question of different cultural languages, which are marked by a set of socio-cultural codes. Of Austria with its "political and cultural individuality" (WIR 11), she states: "The Austrians have participated in so many cultures and have developed another sense of the world compared to the Germans" (WIR 12). Bachmann later went on to make the problematic statement that the destruction of Poland would have never entered the minds of Austrians: "However, the way it ended, I believe, would have never occurred to an Austrian, to have thoughts like the Germans" (WIR 132), a critique especially paradoxical – if not absurd – if one recalls that Hitler himself was Austrian by birth and that many Austrians supported National Socialism. Bachmann is, however, in a double bind because she has to write in her native German, the language of her supposed enemies: "For a long time I have seen the difficulty within myself of writing in German, of being placed in a relationship with Germany only through this language, but left to a wealth of experiences, a wealth of sentiments of another region. I am from Austria, from a small country, to express it subtly, that has removed itself from history and which has an overwhelming and monstrous past" (WIR 63-64). It is not clear in this passage whether Bachmann's description of Austria's "overwhelming and monstrous past" refers to the Austro-Hungarian Empire, Austria's role during the Third Reich, or both. Bachmann writes in the language that both restricts her in binding her to a fascist past and gives her the ability to express her realization of this double bind.[214] She locates the origin of this language in the Bluebeard-like father figure, one that is inseparable from the fascist past and one whose language carries these fascist structures. Jordan, the Bluebeard figure in *Der Fall Franza*, is just one of the father figures in *Todesarten* who embodies fascism. Not only does Bachmann find it difficult to write about her experienced past, but she also finds it almost perverse to employ the language which she has inherited from her parents and her country of origin, one whose culture she believes made the events of the Third Reich possible.

Added to Bachmann's critical observations about her native German language was her dependent yet critical relationship to the German literary and publishing scene which began when she joined the German writers of *Group 47*, and began publishing her works with Suhrkamp and Piper. On June 13, 1953, during a reading trip through Germany, Bachmann was quoted in the German newspaper *Münchner Abendzeitung* as saying that she wanted to live as a freelance author and perhaps move to Germany (WIB 268). Bachmann's two thousand DM poetry award from *Group 47* in May 1953 and the three hundred DM she received for reading eleven poems on the air for the NWDR Hamburg radio station marked the beginning of her career as a freelance author and her relationship with the German literary scene. Weigel, who succinctly states that in Bachmann's memory "literary enterprise and Germany were identical" (WIB 270), points out that Austria did not even acknowledge the young author until a year after she had already been heralded a literary star in Germany (WIB 276). Weigel portrays Bachmann both as an author caught between the competing publishing enterprises of Austria and West Germany and as a young female writer among older male publishers. More importantly, Weigel notes that the literary scenes of Germany and Austria dealt very differently with those Jewish intellectuals and writers who returned after the war from exile or imprisonment. Whereas Germany did not pay much attention to exile literature after 1945, Jewish Austrian authors, such as Hans Weigel who returned to Vienna from Swiss exile in 1945, played a vital role in the Austrian literary and publishing world (WIB 276-278). Reflecting on her first impressions of Germany, Bachmann wrote in 1961: "On the second day I wanted to leave because a conversation which made assumptions I did not understand suddenly led me to believe that I had stumbled upon German Nazis" (WIB 280). Despite Bachmann's dependence on Germany's *Group 47*, the German media that spread her fame, and German publishers such as Piper who supported her work, she remained "suspicious" (WIB 279) of a country she thought synonymous with the Third Reich.

Bachmann's Association of Women with Jews

Bachmann's role as a woman writer, scholar, and intellectual during the Third Reich and in postwar Austria is reflected in her depictions of women throughout her fictional work, especially in the novel cycle *Todesarten*. She uses the Bluebeard tale as a trope for women's experiences during this time by portraying the father figure as an all-powerful, sadistic fascist. As an author, Bachmann perceived herself restricted both as an individual and as an independent author by a society she felt to be male-dominated, a sentiment shared by the female narrator in *Malina*.

Issues facing women in postwar Austria provide a background for Bachmann's portrayal of women's roles in her prose. Universal suffrage in 1918 marked the beginning of political equality for Austrian women who received Equal Rights Status in 1920. After the National Socialist motto "Frau zurück ins Haus" (Woman return home) of the fascist 1930s, women were pushed into agriculture as well as the war industry during the war. Following the annexation in 1938, only ten percent of women were allowed to be part of the university student population, and Austrian girls were placed in government-regulated girls' grammar schools.[215] The focus of the education of girls and young women was primarily on preparing them to care for the home and the family. During a "mandatory year," young women had to complete an unpaid year of working in agriculture, assisting large families, or fulfilling duties in the households of high-ranking National Socialists.[216]

The period of postwar reconstruction after Austria declared itself a neutral country on October 26, 1955 saw little change in women's roles. Many laws were passed that further fixed women's position as mothers and wives. One can imagine that a woman like Bachmann, who had received a doctoral degree in Philosophy from the University of Vienna in 1950 and who scorned marriage, did not find much support in her desire to become a financially independent freelance writer.[217]

Bachmann, however, was not the only woman author to make observations about women's roles, socialization, and language shortly after World War II. Because of their similar experiences as freelance women authors during the postwar years, it is not surprising that one finds striking similarities between the work of Bachmann and that of the American poet Sylvia Plath (1932-1963). Both Bachmann and Plath write about to the fascist father figure, the woman as a victim of a patriarchal society, and the woman writer suffering from mental illness. It is of note, therefore, that Bachmann owned both the 1968 German translation of *The Bell Jar* (1963) and an English edition of *Ariel* (1961) in her personal library.[218] Plath's ambivalent daughter-writer relationship with her father is reflected in the character Esther Greenwood in *The Bell Jar*. The novel refers often to the German heritage of Plath's mother and father, the father's early death, and her brother's fluency in German. Living in the postwar era, Plath was faced with the complex and problematic history of her German heritage and discussed her ambiguous relationship to the German language in her fiction. The character Esther reveals her disgust with German culture: "What I didn't say was that each time I picked up a German dictionary or a German book, the very sight of those dense, black, barbed-wire letters made my mind shut like a clam."[219] For Plath, women especially were victims of society in much the same way that Jews had been victims in the Third Reich. Her poem "Daddy" associates femininity with Jewishness: "I never could talk to you./The tongue stuck in my jaw.//It stuck in a barb wire snare./Ich, ich, ich, ich,/I could hardly speak./I thought every German was you./And the language obscene//An engine, an engine/Chuffing me off like a Jew./A Jew to Dachau, Auschwitz, Belsen./I began to talk like a Jew./I think I may be a Jew."[220] In Plath's poem "Lady Lazarus" the female narrator identifies with a Jew: "A sort of walking miracle, my skin/Bright as a Nazi lampshade,/My right foot//A paperweight,/My face a featureless, fine/Jew linen."[221] The female speaker of the poem becomes the Jew who has been murdered and whose body has been turned into what are normally considered objects of beauty. However, the female narrator also assumes the position of the Nazi who sees the beauty of these "objects," the fine linens and paperweights. Although Bachmann had already written much of *Der Fall Franza* and *Malina* by the time the translation of *The Bell Jar, Die Glasglocke,* was published, the similarities are striking, yet not unusual for the situation of postwar women authors with an awareness of recent European history. In 1968 Bachmann wrote an essay on *Die Glasglocke*, in which she does not discuss the role of the father and language but praises instead Plath's portrayal of mental illness and depression, describing her own reaction to the book as "alarming" and "shocking."[222] Like Plath, Bachmann projected the father figure onto the whole of male-oriented society. Bachmann once said in an interview that male-female relationships were fascist by nature: "Fascism is the first thing in a relationship between a man and a woman" (WIR 144). Both Bachmann and Plath saw their femininity as confined within patriarchal boundaries and restricted by their roles as women, which they perceived as stable and fixed gender roles. The Bluebeard-like father figure is also viewed as the source of language for both writers, carrying with it fascist structures.

Bachmann's references to National Socialism in *Todesarten* raise questions about the validity of such parallels. If Bachmann equates women with Jews in these passages, then can the extermination of over six million victims murdered for their alleged otherness within western European culture – a culture to which Bachmann belonged – be compared to an abusive relationship? Does this comparison not negate the significance of the human tragedy of the Holocaust? The specificity of such a collective and

individual destruction becomes diminished, even loses its singu-
larity, when linked to an intimate act of destruction, such as that
between father and daughter, Franza and Jordan, Fanny and Marek.
By referring to the murder of Jews in her discussion of the
Holocaust, Bachmann also excludes countless other victims of the
National Socialist regime, such as homosexuals and Gypsies. Her
portrayal of the father figure and Bluebeard as the fascist and the
woman as the persecuted Jew in her fictional work must therefore
be read in the context of the psychoanalytic tradition in which such
arguments have been made.

The following discussion is critical for understanding Bachmann's use of the Bluebeard tale in her work as a means of
exploring issues of power and gender. The conclusion Bachmann
draws concerning the desire for women and Jews to be viewed as
victims is disturbing to contemporary readers. Bachmann equates
women with Jews in their position as victims within society, thus
placing the responsibility of victimhood on the victim instead of on
the aggressor. Such an association can easily be misconstrued after
the Holocaust for the very reason that women were never murdered
as a cultural group like the Jews. Early psychoanalysts, for instance
Otto Weininger, Otto Rank and Bruno Bettelheim – who were also
German-speaking Jews – drew parallels between Jews and women
in their works with which Bachmann was familiar when she began
writing her novel cycle *Todesarten*. Her psychology studies in
Vienna from 1946 to 1950 and her internship at the well-known
mental institution *Steinhof* outside of Vienna provided the author
with a formal knowledge of the history and theory of psychoanalysis grounded in the Viennese tradition beginning with Freud,
a tradition which would inform her views concerning women's
position in society.

Although Walther Rathenau had stressed the feminine nature
of the Jew in his 1897 essay "Höre, Israel!" (Listen, Israel!),[223]
Otto Weininger, in *Geschlecht und Charakter* (*Sex and Character*)
published in Vienna in 1903, was the first psychoanalyst to
associate women with Jews as victims of society. For Weininger,
Judaism was a tradition he described as "nur eine Geistesrichtung"

(only an intellectual direction).[224] IIis unflattering views of women are almost legendary, as the following statements exemplify: "a woman of the highest social standing is still far beneath a man of the lowest social standing"[225] and "the largest, the only enemy of women's emancipation is woman herself."[226] In his third chapter concerning Judaism, Weininger summarizes the similarities between Jews and women. Here he holds that both the Jew and the woman lack personality, hold together in groups, function as matchmakers, cannot distinguish the good from the bad, and have no self-esteem.[227] Yet Weininger also writes that whereas women always believe in "their man" and "their child," the Jew does not believe in anything. Jewish women in particular, he argues, capture the "essence" (Idee) of the woman, and Jews and women relate to one another as a "genus" (Gattung).[228] Weininger perhaps speaks of his own fears when he claims that mankind hates what it fears in itself.[229]

In his later work *Taschenbuch* (Paperback, 1919), Weininger continues his tirade: "Hatred against women is still unresolved hatred against one's own sexuality."[230] He further describes women as "lusty" and Jews as "lascivious," yet "less potent" than the "Aryan man."[231] Weininger clearly illustrates the phenomenon of Jewish self-hatred in his own work, a sentiment originating in the hatred of "others" within society. Bachmann's writing is influenced by Weininger's discussion about the "fear of the other." For instance, while Jordan demonstrates hatred for Franza in *Der Fall Franza*, she comes to realize that it is precisely her "otherness" that he desires to extinguish: "Why was I so hated? No, not me, the otherness in me, ..." (FF 400). This otherness seems to be related to Jordan's fear of his own sexuality. While he is threatened by Franza's sexuality, one that he observes in her desire for "English kisses," he abhors and fears this sexuality within himself. Sander Gilman views such self-hatred as the result of accepting the values, social structures, and attitudes of the determining group, in this case views of Austrian society. Gilman does not consider Weininger's association of women and Jews unusual since, as he points out, both Jews and women were becoming more visible on the horizon of European consciousness in the late nineteenth century through their articulated demands for legal and cultural emancipation.[232] Therefore, Bachmann's search for cultural emancipation for women underlies her association of Jews and women in her fiction.

Otto Rank's first book in English, *Beyond Psychology,* published in 1941, also compares women to Jews, and it stresses as well the dominance of the father. Rank's observation of the importance of the father figure in the Judaic tradition can be seen also in Bachmann's portrayal of the father figure in the lives of her women characters in *Todesarten*: "The overwhelming importance of the father, likewise a characteristic of Jewish tradition and mentality, represents the rational aspect of Freudian psychology, whereas the vital relationship to the mother is conceived of as merely an 'infantile' fixation."[233] Although Rank views both Freud's and Weininger's view of women as derogatory because they are based on what he describes "the outgrowth of the patriarchal attitude in the Old Testament," he claims that women "suffered from the very beginning a fate similar to that of the Jew, namely, suppression, slavery, confinement, and subsequent persecution...."[234] Rank traces the analogy of women to Jews to the tradition of Freudian psychology – a tradition that also informed Bachmann's work – which projects a specific Jewish psychology upon the woman "who therefore is depicted as enslaved, inferior, castrated ...."[235] Rank states that it was the Jew who "invented" the first psychology as an explanation of evil in human beings, and further, that it is the Jew who took over the "curse" of being persecuted for all human evils from women, who had historically played the role of scapegoat. Rank traces the "feminine" fate of the Jews to Freud's psychoanalytic tradition: "What Freud attempted unconsciously in his ideology therefore was the projection of those feminine characteristics of the Jew upon the woman, thereby achieving a kind of therapeutic self-healing for the Jewish race."[236]

Bachmann was well read in the Viennese psychoanalytic tradition of Weininger and Freud and familiar with Rank's works which she had in her personal library at the time she was writing

Todesarten. Though she was neither the first nor last author to equate the father figure with a fascist,[237] Bachmann likens her female characters to Jewish Holocaust victims in order to illustrate their murder by the Bluebeard-like father figure. For Bachmann, the father figure and Bluebeard are metaphors for a society dominated by men who control the definition of women and measure the "other," the feminine, using their own self-image as the standard.

James Young shows how the Holocaust affected and informed writers such as Bachmann and Plath and how they would come to perceive their world and society. Young's discussion of the representation of the Holocaust in Plath's work applies to Bachmann's writings as well: "... rather than disputing the authenticity of [Plath's] figures, we might look at her poetry for the ways the Holocaust has entered public consciousness as a trope, and how it informs both the poet's view of the world and her representation of it in verse."[238] Bachmann's work should therefore be read within a socio-historical context in which her portrayal of women as Jews is understood as a reflection of her view of postwar Europe, however problematic this may be for today's reader.

Bachmann's Prose in the Context of Fictional Accounts of the Holocaust

> *And when one asks which tasks an author has – those are usually very rhetorical questions – then I would always say: to bring or pull people into the experiences that writers have and that are taken away from them by the dangerous development of this modern world.*
> Ingeborg Bachmann (WIR 140)

Bachmann's references to the Holocaust in her prose raise many critical questions: What compelled the gentile author Bachmann to equate her main female characters with Jewish and mentally ill victims exterminated in gas chambers and to write about her characters in a way that associated them with the Holocaust? Moreover, how is the character Franza linked to the Holocaust by seeking out a doctor, a former Nazi in the euthanasia project of the Third Reich, to give her the lethal shot that he once forced upon his "patients?" Finally, in which way is the Holocaust linked to Franza's gradual "murder" by her husband and society as illustrated by Bachmann's reference to the Bluebeard tale? Bachmann's allusions to the Bluebeard figure in her literary work are metaphors for patriarchy as well as Nazi domination. Although her literary work was transformed by her own experiences of war and her reactions to the Holocaust, Bachmann's writings have generally not been read in this historical context. The following shows that her fictional work holds an important place in German-language literature after 1945 precisely because of its discussion of the Holocaust.

Berel Lang's collection of essays about Holocaust narratives focuses solely on novels and works written by Jewish authors and historians and does not deal with non-Jewish writers. Where then does a work such as Bachmann's fit into the discussion of Holocaust historiography and fictional narrative? Taking into account Theodor Adorno's much quoted statement that it is barbaric to write poetry after Auschwitz,[239] one must ask whether or not it is also barbaric to write about the Holocaust. Was Adorno perhaps not referring to the inability to write poetic works after the barbaric act of the Holocaust just as Bachmann spoke of her own inability to write after her visit to Poland in 1973? Berel Lang raises the important question whether "the enormity of the Holocaust [is] at all capable of literary representation."[240] Günter Grass, in response to Adorno, perhaps answers this question in his essay "Schreiben nach Auschwitz" (Writing after Auschwitz): "Auschwitz will never be understood, even though it is oppressed by explainable words."[241] Despite the fact that the horrible crimes committed during the Holocaust remain exceedingly difficult to grasp by any imagination, Grass nonetheless saw the need to address the issue of the Holocaust in writing: "There is no promise that writing will end after Auschwitz unless mankind gives up on itself."[242]

Lang's anthology of essays concerns the writing of Holocaust narratives, although certain objections are raised about this practice by its authors and editor. According to Lang, writings about the Holocaust often presuppose a definition of the historical or moral uniqueness of the Holocaust while that definition is still in question. Second, generalizations about the Holocaust, discussing traditional artistic, critical, or ethical themes in the narrative, diminish or obscure the moral significance of the event. Finally, Lang fears that writing *about* this event may lead many readers to distance themselves from the subject of the Holocaust itself.[243] James Young cautions that not only writing about the Holocaust, but also interpreting these narratives, threatens to "supplant the horrible events at the heart of our inquiry."[244] Young makes a case for a critical historiography of the Holocaust in which one explores both the plurality of meanings that these texts generate and the actions that issue from the meanings outside these texts.[245] Lawrence Langer, in his introduction to a collection of essays concerning Holocaust narratives, *Preempting the Holocaust*, cautions that the "Holocaust reality limits rather than liberates the vision of the writer, historian, or artist who ventures to represent it" and states that incorporating the Holocaust "into our moral or historical intuitions about past *or* future remains a challenge to the modern intelligence."[246] Langer insists that readers not search for meaning in what he so aptly calls the "disabling outburst of un-reason we name the Holocaust" and states that literalist discourse about the Holocaust "has the grace to acknowledge that we learn nothing from the misery it finds there."[247] There is, however, a consensus in Lang's collection of essays that in writing an author is acting against a threatening silence, a silence that would in fact signify forgetting or even denying that the Holocaust ever happened. Bachmann's writings counteract this silence by invoking gruesome images from the literary imagination of the Holocaust that do not allow readers to forget atrocities that were committed in reality.

The role of the imagination in historical writings exacerbates the problem of writing narratives dealing with the Holocaust.

Bachmann, for instance, would most likely be criticized by writers of Lang's collection for creating fiction from second-hand information – in other words, from her friendships with Holocaust victims, from literary sources, and from her own imagination. Although this is also applicable to all historical fiction, Young illustrates problems created by fictionalizing the Holocaust in particular: "... the problem with this and other 'documentary fictions' of the Holocaust is that by mixing actual events with completely fictional characters, a writer simultaneously relieves himself of an obligation to historical accuracy (invoking poetic license), even as he imbues his fiction with the historical authority of real events."[248] Young would most likely accuse Bachmann of not striving for "historical accuracy," since in a dream sequence she dresses her female narrator of *Malina* in a "Jewish coat," and then describes her deportation in a truck. The melodramatic scene within this dream, in which the female narrator loses the love of her life when the truck falls into a river drowning its Jewish victims, illustrates the dubious nature of weaving together actual historical events with fictional characters. Although fictionalizing the Holocaust is problematic, Young recognizes that "literary and historical truths of the Holocaust may not be entirely separable."[249] Though it is known that Bachmann read much literature concerning the Holocaust and had access to information from close friends like Paul Celan and Nelly Sachs, she does, however, provide readers with loaded images concerning the Holocaust that are questionable because she appropriates this Jewish past for her own writing. Her work should therefore not be dismissed as unimportant in postwar literature, although her works are often left out of traditional literary canons and collections of works that discuss postwar writings. Instead, her work can be read as a personal history about someone who – although not directly involved in the Holocaust – was deeply affected by it and attempted to come to terms with the events of the Third Reich by writing about them in her fiction.

Bachmann's references to the Holocaust are not based on personal experiences and so may seem melodramatic or even clumsy to some readers. This is the response of many readers to historical fiction in general. In fact, an author's imagination and its confrontation with actual history can be overwhelming and lead to a kind of "helplessness," as Irving Howe writes: "... Holocaust writings often reveal the helplessness of the mind before an evil that cannot quite be imagined, or the helplessness of the imagination before an evil that cannot quite be understood."[250] Bachmann seems to adapt a more "structural approach" in her narratives, one that Saul Friedländer describes as a "liberal view" in which the whole of society is seen as a model fascist society.[251] The "structural approach" stresses the continuity of social structures rooted in nineteenth-century imperial Germany – or in the Austro-Hungarian Empire as in Bachmann's case – that allowed Nazism to emerge. The social structures of nineteenth-century Germany are reflected in Grimms' tales, making the Bluebeard tale an ideal metaphor for Bachmann's writings in which she wished to portray destructive gender and power structures in the postwar era of the twentieth century.[252]

Bachmann's Coming to Terms with the Holocaust

> *What will remain?/I sigh, suffer, search,/and my wanderings/will never end./The dark shadow/that I have followed since the beginning/leads me to a deep winter-loneliness./There I stand still ... ./*
> Ingeborg Bachmann, "Ängste" (Fears; HIB 38)

The discussion of Bachmann's fictional use of the Holocaust and her relationships with its victims provide a context in which to read Bachmann's attempts to come to terms with it in her short story "Unter Mördern und Irren" and in her novels *Malina* and *Der Fall Franza*. Although the proto-fascist figure of Bluebeard is referred to by name only in *Der Fall Franza*, the Bluebeard figure and what he represents prompts Bachmann to write and deal with her life history within the larger history of Austria and eastern

Europe. Like the heroine of the Bluebeard tale, Bachmann sets out to expose the destruction and "bloody chamber" of the Third Reich in her writings.

Bachmann first discusses the issue of the Holocaust victim and postwar life in Austria in her 1961-1962 short story "Unter Mördern und Irren." Ten years after the end of the Third Reich, the male narrator joins his roundtable of male friends at a tavern where discussions about the past take place, in an attempt to come to terms with the events that shaped their lives during and following the war. It is unclear for the most part what each individual at this round table suffered during the war. However, their Jewish background is noted in the narrative. When Mahler states: "We are only three Jews today" (UNT 161), Friedl argues that they really are not Jews: "... in fact he wasn't a Jew and Mahler wasn't either, his father perhaps, his grandfather ..." (UNT 161).[253] The central issue of the short story is the question of victimhood. Friedl concludes that nothing changes for the victim in his or her status as victim, whereas for the murderer, the society and the times change: "Jews were murdered because they were Jews, they were only victims, so many victims, but then not so one would finally realize today to tell the children that they are people? A little late, don't you think? No, nobody understands that the victims were in vain!" (UNT 177). Bachmann asserts that it is the individual labeled a "victim" who should be remembered.

Even though Bachmann later explored the complex and problematic situation of the victim, *Todesarten* positions its female characters as victims who are unable to break out of this mold. In an untitled, unfinished, posthumously published essay, Bachmann criticizes the naming of the victim with the term "Opfer" – with its two German meanings of victim and sacrifice – claiming that no person or country has the right to appeal to its victims and that the right to appeal to its victims yields nothing: "It's not true that the victims warn, bear witness, that is one of the most awful and thoughtless, weakest myths, ... Nobody should appeal to a victim. It is abuse. No country, no group, no idea should appeal to its dead" (OPF 335). In reference to women or victims of the Third

Reich, Bachmann cautions against victimizing by talking *about* the victim. It is questionable whether she observes her own diction. Ingeborg Majer O'Sickey points out that Bachmann suggests "calling victims to witness, no matter the writer's good intentions, not only involves a questionable reconstruction of others' experience but a kind of co-optation of that experience for alien use, resulting in a re-victimization."[254]

Bachmann attempts to avoid such a re-victimization by refusing to identify her fictional characters as Jews in the manner of the Nazis. Labeling a person a Jew according to his or her family heritage was done largely in accordance with the definitions stated in the Nürnberg laws under the Nazi party. In other words, the Nazi act of identification became a matter of life or death for people who happened to fall into certain categories. In "Unter Mördern und Irren," a stranger joins the roundtable and confesses that he was put in a prison camp until the end of the war because he denied this identification by not shooting people who were said to be the "enemy" only on the basis of an abstract definition: "You understand, I could not shoot. If I couldn't shoot at the person, then even less at an abstraction, ..." (UNT 185). In the short story, the soldiers at the war front, for example, who killed others without ever questioning their position as soldiers, sing their war songs at the pub, "as if not a day had passed" (UNT 185). At the close of the short story the stranger is found murdered after having provoked the soldiers, leading the narrator to comprehend the absurdity and futility of the binary identification of murderer and victim.

Bachmann's discussion of "victimization" raises the question whether or not it is even possible to get around such identification processes as a writer. In order to avoid repeating potentially dangerous categorizations, one must explore what each particular identification implies within a framework of a self-reflective discussion. Bachmann's later prose shows her coming to terms with National Socialism in her discussions of the problematic nature of victimization. She achieves this by referring to the elements of power, domination, and murder of the "other" in the

Bluebeard tale and relating them to events of the Third Reich. Before exploring how Bachmann uses elements of the Bluebeard tale in her prose to come to terms with the Third Reich, the following will provide a context in which to view Bachmann as an author affected by this history, and a writer using history in her fiction.

References to Events of the Holocaust in *Malina* and *Der Fall Franza*

> *"It's called 'The Third Man.'"*
> *"A novel, Mr. Martens?"*
> *"A murder story. I've just started it. It's based on fact."*
> "The Third Man" (1949), film directed by Carol Reed, screenplay by Graham Greene.

Events of the Holocaust are staged throughout *Todesarten* in dream narratives in which the female characters are murdered by a Bluebeard-like father figure. From the original domination by the father, one can trace a vein running through *Todesarten* that branches out to larger political power structures like fascism. The central dream chapter in *Malina*, in which the father attempts to exterminate his daughter in a gas chamber, clearly alludes to fascism:

> My father calmly takes a first hose down from the wall, I see a round hole which he blows into, and I duck, my father continues to take down one hose after the other, and before I can scream, I am breathing in the gas, more and more gas. I am in the gas chamber, that's what it is, the largest gas chamber of the world, I am in it alone. One can't fight the gas. My father has disappeared, he knew where the door is and didn't show it to me, and

while I am dying, my wish to see him again and to
tell him that one thing is dying, My father, I tell
him, who is no longer there, I wouldn't have told
on you, I wouldn't have told anyone. You can't
fight it here. (MAL 175-176)

In *Der Fall Franza*, Franza also has a dream in which Jordan
exterminates her in a gas chamber: "Tonight I dreamt I am in a gas
chamber, all alone, all the doors are locked, no window, and Jordan
tightens the hoses and lets the gas flow in and, how could I dream
such a thing, ... " (FF 407). Although gas chamber motifs have
traditionally been read as the female narrator's identification with
a Jewish victim of the Holocaust, Bachmann does not specify with
whom the dreamer is identifying in the gas chamber. She does,
however, make a connection specifically to the murder of Jews in
her Kagran tale, as described in the first chapter. The gas chamber
motifs in both *Malina* and *Der Fall Franza*, as well as references
to other events of the Holocaust found in *Der Fall Franza,* show
Bachmann's awareness of the history of National Socialism.

In *Der Fall Franza*, Franza's psychiatrist husband Jordan, who
has made her into one of his cases, represents National Socialism
in that he dominates and destroys her for her alleged otherness. She
begins to understand her husband's torturous and fascist treatment
of her, as she recounts: "He must be insane. And there is nobody
who seems more rational. I can't explain to anyone, can't go
anywhere and prove that it is really him. How horribly he has
tortured me, but not spontaneously or only rarely, no, with purpose, everything was planned, tactics, tactics, how can one be so
calculating?" (FF 404). The perspective shifts here when Franza
portrays Jordan as insane because of his manipulative and cruel
behavior. Whereas the narrator Martin often refers to his sister as
insane (FF 370-371) and Jordan describes her actions as mentally
unstable in his "case study" (FF 383-384) of her, Franza is later
aware that these descriptions of her person are what lead to her
destruction.

Jordan, who had written a study "About the Experiments on

Female Prisoners. On the Consequences" (FF 455), continues to carry out experiments on his wife as he both causes and observes her mental unraveling. It is in fact Franza's collaboration on Jordan's project concerning medical experiments on women during the Third Reich that contributes greatly to her destruction as she concludes: "I also became ill because of that" (FF 456).[255] Like the heroine in the Bluebeard tale, Franza exposes the murderous characteristics of her husband's destructive Bluebeard-like behavior and also unmasks the true identity of another highly respected doctor.

Bluebeard's Bloody Chamber: Euthanasia during the Third Reich and Bachmann's Association of the Mentally Ill with Women Intellectuals

> *Because what does it mean exactly to describe all of society, the state of consciousness of one time period? It doesn't mean that one repeats the sentences that this society speaks; instead one has to show them differently. And it has to be shown in a radically different way because, otherwise, one will never know what our time period was. And the illness, the torture therein, and the sickness of the world, and the sickness of this person [female narrator in the novel* Malina] *is the sickness of our time for me. And if one cannot see it this way, then my book [*Malina]*has failed. But if it can be seen therein, then perhaps not.*
>
> Ingeborg Bachmann (WIR 72)

Bachmann's detailed references to the euthanasia program during the Third Reich in *Der Fall Franza* show that she knew about the mechanics of the program and against whom it was directed. Her discussion of the Holocaust pertains largely to crimes committed against the mentally ill during the Third Reich in Germany and Austria. Bachmann associates these crimes with "crimes" committed by postwar society against women intellectuals. However, as in Bachmann's association of Jews during the Third Reich with women as victims of a patriarchal society, the events of the Holocaust become a highly questionable metaphor for victimization. Bachmann owned a 1960 edition of Mitscherlich's documentation of the Nuremberg Trials *Medizin ohne Menschlichkeit* (1949, *The Death Doctors*, trans. 1962). The tenth chapter of this study, entitled "Euthanasia Program," discusses these "mercy killings," the murders of the incurably ill, and the elimination of those declared to be "racially inferior:" Poles, Russians, Jews, and Gypsies.[256] A brief account of the euthanasia program provides a context in which to read Bachmann's prose as a coming to terms with the murder of Jews and the mentally ill.

The euthanasia program was first directed against the mentally ill and the elderly who were confined to sanatoria and nursing homes throughout Germany. The euthanasia law, "to permit the extinction of lives not worth living," was decreed under Hitler as early as 1932 and was by order kept a secret from the public. In this program the mentally ill were gassed and/or poisoned in the Grafeneck Castle and Hadamar, under the direction of Dr. Schumann as well as in the Irrsee Institution directed by Dr. Falklhauser. The mentally ill were transferred from sanatoria to "observation stations" such as Eichberg where most of the "patients" were killed within twenty-four hours. After each murder, a letter was sent to the "patient's" relatives, stating that he or she had died under mysterious circumstances, by accident or of an illness. The secret, however, did not last long. In fact, when the mentally ill arrived at Hadamar, local school children would even call out, "Here comes the murder truck again,"[257] or "There they go again for gassing."[258] In Austria, at least twenty-five thousand individuals fell victim to the euthanasia program and approximately ten thousand victims suffered forced sterilization. The National Socialist regime initiated its euthanasia murders in Austria with mentally and physically disabled children. Hundreds of children were murdered in Vienna's *Steinhof* clinic *Am Spiegelgrund* by poison, injections, or starvation. In 1940, the majority of patients in psychiatric clinics and in geriatric care facilities were murdered during the "T4" euthanasia program. The "T4" program officially ended in 1941; however, the murders in Austria continued until 1945. In an issue of the National Socialist paper, *Volksdienst*, Professor Kranz wrote that one million "patients" were slated for elimination.[259] Karl Brandt, the chief defendant in the Nuremberg trials, believed the number to be closer to three million. This euthanasia program is referred to throughout the trial as "14F13," although it is not clear from the text what this number specifically signified. From this fact, however, one can infer that this code number was meant to conceal the planned murder of over three million victims in the euthanasia program of the mentally ill.

A brief review from the Nuremberg trial reminds readers that gas chambers were first used to murder the mentally ill and later extended to Jews and finally to other inmates in work and concentration camps.[260] In his testimony on January 17, 1947, under examination by Brandt's defense counsel, Dr. Mennecke participated in the following dialogue. When the judge asked Mennecke: "So at first it was a matter of people of unsound mind?" Mennecke answered, "It was a medical matter." To the next question, "Then later it became a political and racial matter?" Mennecke only replied, "Yes."[261] Hitler ordered the termination of the euthanasia procedures in the summer of 1941, but no one could attest to this fact at the trial. It is known that some of the gas chambers dismantled at Hadamar were re-erected in the eastern city of Lublin where Polish Jews were murdered. "Idiotic and deformed children," however, were exterminated until the end of the war. The leaders of the euthanasia program were tried at Nuremberg, and many were sentenced to death. Because Hitler's orders were never made public or published anywhere and very few people had access to documents concerning these matters, it was unclear at that time which other individuals were actually involved.[262]

Simon Wiesenthal documents the euthanasia project and those responsible in his 1989 memoir and historical record *Justice Not Vengeance*. He describes Hartheim as an old Renaissance castle not far from the Mauthausen concentration camp in Upper Austria, one of the four "sanatoria" of the Third Reich. The others were Hadamar near Limburg, Sonnenstein in Saxony, and Schloss Grafenegg in Brandenburg. The program was under the supervision of Dr. Werner Heyde, professor of psychiatry at the University of Würzburg, Germany. "T4 experts" would form their opinions about patients and mark a cross at the bottom of a patient's file. The "sanatoria" became pilot programs for the mass murders committed in Treblinka and Auschwitz.[263] The laboratory was in the cellar of the castle and was linked to a small crematorium. The commandant of Hartheim, Captain Christian Wirth, first murdered people by poison gas.[264] Wirth's successor, Franz Stangl, was imprisoned after the war in 1949, escaped, was recaptured in 1967, put on trial in 1970 and died in prison the following year.[265] Wiesenthal explains that some doctors felt they had earned the right to decide about life and death, but he questions how they were able to reconcile the murder of patients with the Hippocratic Oath. As he observes: "It takes a strong psychological impulse to make that ambition turn into its opposite and to make a physician, who would normally try to save a patient weakened by sickness with an injection, turn into a murderer who kills with an injection."[266] Bachmann makes a similar observation in *Der Fall Franza* when Franza seeks out the (fictional) former "SS-Hauptsturmführer," Dr. Kurt Körner, while on vacation in Egypt. Körner, an Austrian who had murdered people by injection in the euthanasia program of the Third Reich, is regarded as a German "wonder-doctor" in exile (FF452) by the locals and visiting tourists. It is because of her work on her husband Jordan's euthanasia study that Franza recognizes Körner as one of the "Death Doctors" of the euthanasia program in Dachau and Hartheim. Franza, who identifies with the victims of this euthanasia program, pleads with Dr. Körner that she might be "eradicated" by the same fatal injection he administered to his victims during the Holocaust: "I want you to do it again ... Give me a shot ... How could she make it clear to him that she wanted to be eradicated? Yes, eradicated, that was it" (FF 462). This request seems incomprehensible to the doctor, and Franza is once again classified as insane by yet another man, Dr. Körner, as he judges her: "You are insane" (FF 462). Only Franza seems to realize the hypocrisy of the situation as she says of Dr. Körner: "... I ask him for something that he used to do voluntarily and without being asked to do, and now someone comes and can't even beg and pay for it. What kind of a world is this?" (FF 462). Franza's desire to be sacrificed and destroyed surfaces once again as she begs to be murdered as so many countless victims of the Holocaust were.

When she first makes it known that she recognizes Körner as a former Nazi "death doctor," Franza apologizes for having discovered his secret past. Franza, however, suddenly recalls a passage from the Nuremberg trials in which the tortured and castrated "Witness B." apologizes for his silence and tears on the witness stand: "Witness B. had lost his ability to speak, no, it was as if he had vanished from the page, swallowed up by the paper and print" (FF 458). Franza realizes that, just as she had apologized to Körner, only the witness and victim at the trial had apologized, never the doctors who had committed the crimes. Franza, empowered the second time she goes to Körner's office, becomes the silencing agent when confronting him with his past, for he flees in fear as soon as she has divulged his secrets: "Körner had really driven away, because of her, because he was afraid of her. Someone had been afraid of her, for the first time someone was afraid of her and not she of someone ... But I have finally also frightened someone. One of them. Yes I have" (FF 464). Franza, like the heroine in the Bluebeard tale, gains power over Dr. Körner by discovering his atrocious secrets and thus becomes empowered by her success in exposing and silencing the murderer. However, at the conclusion of the novel, it becomes clear that her momentary success has come too late actually to save her.

Bachmann, who was well read in the history of the mentally ill during the Third Reich, was aware of the gas chamber procedures used to murder them in the manner described in the Mitscherlich study. The gas chamber narratives in *Malina* and *Der Fall Franza* can therefore be read not only on a parallel level as a reference to the murder of Jews, but also as depictions of the situation of women who were labeled mentally insane by a society Bachmann portrayed as patriarchal.

The catalog *Frauenleben 1945–Kriegsende in Wien* (Women's Lives 1945 – The End of the War in Vienna), published by the Historical Museum of the city of Vienna, makes evident that women intellectuals, artists, scientists, and politicians were expelled from Austria or were murdered in concentration camps.[267] The Austrian author Erich Fried offers a biting criticism of Austria's expulsion of intellectuals in his 1986 essay "Die Vertreibung des Geistigen aus Österreich" (The Expulsion of Intellectuals from Austria).[268] The author states that this process of expulsion did not begin with Adolf Hitler, nor has it come to an end in the present. Fried believes that the "expulsion of the spirit" does not always correlate with the exile of those carrying such a spirit. Instead, the authors' spirits are shattered because they are either not welcomed back to their homeland or are ignored completely. Although he does not mention Bachmann by name, he lists an astounding number of Austrian writers and intellectuals who, he writes, were "driven out," "exterminated," "kept small," and "discriminated against."[269]

The gas chambers Bachmann describes in her novels show that she knew of the fate of the mentally ill during the Third Reich. During the Nuremberg trials it was stated that the gas chambers at locations such as Hadamar and Schloss Grafenegg were of the same size and appearance of any other room in the institution, so that the "patient" would find the room familiar and would not be afraid to enter it. The patients were introduced into the room naked and were then poisoned with carbon monoxide gas.[270] The gas chambers of work and concentration camps, however, were used to murder larger groups of people. In the first dream sequence of the chapter "Der dritte Mann" in *Malina*, for instance, the "chamber" which the female narrator enters is described as "large and dark, no, it is a ward, with filthy walls, it could be in the castle of the Hohenstaufen in Apulia. Because there are no windows and no doors" (MAL 175). The term "chamber" (Kammer) denotes a small room, and suggests that the narrator's initial response to the room was that it was "homey," i.e., familiar. The term "ward" (Saal), typically used to refer to a hospital ward, signals its reference to a mental institution with which the female narrator also seems familiar. More important though is the description of the Hohenstaufen castle, most likely alluding to one of the castles in Sicily once belonging to the German Staufen family, which Bachmann might have visited when she lived in Italy. The imagery of the medieval castle can be associated with the castles such as Grafenegg where the mentally ill were gassed.

In the passage directly following the gassing scene, the narrator describes herself as insane, or rather, as having been driven insane: "When it begins, the world is already all mixed up, and I know that I am insane," (MAL 176) whereupon she has a series of hallucinations in which her father torments her throughout. Again the narrator describes the world as one in which she is insane and where the world itself has come to an end (MAL 178). As the narrator comes out of her hallucination, she realizes that she has been given electroshock treatment as described by Franza: "... I have little metal plates on my shaved head and I look around in amazement ... They have given me electroshocks" (MAL 178). Electroshock, a common treatment for depression and other mental illnesses when Bachmann wrote her novels in the 1960s, is said to be often painful and disorienting for the patient and is now only used in very serious cases of mental illness.

Bachmann's prose, which not only deals with Jews and other victims of the Third Reich but also the treatment of the mentally ill, raises some compelling questions: Was Bachmann then referring to the plight of female writers and female intellectuals who were viewed as mentally ill by a conservative and traditional postwar society?[271] Is it then a Jew who is murdered by a Nazi in *Malina* and *Der Fall Franza,* or is it a mentally ill patient who is being exterminated by her doctor? A distinction between these two allegories would not make these horrifying acts any less shocking or disturbing to readers. Bachmann's gas chamber dreams become a powerful yet highly problematic portrayal of the psychological

life of a woman and writer who is viewed as unfit and insane by
her society and one who is exterminated because of her purported
otherness.

"Unfit" Women and "Unfit" Mothers in *Der Fall Franza*

The narrative passage in *Der Fall Franza*, in which Franza
tells of the abortion forced upon her by her husband and other male
physicians in a Viennese hospital, also alludes to the euthanasia
project of the Third Reich by illustrating the consequences of
nonconformity in what Bachmann portrays as a male-oriented
society.

Gisela Bock's study *Zwangssterilisation im Nationalsozialismus* (Forced Sterilization during National Socialism) notes
that under National Socialism the mentally ill were forbidden to
marry or bear children. As early as 1929, before the advent of
National Socialism, all mentally ill patients were part of a
sterilization program for "inferior" people (Minderwertige).[272]
Although abortion was not forbidden after 1935, women's
reproductive rights were determined by the state.[273] Bock states
that the first victims of "Anti-natalismus" (anti-birth) were patients
suffering from schizophrenia, manic depression, and epilepsy and
were all sterilized under the same generalized diagnosis of
"Schwachsinn" (feeble-mindedness).[274] Mandatory sterilization
and forced abortions became routine by 1935. Under this same
law, for example, abortions were performed on women whose
children would have been considered not "reinrassig" (racially
pure) but "schlechtrassig" (racially inferior).

In *Der Fall Franza,* Jordan forces his wife Franza, whom he
considers mentally unstable and therefore an "unfit" woman and
mother, to have an abortion. In the passage of *Der Fall Franza*
describing the forced abortion, Franza kneels and pleads with the
head surgeon to allow her to take part of her fetus home with her
to Hietzing in a pickling jar since it *may not* live: "... nevertheless
you must leave me a part of him, then I want to be able to eat it,

one piece, then I want to think that could have become his heart, because you cannot take it all from me, then I would rather devour it, if *it should not live*" (FF 420, italics my emphasis). Franza wants to devour her child, to incorporate it physically and internalize it emotionally, in an attempt to spare it from the crematory. Franza's act can be read as an attempt to save the memory of her child by placing it in a pickling jar. During Franza's trip through Egypt she promises her brother Martin that she will forget her memory of this "incident," and says that she has metaphorically "devoured" her fetus between Cairo and Suez, an empowering mental act which Franza believes has given her the strength never to kneel before anyone again. Franza asserts herself by stating: "I will never again fall on my knees, not for anyone, not for any people in white" (FF 421), who represent psychiatrists or surgeons in this passage. Franza, however, cannot ignore her memories and is ultimately destroyed by her past passivity, as becomes evident in her death by suicide, at the conclusion of the novel when she bashes her head against a wall in Egypt.[275]

From the point of view of the surgeons, Martin and the third-person narrator, Franza's desperate plea to eat her child is viewed as an abominable cannibalistic act, described by the narrator as a "monstrosity,…that could not be repeated on any telephone…" (FF 420). Martin judges his sister's mental stability by questioning: "Who still knelt in front of someone, … one risked being shipped off to an insane asylum" (FF 420). Martin's unsympathetic and horrified reaction represents the general reaction of shock and disgust at the possibility that a woman might eat her child: "… she had done and said something so horrifying…" (FF 420). Franza's so-called insanity demonstrates just one way (Todesart) in which she is destroyed by the Bluebeard figure Jordan. By alluding to the forced abortions of the euthanasia projects, Bachmann makes the problematic association of the horrors of private relationships, such as Franza's and Jordan's, with the atrocities committed during the Third Reich.

The previous chapter showed how Bachmann comes to terms with her experiences during the Third Reich as well as her knowledge of the atrocities committed during this time, by channeling her emotional reaction to the Holocaust into the artistic expression of writing fiction. Bachmann's references to images of domination and violence in the Bluebeard tale are a comment on the socio-cultural history of Austria. This was also made evident by her association of women in a male-oriented society with Jewish victims of the Holocaust, a view shared with the Austrian psychoanalytic tradition she had studied. The scenes in which the father attempts to murder his daughter in a gas chamber and the passage in which Jordan forces Franza to have an abortion illustrate how Bachmann's female characters in *Todesarten* are perceived as "other," and are defined as "insane" by society, a role which ultimately destroys them. Through her female characters in *Todesarten*, Bachmann demonstrates how women take refuge in depression and madness when they are forbidden to express anger at their lack of power, control, and self-expression.[276] Although Bachmann's association of patriarchal society with the atrocities of the Holocaust in *Todesarten* are problematic, her work shows how her reaction to the Third Reich informed her writing and how the Holocaust has entered the postwar literary imagination.

Bachmann's portrait of Austrian society in the 1950s is one in which women are socialized to be passive and submissive, and in which their attempt to get at knowledge and social standing-in other words, entering Bluebeard's secret chamber – is viewed as a threat to the male-oriented society. Like the heroine of the Bluebeard tale who exposes the murderous acts of her husband, Bachmann exposes the monstrous acts that took place during the Third Reich.

Chapter Four

"A Step towards Gomorrah": Bluebeard, Gender, and Power

> *Orlando had become a woman – there is no denying it. But in every other respect, Orlando remained precisely as he had been.*
>
> Virginia Woolf, *Orlando*, 1928[277]

The previous chapter explored how Bachmann refers to gender relations, power, and destruction in the Bluebeard tale to express her reactions to the events of the Third Reich. In Bachmann's short story "Ein Schritt nach Gomorrha," however, it is not a male figure who takes on the identity of Bluebeard. Instead, Bachmann rewrites the Bluebeard tale by depicting Charlotte as a female Bluebeard in order to explore social issues of gender, language, and female identity. "Ein Schritt nach Gomorrha" narrates the course of one evening in which Charlotte and Mara establish what has been construed as a lesbian relationship in order to create alternative roles for themselves as women.[278] The two female characters are propelled towards each other by a desire for power rather than sexual gratification. The tale, narrated in the third person and reflecting Charlotte's point of view, explores her ideas about gender construction and her role as a woman and wife.

In order to saturate the narrative with images of anger, passion, and death, Bachmann's short story is flooded with references to the color red. Charlotte finds herself alone in her apartment after a party with an enthusiastic and enamored Mara, whose red skirt seems to intensify the redness of Charlotte's room, prompting the hostess to face a moment of intense recognition: "for one single moment the world was red" (GOM 188). The color red, traditionally a metaphor for such abstract notions as love, passion, hatred, anger, death, and hell, becomes more specifically the "deathly red" (GOM 188) of Mara's skirt, as well as the "hellish red" (GOM 190) of the bar where Mara dances for Charlotte. The image of the red skirt, which frames the short story, forewarns of Charlotte's charged, existential situation in which the revelation of her constructed gender prompts her to attempt a withdrawal (Austritt) from this mold, and forewarns also of the subsequent realization that there is no exit from the bipolar gender construct of domination and subjugation. The red skirt becomes a symbol of possibilities (Möglichkeiten) to escape the rut of everyday marital life and prescribed female roles within society.

The short story unfolds with the red skirt seductively hanging over Mara's knees, sweeping the floor like a bullfighter's provocative throw, "the wide skirt with the deathly red, to which drums should have sounded" (GOM 188). Toward the end of the narrative, Charlotte glimpses the possibility of a new way of existence by recalling the image of the red scarf: "...to carry out the withdrawal when the drum sounds, when the red scarf trails on the ground and nobody knows how it will end" (GOM 212). The verb "trailing" (schleifen) within the context of the metaphor of a bull fight, captures the image of a provocation that might prompt an aggressive move of some kind. Instead, the narration concludes with the red skirt crumpled at the foot of the bed, in which Charlotte has resigned herself to lying beside the passive Mara: "When they were both in the bedroom, Charlotte knew that it was too late for everything. ... They were both dead and had killed something" (GOM 213). Both women "kill" the possibility of entering a new dimension of existence and gender by falling into old patterns of socialized male and female roles. The reference to the color red also suggests the image of Bluebeard's bloody chamber and forewarns the trespasser Mara of the punishment she will have to endure for having crossed into this forbidden domain.

Death becomes an imminent factor in the short story as both women are projected into inevitable failure when they attempt to leave their stagnant situations. Once again, for Bachmann the figure of Bluebeard becomes a trope for male gender. This time, however, it is Charlotte who takes on this villainous persona in order to commit her previous lovers to memory and remind herself of the unsatisfying and unsuccessful role these previous relationships have played in her life: "She saw neither Mara nor the room in which she was, but her farthest, secret room that she had to lock up forever ... They were dead ... Mara would never find out, would never be able to find out, what a room full of dead people was and under which omen they had been killed. ... The key to the room, she still knew that, she wore under her shirt" (GOM 212). Charlotte's image of Bluebeard's chamber in which she has buried all seven previous male lovers becomes a secret domain, one she can lock up from the future. Charlotte swears that Mara must never discover the origin or existence of this chamber of dead lovers, or ever ask about it. Unlike the traditional Bluebeard figure, Charlotte keeps the key to the secret chamber hidden from Mara. She fears that Mara would also be among those dead and that she too will have been unsatisfactory as a lover and partner. Again, the nature of Charlotte's relationships to her previous male lovers and to Mara becomes a power issue. By keeping her lovers in the secret chamber, she maintains control and power over them, just as she wishes to keep Mara as her "creature" (Geschöpf) and in her power. Immediately following Charlotte's oath, Mara speaks the inevitable: "I am dead ... I can't go on. Dead, I am so dead" (GOM 212). Even Charlotte's fervent hope to succeed in this "new" relationship – so seemingly different from the memory of her lovers and her marriage – comes too late as Mara rejects Charlotte's positive attitude towards this relationship: "I can't drink anymore, walk anymore. I am dead" (GOM 213).

Bachmann's image of sleep at the conclusion of the short story illustrates that both women desire to awaken only when society no longer has prescribed gender roles that are based on the opposition of "Perpetrator/Victim" (Täter/Opfer). Earlier in the short story, Charlotte invokes the tale of "Sleeping Beauty" to illustrate her desire to be awakened by "another hand" and not by a prince: "Come, that I may awaken when this doesn't mean anything anymore – man and woman. When it is over one day!" (GOM 202). In Bachmann's short story, the image of the woman needing to be brought into consciousness by a male savior is replaced by a woman's plea for sleep so she can wake up to a transformed and emancipated world. Charlotte's wish for sleep is granted as she and Mara fall asleep, exhausted from their attempt to establish a new kind of existence, surely only to be awakened by an unpleasant encounter with the housekeeper and husband. The red skirt that represented a challenge to convention and expressed female power at the end lies "crumpled and insignificant" at the foot of the bed, suggesting that Charlotte and Mara were unable to escape their fixed gender roles (GOM 213).

In her narratives, Bachmann explored feminist issues such as the differences between sex and gender, which have only recently come into more formalized discussions. The author discusses the notion of men and women engaged in a "gender-battle," a view commonly associated with early German-speaking feminist dis-course of the 1950s through the 1970s. Bachmann brings this into greater focus by projecting the issue onto two women. The character Charlotte, for example, is quite conscious of the fact that Mara is of the same sex: "She is out of the same material of which I am made" (GOM 194). In her quest to create a different type of existence for women, Charlotte observes that gender is constructed and socialized, and not based on biological differences. This is illustrated by the fact that she assumes the dominating persona of Bluebeard and of the father figure in *Todesarten* by using what she views as a typical male language. Rather than focusing on the sexuality of her female characters in this short story, Bachmann uses their sexual relationship to explore the socialization of men and women and their role as individuals in society. In their first moment of physical contact, Charlotte, for example, does not derive sexual pleasure from kissing Mara's lips. Instead she observes how men might perceive her own mouth: "So this is how her own lips were, this is how they met a man, thin, almost without resistance, almost without muscle – a tiny snout, not to be taken seriously" (GOM 196). Clearly, she establishes that the power relationship is created from the very beginning. A woman's lack of power is represented as an integral part of her body and the application of her language. Moreover, Charlotte observes all of Mara's actions as typically feminine, qualities normally associated with stereotypical and negative descriptions of women. Mara, for instance, pouts, whines, whimpers, cries, begs, and pleads with Charlotte to love her, to stroke her, to desire only her. Mara pouts: "I am not rational" (GOM 195) and begs Charlotte to think for her: "My poor head! You have to feel sorry for it, have to stoke it, tell it what it should think" (GOM 199). Charlotte realizes that those characteristics she observes in Mara reflect the way men must have perceived her own actions in the past: "She had so often rambled on, especially in the beginning with Franz; she had also taken on this tone with Milan, had made her voice frilly; he had been forced to listen to this sing-song full of irrationality, with a distorted mouth she, the weak, helpless, and unintelligible one had babbled at him, the strong and reasonable one. She had played out the same weaknesses for him that Mara now played out for her, ..." (GOM 199). The impact of language on the construction of individuality, gender, and identity becomes a crucial element in Charlotte's utopian vision of a new order within society. She typically views human beings as speaking a logical, rational language, one that enables men to dominate while women are subjugated because of their incomprehensible "babbling." This is exemplified by Charlotte's description of Mara's mode of speech: "I am always unsure what she is speaking about. The language of men was always such that one could depend on it in those hours. I cannot listen to Mara, her unmuscular words, these insignificant small words" (GOM 198). Bachmann's description of Mara's "unmuscular" and "insignificant" words illustrates how language expresses and confirms gender stereotypes, and supports the assumption that men and women cannot improve their society without a "new" language.

Bachmann explores the concept of a "new language" in her collection the *Das dreißigste Jahr*, in which the protagonists are struck by the revelation that changing or creating a new language might enable them to begin a new life and progress beyond their dreary existence. The protagonist of the short story "Das dreißigste

Jahr" seeks to establish a new language outside of the current "Gaunersprache" (language of swindlers) by stepping out of the given order of polarities and prescribed gender roles. Like Charlotte, who finds herself living in a "bright order" (GOM 200), the protagonist of "Das dreißigste Jahr" compels himself and the reader to change the world: "Then jump up and tear at the old disgraceful order. Then be different, so that the world can change itself, so that it can change its direction, finally! Then, you take the first step!" (DRE 114). The introspective father of "Alles" experiences a similar revelation and hopes that he can change his world by teaching his newborn son a different language:

> And suddenly I knew: everything is a question of language and not only this particular German language that was created with others in Babylon to confuse the world. Because underneath it grows another language that reaches into the gestures and glances, the unwinding thoughts and the passage of emotions, and all our misfortune already lies within it. Everything was a question of whether I could save the child from our language until it had created a new one and could usher in a new age. (ALL 143)

Instead of the "language of swindlers," the father wishes to teach his son a new language that would communicate the "unspoken language" of "gestures, "glances," and "emotion," thus emphasizing a modus of communication related to sign language, telepathy, and the intuitive powers of the "sixth sense." The narrator calls this language a "Schattensprache" (language of shadows) which might create a new order: "Teach him the language of shadows! The world is an experiment, and it is enough that this experiment has always been repeated in the same manner with the same result. Try another experiment!" (ALL 145). This "language of shadows" would then also reflect the possibility of "another experiment" in which the voices of all individuals might find opportunities of expression. As all of Bachmann's protagonists come to realize, language and humankind's experience confine him/her to repeat those structures that bind him/her to certain social and gender roles. The narrator of "Alles" gives up his quest for a new language because he cannot find "words from such a language" and "cannot go beyond its borders" (ALL 145). For Bachmann, a person's experiences represent the limitations of language, as illustrated in her observation on traditional Western, hierarchical thought, which is "always divided in up and down, good and bad, light and dark, number and goodness/purity, friend, and foe (ALL 148), images which are then carried over to prescribed gender roles as well. "Alles" concludes with the son's accidental death after his father distances himself emotionally from both his son and his wife because he cannot create a new order by way of language through his son. It becomes clear that the father ironically attempts to apply the same structures of domination and control to his son that he has observed in general society. The language that the father attempts to teach his son, the "language of shadows," is an ambiguous term. At first glance, such a "language of shadows" seems to constitute a "natural" language, derived from observing nature, as the father recollects: "and when the trees cast their shadows I thought I heard a voice: teach him the language of shadows!" (ALL 145). This language, however, would in fact not be new, but a *shadow* of the existing language, thereby raising the question whether or not there can even be such a thing as a fundamentally *new* language. The conclusion of "Alles" once again provokes the reader with false hopes of being able to change the world through a "different tongue," as the father proclaims: "You learn the language of shadows! Learn it yourself!" (ALL 157).

Similarly, in "Ein Schritt nach Gomorrha," Charlotte takes on a role she perceives as different, as a "new beginning," as something "that had become possible," (GOM 203) with the same enthusiasm as the father in "Alles." She views her new role as one in which she will make Mara her "creature" (Geschöpf): "I want to decide who I am, and I also want to make my creature, my tolerating, shadowy partner. I do not want Mara because I want her mouth, her gender – my own – Nothing of the kind. I want my creature and I will create it for myself" (GOM 205). When Mara becomes her "creature," a term with derogatory implications, it will be Charlotte who creates a new language in which to live: "She would no longer be the chosen one, and she could never again be chosen in this language" (GOM 205). On the one hand, Charlotte, like the father in "Alles," foresees that language will recreate itself as something different from the prescribed language which automatically determines social and gender roles: "She had always abhorred this language, every stamp that had been pressed onto her, and that she had to press on someone – attempted murder of reality. But when her kingdom came this language would no longer count, then this language would fix itself" (GOM 208). On the other hand, just as the father in "Alles" wants to teach his son the "language of shadows," Charlotte has already internalized the structures of control, subjugation, and domination, by wanting to dominate and teach Mara *her* language: "... she would teach Mara how to speak, slowly, precisely, and not let any darkening occur through the usual language" (GOM 209). Charlotte, however, falls into the trap that Bachmann has laid out for all her protagonists. Once Mara agrees to become the Bluebeard Charlotte's submissive "creature," Charlotte realizes that she has finally found *her* creature: "Charlotte grabbed Mara's wrists. Now she had her just where she wanted her. She appraised her prey and it was useful, was good. She had found her creature" (GOM 211). For Bachmann, the binary nature of domination and subjugation leads Charlotte to see herself as having no choice but to take on a traditionally male role, bringing with it the structures that cause men to dominate the world, to create law, and to create images: "It was a shift change and now she could take over the world, name her partner, lay down the laws and duties, make the old images invalid and create the first new one " (GOM 211). By taking on a traditionally male role with this "shift change," and by dominating Mara, Charlotte becomes like the destructive Bluebeard and father figure in *Todesarten*. Bachmann's characters Charlotte and Mara therefore represent women who cannot go beyond the relationship of subjugation and domination because of their socialization. The role of the dominating and destructive Bluebeard figure assumed by Charlotte is reflected in her observations on certain behaviors exhibited by her husband and her previous lovers, as well as on her own socialization within society.

Bachmann refers to the Bluebeard tale in "Ein Schritt nach Gomorrha" to explore issues of gender, language, and identity. No longer do men like Jordan and the father figure from *Todesarten* take on Bluebeard's role in this short story. Instead, it is Charlotte who becomes an exemplary female Bluebeard, having taken on those negative stereotypes of male gender she had observed in men. In Bachmann's short story, Charlotte struggles but fails to escape the traditional binary structures of male and female language and gender. Bachmann shows that the destructive figure of Bluebeard is not necessarily male, but rather a figure or group which dominates and destroys those defined as "other." Thus, for Bachmann, the gender issue seems ultimately to be a question of power. It is precisely this power-struggle from which Charlotte is unable to escape.

Conclusion

> ... *(B)oth the oral and the literary forms*
> *of the fairy tale are grounded in history:*
> *they emanate from specific struggles to*
> *humanize bestial and barbaric forces,*
> *which have terrorized our minds and*
> *communities in concrete ways, threat-*
> *ening to destroy free will and human*
> *compassion. The fairy tale sets out to*
> *conquer this concrete terror through*
> *metaphors.*
>
> Jack Zipes, *Spells of Enchantment*[279]

> *Don't tell us any tales!*
>
> Ilse Aichinger, *Die größere Hoffnung,*
> 1948[280]

Bachmann once stated: "Usually, literature is well ahead of life" (HIB 153),[281] thereby remarking on the timeliness of her own work. Her writings address contemporary and controversial topics such as gender roles, xenophobia, fascism, and the atrocities of war that have been more readily discussed at the close of the twentieth century than they were in the 1950s when she began her career as a freelance writer. Bachmann's words have inspired novels, musical compositions, theater performances, films, and multi-media shows in Austria and throughout the world.[282] In Austria, a train, the *Inter City* 594 from Salzburg to Vienna, now bears Bachmann's name, carrying passengers across a country that could not fully appreciate her work during her lifetime. In her hometown of Klagenfurt, *The Klagenfurt Jergitsch Gymnasium* was renamed the *Ingeborg Bachmann Gymnasium* in 1995, at last honoring its citizen who dared to criticize Austria's involvement with the Third Reich. In celebration of her poetry and love of music, the contemporary musician Friedrich Cerha composed a piece entitled "Für K," which premiered in St. Pölten on September 25, 1993, and was inspired by Bachmann's short story "Ein Wildermuth" (1957). On November 11, 1995, the theatrical production of Bachmann's life and work *Ingeborg Bachmann. Wer?* premiered at the *Burgtheater*, the Austrian National Theater in Vienna, under the direction of Claus Peymann. Even though many of the productions directed by Peymann had been criticized as controversial and flouting the tradition of the *Burgtheater*, the dramatization celebrating Bachmann's *oeuvre* nonetheless legitimized her work in the eyes of the general Austrian public. This production by director Peymann and writers Hermann Beil and Jutta Ferbers interprets Bachmann's life as emotionally tumultuous, yet it manages to portray the sometimes vain, fashionable, girlish, and humorous side of the Austrian writer otherwise known for her battle with depression, and her tragic death. Peymann's portrayal of Bachmann has enabled the Austrian public to embrace her work, even though her words often unmask the hypocrisies of twentieth-century Austria and western European culture. Bachmann demonstrated foresight when she stated that texts such as her own were to be interpreted differently by every generation: "In any case, one has to be able to read a book in different ways and to read it differently today than tomorrow" (WIR 100). Because contemporary readers have come to appreciate the historical relevance of Bachmann's works, her fictional and political writings are featured in current studies on Austrian women's literature and history.[283]

While I was completing this book about the historical significance of Bachmann's prose, several important works have been published that offer a new perspective on Austrian women's history, Jewish studies in Austria and, more specifically, Bachmann's life and work. These studies, published primarily in the German language, have focused largely on Bachmann's works as important cultural reflections of history and intellectual thought. While I have included much of the material from the more recent studies in this book, the publication of previously unpublished poetry and letters allows for varied readings of Bachmann's poetry and prose.[284]

Höller's 1998 study *Ingeborg Bachmann. Letzte unveröffent-*

lichte Gedichte, Entwürfe und Fassungen (Last Poems, Drafts, and Versions) allows for a more socio-historical reading of Bachmann's last, unpublished poems, written during her stay in Berlin from the spring of 1963 to the end of 1965. Although she had stated in an interview with Kuno Raeber in January of 1963 that she had "stopped writing poems" (WIR 40), Bachmann continued to write and revise numerous poems during the time she was writing *Todesarten* until the end of 1967. Featured are "Böhmen liegt am Meer" (Bohemia Lies on the Ocean), "Keine Delikatessen" (No Delicacies) and "Enigma" (LUG 7). "Böhmen liegt am Meer" and "Enigma" were written after her travels to Prague in January and February of 1964, a time she recalled as "wondrous" despite her separation from Max Frisch and her bouts of depression (LUG 8). Höller compares the many variants and revisions of the poems to the pluralistic unity of prose variations in *Todesarten*. "Enigma," for instance, exists in at least twelve versions and was revised over a period of three years (LUG 12).

It is, however, Bachmann's collection of shorter poems that address more urgently her coming to terms with the history of the Holocaust in her fictional work. The short poem "In Feindeshand" (In the Hands of the Enemy) is hand-written on a small piece of notepaper without any visible corrections. The poem describes the violence of war and recalls images of the Holocaust by directing the voice at a reader who becomes an unwilling object of the hatred of an unidentified perpetrator: "You are in enemy hands, /they are already grinding your /bones, they are stomping out/your vision/they are stepping on your vision/with their feet/trill in your ear/ with alarm whistles/Alarm" (LUG 20, 35). This image of the tortured victim is a recurring subject throughout *Todesarten*, her short story "Three Paths to the Lake," and her poem "Keine Delikatessen" (LUG 36-37). Bachmann's poem "Jüdischer Friedhof" (Jewish Cemetery) from 1964 depicts the graveyard as "an enclave of peace and of a friendly concept of death" (LUG 40). The graveyard itself is described as a tranquil and humble resting-place, "stone forest, no flashy graves, nothing to kneel in front of/and not for flowers. A stone so tightly placed there, as if/one were embracing the other; one can't imagine one without the other,/" and concludes on an exuberant note: "and for the living a crack through which they are allowed,/without mourning, he who reaches the exit, has not death/but the day in his heart" (LUG 40). Bachmann's poetic image of the graveyard recalls a meditative locus in which the dead have found the peace they were unable to experience on earth. It evokes the utopian and hopeful phrase from *Todesarten*, "A day will come," one of peace and love, even if it is in death.

Höller's recent Bachmann biography (1999) emphasizes the historical relevance of her poetry and prose and presents her writings as embedded in the larger history of World War II, the postwar era, and the Cold War. Höller celebrates the immediacy of Bachmann's work by showcasing the aria "Freies Geleit (Aria II)" (Safe-Conduct) from her libretto for Hans Werner Henze's opera *Der Prince von Homburg*, "the most beautiful poem ever written against nuclear war" (HIB 112). The poem introduces a romantic and spiritual vision of the world: "With sleep-drunken birds/and wind-whipped trees/the day rises, and the ocean/empties over it a foaming cup.//" It implores the reader to accept and protect the natural wonders of the world, "the king fish," "the fire-prince salamander" and the corals "she [the world] plants for us in the ocean." Bachmann further exhorts: "The earth does not want to carry a mushroom cloud/no being, spit out before the heavens/to rid with rain and angry glances/the unheard – of voices of ruin/" and concludes by stating that the earth wants a "safe passage" as it travels through the universe. In an effort to share Bachmann's work with a more contemporary audience, Höller describes Bachmann's collection of short stories entitled *Simultan*, as a revision of her portrayal of gender roles, her depiction of women in society and her relationship to writing (HIB 15). In a letter to the Piper publishing house, referring to *Simultan*, Bachmann writes that her work-in-progress "Wienerinnen" (Viennese Women) pays homage to "something she had very much neglected," "to women who also exist while she had been busy for decades with controversies, ideas, and the men they have" (HIB 151). She writes that while she had been preoccupied with *Todesarten*, she had begun "to write strange stories about women" in whose company she felt she had entered and "whom she had always observed from the outside and continues to see that way" (HIB 151). Bachmann insists that she wants the long-lost "magic" and "charm" to "begin again," "to accompany both sexes" (HIB 153). By giving her Viennese women a "chance to reestablish the magic and not the separation" (HIB 153), Bachmann hopes to empower the female protagonists in her later work. The revised vision of women and male-female relationships in the fragments of Bachmann's prose is therefore not so much in contrast to those female protagonists portrayed as "murdered" in *Todesarten*, but more a development out of her more rigid view of men and women as confrontational polar opposites.

An additional study that complements my reading of Bachmann's work within the context of World War II and the Holocaust is Karen Remmler's *Waking the Dead: Correspondences between Walter Benjamin's Concept of Remembrance and Ingeborg Bachmann's "Ways of Dying"* (1996), written for an anglophone audience. Remmler explores the dilemma of remembrance and representation in Bachmann's *Todesarten* by drawing on Walter Benjamin's concept of *Eingedenken* (insightful remembrance), which calls for the interrelationship of collective history and personal experience. Remmler shows how Bachmann's female protagonists are unable to express their pain publicly but also examines their refusal to differentiate their own suffering from that of others. As Remmler reminds her readers, it is precisely this absence of the process of public mourning in postwar Austria that led to the dismissal of the memories of the victims of the Holocaust, as well as their isolation. Although Bachmann's female protagonists voice their memories by refusing to conform to repressive forms of misremembrance, Remmler points out that this does not erase their complicity in monumental history. Bachmann never explicitly mentions remembrance in her texts and essays, yet she shares Benjamin's interest in a non-violent representation of suffering and thus commits herself to overcoming the separation between personal memory and history in her work. Remmler also questions Bachmann's appropriation of images of the Holocaust in representing female suffering and victimization. She argues, however, that Bachmann refers to the Holocaust in order to depict the structural continuity of social oppression in *Malina*, therefore remembering the victims of the Third Reich as Benjamin attempted to do with his concept of *Eingedenken*. Remmler concludes that *Todesarten* portrays the fatal consequences of dismissing personal memories for the sake of monumental history by mourning the absence of a public memory based on the interrelationship between subjective experiences and history.

Sigrid Weigel's 1999 study *Ingeborg Bachmann* reveals surprising and fascinating evidence that underlines my own reading of Bachmann's relationships with Jewish intellectuals and Holocaust survivors during the postwar period. Weigel was able to trace Bachmann's correspondences in the posthumous collections of scholars and writers like Gerschom Scholem, Theodor Adorno, Hannah Arendt, and Wolfgang Hildesheimer. Weigel demonstrates that Bachmann's work is a result of a vibrant exchange of ideas about victimhood, punishment, and justice in the wake of World War II and the Holocaust.

Although many issues were discussed during her lifetime, especially political issues such as the statute of limitations on murder committed by Austrian and German Nazi war criminals, Bachmann questioned many of the perceptions of her time by always emphasizing that history is a continuity of actions by individuals spanning the past, present, and future. Bachmann's work can be appreciated today primarily because the issues she deals with: violence in everyday life, victimhood, and justice are an integral part of current events. Bachmann hoped for a literature "ohne Phrasen," without clichés and superficialities. She realized that as an author her work "could not change the world," but that her explorations of individual responsibility and her empowering phrase "a day will come" would emphasize that even what seemed the most insignificant interpersonal relationship becomes an integral action in the larger history that all individuals share.

Readers of Bachmann's work come away burdened by the everyday violence of contemporary society, but empowered by the hope that individuals can – and do – affect the outcome of history through acts of compassion and kindness. For Bachmann, love is a healing agent, while the act of writing is an act of hope. Bachmann's phrase "a day will come" reappears throughout *Malina* like a fervent prayer or mantra, tantalizing the reader with the hope of salvation and the traditional "happy end" of fairy tales.

By referring to fairy-tale elements and motifs in her prose, Bachmann-like Aichinger, whose character from *Die größere Hoffnung* demands the truth by admonishing us "don't tell us any tales!" – exhorts the reader not to succumb to false hopes and dreams of salvation as do her female narrators, who are "murdered" by their hopes for a utopian existence. Bachmann uses fairy-tale elements in her prose to explore subjects such as gender relations and events of the Third Reich that were taboo at the time she began writing in the 1950s. Although Bachmann's criticisms of war, xenophobia, social oppression, and gender relations have been discussed in recent literature by women, she was one of the first postwar, German-speaking authors to address these issues with such insight, empathy, and candor. By referring to Austria's historical tradition of psychoanalysis, the social history of women in postwar Austria, the history of feminism in German-speaking countries, and the historical events of the Third Reich, I have presented Bachmann's work in the socio-cultural and socio-historical context of the Austrian postwar years. Relevant for readers at the dawn of the twenty-first century, Bachmann's work can be better appreciated in light of historically significant events of the Third Reich and can therefore be read as historical fiction.

Bachmann's critical use of fairy-tale elements in her prose and her discussion of the historical events of the Third Reich demonstrate how her work, especially *Todesarten*, can be read as a critical and crucial socio-historical narrative. For Bachmann, the personal was political and the political was personal. When the protagonist Franza in *Der Fall Franza* demands to know where her personal (his)story comes together with the larger history, I contend that the personal and larger history unite precisely in such a work as *Todesarten* (FF 433). Bachmann's writing illustrates that personal experiences are affected and altered by history and that, in turn, personal experiences (and personal responsibility) affect and alter the "larger" history. Her experiences during the Third Reich as a young woman, her relationships with Jewish intellectuals and Holocaust survivors, her role as a young female writer supported by older male publishers, and her life as an Austrian writer living in Germany, Switzerland, and Italy, all informed the way she would perceive and write about her past, and about Austrian history and culture.

After World War II, many women authors along with Bachmann wrote fiction in order to portray the events they had experienced, intending to recall and come to terms with their personal histories. These authors described the act of writing as imperative for their emotional and psychological survival during and after the Third Reich. One of Bachmann's earliest memories was the knowledge that she had to write *Todesarten* for herself: "For me it is one of the oldest, yet almost buried memories: that I always knew I had to write this book – already early on, even while I was writing poems" (WIR 99). Ilse Aichinger, Bachmann's contemporary, also said that writing *Die größere Hoffnung* was imperative for her. In an interview, Aichinger described the role of writing in her life: "It made it possible for me to stay in this world. I believe that it was necessary for me, otherwise I would not have done it. In the novel *Die größere Hoffnung*, for example, I thought at first I would write a report so that one will know what happened. It was not that. It was necessary, for me anyway."[285] Marlen Haushofer, an Austrian postwar writer engaged in portraying the experiences of women in Austria in the 1950s and 1960s, wrote in her diary on January 27, 1968, while suffering from cancer: "Actually I can only live when I am writing and because I am not writing currently, I feel dissolute and disgusting."[286] She died two years later. Her well-known novel *Die Wand* (The Wall, 1968) tells the story of a woman reconciling her past life with her new sense of independence.

Although the works of these Austrian women writers were innovative and highly critical for their time, Bachmann, Aichinger, and Haushofer did not gain popularity until the 1970s because their portrayal of the female perspective and experience differed from the more confessional literature popular during the immediate postwar era of the 1950s. Nonetheless, Bachmann, like Aichinger and Haushofer, reconstructed history from a female perspective and thus freed historical discourse from more traditional male paradigms.[287]

The image of "freeing" oneself or wishing to liberate oneself from social structures or dominant discourses is evident in works by women authors like Bachmann, writing *about* the experiences of women authors. Much the same thing can be seen in the the the nineteenth-century short story "The Yellow Wallpaper" (1892) by Charlotte Perkins Gilman, where a woman is confined to an attic room by her husband because of her desire to write, an activity which, at that time, was said to cause insanity in women. The female narrator, who "did write for a while in spite of them [her husband and caretaker Jane [K. K.],"[288] begins to see the image of an old woman creeping behind the torn wallpaper of her "prison" room. Believing that the "woman gets out in the daytime,"[289] she frees the imagined woman and thus herself, warning her husband in the end: "I've got out at last, in spite of you and Jane. And I've pulled off most of the paper, so you can't put me back!"[290] At one point the female narrator in Perkins Gilman's story sees many women creeping behind the wallpaper and speculates: "I wonder if they all come out of that wallpaper as I did?"[291] Perkins Gilman describes the situation of many female writers of the past and foreshadows a later generation of writers like Bachmann's female narrator in *Malina*, who does not "come out of the crack in the wall" as does the narrator in "The Yellow Wallpaper." Instead, Bachmann's female narrator cannot escape her confinement in the wall which "is a very old, a very strong wall, out of which nothing can fall, that nobody can break open, out of which nothing can ever be heard" (MAL 337). However, unlike the female narrator in *Malina*, Bachmann was able to write *herself* free from the confinement of expectations about a novel's structure and a narrator's perspective.

For Bachmann, as well as for the many other authors of her time, transforming memory and personal history into literary fiction becomes a source of liberation for her personal story and her perspective. Like the heroine in the Bluebeard tale, who dares to explore the world beyond the confines of social definitions and roles for women, Bachmann frees herself from the past in her fiction by exposing the bloody chamber of history and the criminal in all Bluebeard figures. As a storyteller, Bachmann identifies with the character Scheherazade from *The Thousand and One Nights* who recounts tales in order to prolong her life: "so that one escapes, that the deadline is extended."[292] By telling stories, that is by writing and by rewriting history, Bachmann, like the Persian princess, is able to liberate herself and therefore survive the murder scene of society and history.

Notes

Introduction

[1] "The Fairy Tale in Our Day," Horváth's literary tale, is undated. Elisabeth Borchers, ed. *Märchen Deutscher Dichter* (Frankfurt a. M.: Insel Verlag, 1972), 11.

[2] Hilde Spiel, "Ingeborg Bachmann: Keine Kerze für Florian" (No Candle for Florian) *Kleine Schritte: Berichte und Geschichten* (Munich: Edition Spangenberg, Ellermann Verlag, 1976), 158-163.

[3] Bachmann had completed the drama *Carmen Ruidera* in 1942 and the story *Das Honditschkreuz* in 1943.

[4] Höller points out that this group of Austrian writers differentiated itself from the German *Group 47* who believed that literature of the postwar should begin with a "tabula rasa," at the "Stunde Null" (the zero hour). The libraries and publishing companies in Vienna were not destroyed as they had been in German cities during the war, and it was suggested that the Austrian capital become the new center for the publishing of German-language literature (HIB 43-45).

[5] The editors of Bachmann's collective works, Christine Koschel and Inge von Weidenbaum, have since stated that Bachmann did not die from the complications of burns alone, but also because the prescription medication she had been taking for a depression disorder was withheld from her at the hospital. Before her accident Bachmann had been in various clinics to overcome her addiction to this medication, but doctors treating her burns were unaware of this situation at the time of her accident. Corinna Caduft, "Chronik von Leben und Werk," *du–die Zeitschrift für Kultur*, n. 9, Sept. 1994: 87. See also HIB 156-157.

[6] Monika Albrecht, in her article "Text-Torso oder Trümmerfeld," writes that the novel-fragments from the *Todesarten*-Project (named Goldmann/Rottwitz novel) were written at the same time as *Malina*. Irene Heidelberger-Leonard, ed. *"Text-Tollhaus für Bachmann-Süchtige?"* (Opladen/Wiesbaden: Westdeutscher Verlag, 1998), 29.

[7] Much of Bachmann's work, so influential to her writing, is inaccessible due to the fact that all letters, many fragments of her work, as well as her collection of newspaper clippings at the National Austrian Library will not be available to the public until after January 1, 2026. There are over 10,000 written and typed sheets of paper in Bachmann's

collection at the *Handschriftensammlung*, 5,000 of which were used to compile and publish the *"Todesarten"-Projekt* in 1995.

[8.] Primo Levi, *Die Atempause*, trans. Barbara and Robert Pichl (1963. Munich: Deutscher Taschenbuch Verlag, 1994), 53. I have translated the passage from the German edition. It is interesting to note that, although Bachmann did not own *La tregua* or the translated *Die Atempause* (1963, 1976, 1991) in her private library, she certainly must have read Levi's novel in 1963 because of her interest in both the Holocaust and Italian literature (She had translated Giuseppe Ungaretti's collection of poems from Italian into German in 1961). This information was shared with me by Professor Robert Pichl at the University of Vienna, Austria, and taken from his personal catalog of Ingeborg Bachmann's private library.

[9.] Hans Höller, *Geschichtserfahrung: Das Werk Ingeborg Bachmanns von den frühen Gedichten bis zum Todesarten-Zyklus, Habilitationsschrift*, Universität Salzburg, 1984, 293.

[10.] See for example, Heidi Borhau's study *Ingeborg Bachmann's 'Malina.' Eine Provokation?* (Würzburg: Königshausen & Neumann, 1994), "Ingeborg Bachmann" in *Text und Kritik* 6 (1971); Holger Pausch, *Ingeborg Bachmann* (Berlin: Colloquium, 1975); Günter Blöcker, "Auf der Suche nach dem Vater," *Merkur* 25 (1971), 395-98.

[11.] Heidi Borhau, *Ingeborg Bachmann's 'Malina'': Eine Provokation?*, gives a detailed account concerning the mixed reviews of Bachmann's *Malina*, 39 and 66-154.

[12.] Hans Höller, *Habilitationsschrift*, 330.

[13.] Barbara Kosta, *Recasting Autobiography: Women's Counterfictions in Contemporary German Literature and Film* (Ithaca: Cornell University Press, 1994), 35.

[14.] Borhau, 36, 76-77.

[15.] Kosta, 37.

[16.] Kosta, 37.

[17.] Kosta, 40.

[18.] Kosta, 42.

[19.] Borhau, 107.

[20.] Borhau, 109.

[21.] Christa Wolf, "Vierte Frankfurter Poetik-Vorlesung: Ein Brief über Eindeutigkeit und Mehrdeutigkeit, Bestimmtheit und Unbestimmtheit; über sehr alte Zustände und neue Seh-Raster; über Objektivität. [1983]," eds. Christine Koschel and Inge von Weidenbaum, *Kein Objectives Urteil–Nur ein Lebendiges: Texte zum Werk von Ingeborg Bachmann*

(Munich: Piper, 1989), 536. Also quoted in Borhau, 110.

22. Hans Höller as quoted by Borhau, 110.

23. Borhau, 106.

24. Karen Achberger, *Understanding Ingeborg Bachmann* (Columbia: University of South Carolina Press, 1994), 107.

25. Achberger, *Understanding Ingeborg Bachmann*, 128.

26. Achberger, "Beyond Patriarchy: Ingeborg Bachmann and Fairy-tales," *Modern Austrian Literature* 18.3-4 (1985) : 211-221.

27. Achberger, "Beyond Patriarchy," 212-213.

28. Angelika Rauch, "Sprache, Weiblichkeit und Utopie bei Ingeborg Bachmann," *Modern Austrian Literature* 18.3-4 (1985) : 21.

29. Rauch, 27.

30. Rauch, 33.

31. Achberger, "Beyond Patriarchy: Ingeborg Bachmann and Fairy-tales," 216.

32. Achberger, "Beyond Patriarchy: Ingeborg Bachmann and Fairy-tales," 216.

33. Achberger, "Beyond Patriarchy: Ingeborg Bachmann and Fairy-tales," 215.

34. Donald Haase, "Verzauberung der Seele. Das Märchen und die Exilanten der NS Zeit," *Akten des VIII Internationalen Germanisten-Kongresses* (Tokyo, 1990), 48-49.

35. In an interview, Bachmann once said she did not feel herself to be in exile in Italy, but instead that she led a "double life" in which part of her was always in Italy, the other always in Austria (WIR 121).

36. Jack Zipes, "The Grimms and the German Obsession with Fairy-tales," *Fairy-tales and Society: Illusion, Allusion, and Paradigm*, ed. Ruth B. Bottigheimer (Philadephia: University of Pennsylvania Press, 1986), 281 and 275. In 1944 W. H. Auden proclaimed that the Grimms' tales were "among the few indispensable, common-property books upon which Western culture can be founded" and continued that it was "hardly too much to say that these tales rank next to the Bible in importance." W. H. Auden, "In Praise of the Brothers Grimm," *The New York Times Book Review* (12 Nov. 1944): 1,28.

37. Zipes, "The Grimms and the German Obsession with Fairy-tales," 279.

38. Zipes, "The Grimms and the German Obsession with Fairy-tales," 282.

39. Zipes, "The Grimms and the German Obsession with Fairy-tales,

284.

[40] Zipes, "The Grimms and the German Obsession with Fairy-tales," 284-285.

[41] As Torborg Lundell points out in her study *Fairy-Tale Mothers*, the Grimms attempted to break up strong mother-daughter relationships in their fairy tales because such social structures might endanger the patriarchal social order. Whereas positive male figures such as the father, the brother, or the prince aid Bluebeard's bride in the more traditional Bluebeard tales, it is the mother who intervenes in Carter's tale to save her daughter from an otherwise certain death. In: Torborg Lundell, *Fairy-Tale Mothers* (Frankfurt a. M.: Peter Lang, 1990).

[42] Sigrid Weigel, *Die Stimme der Medusa* (Reinbek bei Hamburg: Rowohlt, 1989), 308.

[43] Weigel, 309.

[44] Hanne Castein, "Grass and the Appropriation of the Fairy-Tale in the Seventies," *Günter Grass's Der Butt: Sexual Politics and the Male Myth of History*, eds. Philip Brady, Timothy McFarland and John J. White (Oxford: Clarendon Press, 1990), 99.

[45] Filz, 20.

[46] Filz, 124.

[47] Filz, 67.

[48] Filz, 69-70.

[49] Bachmann, 172. Beilage, K-Zahl 7224-7242, #1803, *Handschriftensammlung*, Austrian National Library, Vienna, Austria.

[50] Bachmann, 172. Beilage, K-Zahl 7224-7242, #1805, *Handschriftensammlung*, Austrian National Library, Vienna, Austria.

[51] In many North American Indian folk tales, traditional figures such as the "trickster" have equally good and bad characteristics. See Paul Radin, *"The Trickster": A Study in American Indian Mythology* (New York: Philosophical Library, 1956).

[52] Although Bachmann views such polar structures as negative, she does not offer an alternative to polarity in her fiction, raising the question whether or not such polar structures are completely unavoidable.

[53] Marie-Luise Gättens, "Die Rekonstruktion der Geschichte: Der Nationalsozialismus in drei Romanen der siebziger Jahre," *Frauen-Fragen in der Deutschsprachigen Literatur seit 1945: Amsterdamer Beiträge zur Neueren Germanistik* Band 29-1989, eds. Mona Knapp and Gerd Labroisse (Amsterdam, 1989), 111.

[54] Gättens, 111-112.

[55] In Elaine Martin, ed, *Gender Patriarchy and Fascism in the Third Reich: The Response of Women Writers*. Detroit: Wayne State University Press, 1993.

[56] Other authors include Erika Mitterer, Marie-Thérèse Kerschbaumer, Elfriede Jelinek, Brigitte Schwaiger, Elisabeth Reichart, and Waltraud Anna Mitgutsch.

[57] Elaine Martin, ed. *Gender Patriarchy and Fascism in the Third Reich: The Response of Women Writers*, (Detroit: Wayne State University, 1993), 244-246.

[58] Further texts include Ursula Hegi's *Floating in my Mother's Palm* (1990) and *Stones from the River* (1994), Elisabeth Reichart's *Nachtmär* (Nightmare, 1995), and Anna Mitgutsch's *Ausgrenzung* (Shut-out), 1992 and *Abschied von Jerusalem* (Farewell from Jerusalem), 1995.

[59] Ruth Klüger, *weiter leben Eine Jugend* (1992. Göttingen: Wallenstein Verlag, 1994), 12.

[60] Aichinger and Bachmann were friends in Vienna during the postwar years and collaborated with *Group 47*. But while Aichinger's only novel, *Die größere Hoffnung,* was celebrated in 1948, Bachmann's novel *Malina* was not published until 1971, and her other novel fragments would not be published until after her death. Richard Reichensperger, *Die Bergung der Opfer in der Sprache: Über Ilse Aichinger - Leben und Werk* (Frankfurt a. M.: Fischer, 1991), 12.

[61] Figures and dates taken from *Jewish Vienna: Heritage and Mission* (Vienna: Vienna Tourist Board, 1995), 12-13; Bundespressedienst, ed. *Österreich-Dokumentation: Jüdisches Leben in Österreich* (Vienna, 1994); *1938: NS-Herrschaft in Österreich. Texte und Bilder aus der gleichnamigen Ausstellung* (Vienna: Bundesministerium für Inneres, Dokumentationsarchiv des österreichischen Widerstandes, 1998); and *Frauenleben 1945 - Kriegsende in Wien.* (205. Sonderausstellung des Historischen Museums der Stadt Wien, 21. September - 19 November, 1995. Vienna: Eigenverlag der Museen der Stadt Wien, 1995).

[62] Jean-François Lyotard, *Instructions païennes* (Paris: Galilee, 1977), 39.

[63] Hayden White, *The Content of the Form: Narrative Discourse and Historical Representation* (Baltimore: The Johns Hopkins University Press, 1987), 47.

[64] White, 57.

[65] *The Thousand and One Nights* is also known as *The Arabian Nights' Entertainment*.

^{66.} Bachmann, K-Zahl 7955-8009, 195. Beilage, # 4483, Rot (7), Bachmann's *Handschriftensammlung*, Austrian National Library, Vienna, Austria.

^{67.} Bachmann discusses this "murderous" and criminal society in her introduction to *Der Fall Franza* (FF 341-343) and in *Malina* (MAL 276).

Chapter One

^{68.} "...mit einem Blick auf Utopia..." JUG 93

^{69.} Bachmann, NL, 172. Beilage, K-Zahl 7224-7242, #2625 Bachmann's *Handschriftensammlung*, Austrian National Library, Vienna, Austria.

^{70.} Achberger, "Beyond Patriarchy: Ingeborg Bachmann and Fairytales," 216.

^{71.} Achberger, 216.

^{72.} Achberger, *Understanding Ingeborg Bachmann*, 7.

^{73.} Kohn-Waechter, *Das Verschwinden in der Wand: Destruktive Moderne und Widerspruch eines weiblichen Ich in Ingeborg Bachmanns "Malina"* (Stuttgart: J. B. Metzlersche Verlagsbuchhandlung, 1992), 43.

^{74.} Kohn-Waechter, *Das Verschwinden in der Wand*, 102.

^{75.} "That the story ends with the death of the princess was mostly disregarded." Kohn-Waechter, 43.

^{76.} Kohn-Waechter, *Das Verschwinden in der Wand*, 63.

^{77.} Kohn-Waechter mentions that the narrator in the dream meets the stranger while he is being deported to a concentration camp, instead of meeting him under a windowsill as the utopian narrative of the "Princess of Kagran" had promised. Kohn-Waechter, *Das Verschwinden in der Wand*, 101.

^{78.} Walter Filz, *Es war einmal? Elemente des Märchens in der deutschen Literatur der siebziger Jahre*, 66.

^{79.} Filz, 67.

^{80.} Friedrich Ruthmaner, "Gründung von Prag: Libussa," *Österreichische Volkssagen* (Vienna: Attenkofersche Verlagsbuchhandlung, 1914).

^{81.} Bachmann, NL, 66 Beilage, K-Zahl 2922-2982a., Blatt 2507, 13, Bachmann's *Handschriftensammlung*, Austrian National Library, Vienna, Austria.

^{82.} Bachmann, NL, 66 Beilage, K-Zahl 2922-2982a., Blatt 2529, 14,

Bachmann's *Handschriftensammlung*, Austrian National Library, Vienna, Austria.

[83] Bachmann, NL, 65 Beilage, K-Zahl 2818-2921, Blatt 2509, rot: 22, Bachmann's *Handschriftensammlung*, Austrian National Library, Vienna, Austria.

[84] In other text versions, however, Bachmann refers to the coat as "siderisch," sidereal, or one having to do with the stars.

[85] The Martagon lily, from the Latin botanical name "Lilium Martagon," is a striking red-purple lily found in both Eastern and Western European countries, North, South, and Latin America, as well as the African continent.

[86] Although it becomes clear that the female narrator in *Malina* is disturbed by the gender, class, and race relations in her everyday life, the sequence describing the deportation of Jews portrays the Holocaust as one historical instance of these gender, class, and race relations in the twentieth century discussed in the novel cycle. Bachmann also discusses issues of race and gender in *Der Fall Franza*, where the character Franza identifies with the indigenous and colonized peoples of Papua New Guinea, "I am a Papua" (FF 414).

[87] In Bachmann's *Todesarten*-cycle, as well as in most of her prose, the mother figure is strangely absent from the lives of her narrators. In *Malina*, for instance, the mother figure is complicit in the crimes of the father in the chapter on nightmares, "Der dritte Mann," and is not further discussed in the novel. In *Der Fall Franza,* the absence and early death of Franza's mother during World War II is noted during Franza's narration. In *Requiem für Fanny Goldmann,* Fanny's mother is mentioned only in relation to her husband who had committed suicide. The marginality of the maternal figure is furthermore emphasized by the strong prevalence of the father figure throughout Bachmann's prose.

[88] Robert Pichl, "Voraussetzungen und Problemhorizont der gegenwärtigen Ingeborg Bachmann Forschung," 77-93, 90.

[89] *Mythen und Sagen aus dem steirischen Hochlande* (1880. Vaduz, Liechtenstein: Sändig Reprint Verlag, 1985), 203-204.

[90] Gustav Gugitz, *Sagen und Legenden der Stadt Wien* (Vienna: Verlag Brüder Hollinek, no date) and Leander Petzoldt, ed. *Sagen aus der Steiermark* (Munich: Eugen Diederichs Verlag, 1993).

[91] Barbara Kunze, "Ein Geheimnis der Prinzessin von Kagran: Die ungewöhnliche Quelle zu der 'Legende' in Ingeborg Bachmann's *Malina,*" *Modern Austrian Literature* 18.3-4 (1985) : 105-119.

⁹² I could find no reference to this "legend" in any Austro-Hungarian, Czech or German folklore and fairy-tale collections.

⁹³ Tales of a man who saves Klagenfurt abound in collections of Austrian fairy tales and legends, such as "Der Lindwurm von Klagenfurt" Kurt Benesch, *Sagen aus Österreich: Oberösterreich. Steiermark. Kärnten* (Vienna: Verlag Kremayr & Scheriau, 1985), 167-171, and "Der Kampf mit dem Lindwurm" in Hans Fraungruber, *Österreichisches Sagenkränzlein* (Vienna: Loewes Verlag, n.d.), 146-147, and "Das Klagenfurter Stadtwappen" in Georg Graber, ed. *Sagen aus Kärnten* (Graz: Leykam Verlag, 1944), 310-312, and "Drachen und Lindwürmer" in Leander Petzoldt, ed. *Sagen aus der Steiermark* (Munich: Eugen Diederichs Verlag, 1993), 274-275.

⁹⁴ Robert Pichl, "Voraussetzungen und Problemhorizont der gegenwärtigen Ingeborg Bachmann Forschung," 90.

⁹⁵ By referring to the fairy-tale character of "Thrushbeard," or the German fairy-tale figure "Drosselbart," the female narrator makes the correlation between Malina and the Bluebeard figure, as one who strangles the female narrator (sie erdrosselt), thereby silencing her, as Malina does at the end of *Malina*.

⁹⁶ Ingrid Riedel's Jungian interpretation, for example, views the tale as the female narrator's animus projection. ["Auf der Suche nach weiblicher Identität," in "Im Sattel der Selbstbehauptung: zur Funktion der Autobiographie," ed. Ev. Akademie Hofgeismar, *Protokoll* 91 (1971) : 13] Whereas Ellen Summerfield reads the tale as a reflection of the narrator's relationship with Ivan [*Ingeborg Bachmann: Die Auflösung der Figur in ihrem Roman "Malina"* (Bonn: Bouvier, 1976), 14-15], Marlies Janz and Stephan Sauthoff identify the stranger in the tale as Bachmann's friend Paul Celan by comparing the biographies of the stranger and of Celan, as well as by tracing references to his poetry in Bachmann's tale. [Marlies Janz, *Vom Engagement absoluter Poesie: Zur Lyrik und Ästhetik Paul Celans* (Frankfurt a. M.: Syndikat, 1976), 218, footnote 47, and Stephan Sauthoff, *Die Transformation (auto) biographischer Elemente im Prosawerk Ingeborg Bachmanns*(Frankfurt a. M.: Peter Lang, 1992), 65-78]. Manfred Jurgensen reads the text as one in which Bachmann places herself in the mythical role of Undine, a figure often associated with Bachmann as a writer in the Romantic tradition. [Manfred Jurgensen, *Ingeborg Bachmann: Die neue Sprache* (Bern: Peter Lang, 1981), 77.] Kurt Bartsch criticizes readings in which Bachmann is associated with the poetic figure Undine, claiming that such correlations lead to mis-

understandings and trivial labeling. [Kurt Bartsch, "Affinität und Distanz. Bachmann und die Romantik." *Romantik - Eine lebenskräftige Krankheit: Ihre literarischen Nachwirkungen in der Moderne. Amsterdamer Beiträge zur Neueren Germanistik* vol. 34 (Amsterdam: Rodopi, 1991), 209-234, 209]. Robert Steiger defines the narrative as the female narrator's "Wunschdenken," "wishful thinking." *"Malina": Versuch einer Interpretation des Romans von Ingeborg Bachmann* (Heidelberg: Winter, 1978), 109.

[97] Kohn-Waechter, *Das Verschwinden in der Wand,* 51.

[98] Kohn-Waechter, *Das Verschwinden in der Wand,* 50.

[99] Kohn-Waechter, *Das Verschwinden in der Wand,* 59.

[100] Kohn-Waechter, *Das Verschwinden in der Wand,* 59.

[101] Kohn-Waechter, *Das Verschwinden in der Wand,* 65.

[102] Kohn-Waechter, *Das Verschwinden in der Wand,* 73-74.

[103] "Alle Mährchen sind nur Träume von jener heymathlichen Welt." Novalis, *Dichter über ihre Dichtungen,* vol. 15, *Novalis,* ed. Hans-Joachim Mähl (Passau: Heimeran Verlag, 1976), 170.

[104] "Ein Märchen ist eigentlich wie ein Traumbild – ohne Zusammenhang – Ein Ensemble wunderbarer Dinge und Begebenheiten. "Novalis, *Dichter über ihre Dichtungen,* 129.

[105] "Es sollte mir lieb seyn, wenn ihr Roman und Märchen in einer glücklichen Mischung zu bemerken glaubtet, und der erste Theil euch eine noch innigere Mischung im 2ten Theile profezeyhte. Der Roman soll allmälich in Märchen übergehen." Novalis, *Dichter über ihre Dichtungen,* 92.

[106] Georg Lukács, "Die Romantik als Wendung in der deutschen Literatur," *Romantikforschung seit 1945,* ed. Klaus Peter (Königstein: Verlagsgruppe Athenäum, 1980), 40-52, 40. Hanne Castein discusses this in his essay "Arbeiten mit der Romantik heute: Zur Romantikrezeption der DDR, unter besonderer Berücksichtigung des Märchens," *Deutsche Romantik und das 20. Jahrhundert,* Londoner Symposium 1985, eds. Hanne Castein and Alexander Stillmark (Stuttgart: Akademischer Verlag, 1986), 5-23.

[107] Adolf Haslinger, "Romantik in der Österreichischen Gegenwartsliteratur: Rezeptionsprobleme und Rezeptionsbeispiele," *Deutsche Romantik und das 20. Jahrhundert,* 160. Haslinger supports his model of identifying Romantic elements in contemporary literature with three points from René Wellek's essay "Romanticism Reexamined." First, poetry is regarded as a complete means of "realization" (Erkenntnis).

Second, nature is conceived to be an organic unity in which the duality of subject and object is suspended. Third, poetry expresses this organic unity through mythology and symbols. René Wellek, "Romanticism Re-examined," *Concepts of Criticism*, ed. Stephen Nichols Jr. (New Haven and London: Yale University Press, 1963).

[108] Bartsch describes Bachmann's use of montage as an intentional act, "whereby she writes in the modern tradition because she lets her reader know 'what she is doing and that she is doing it' by using quotes in a 'montage' form." Bartsch, 217.

[109] Bartsch lists Wolfgang Gerstenlauer's "Undines Wiederkehr. Fouqué-Giraudoux-Bachmann," *Die Neueren Sprachen N.F.* 19 (19-70): 514-527; Hans Joachim Beck's "Malina oder die Romantik," *Germanisch-Romanische Monatsschrift*, ed. Conrad Wiedemann, vol. 38, (1988): 304-324; Erika Tunner, "Von der Unvermeidbarkeit des Schiffbruchs. Zu den Hörspielen von Ingeborg Bachmann," *Ingeborg Bachmann. L'oeuvre et ses situations: Actes du colloque* (Nantes, 1986): 82-99. Bartsch, 214.

[110] Beck claims that Bachmann's *Todesarten* trilogy, in the order of *Malina, Der Fall Franza* and *Requiem für Fanny Goldmann*, reflects a montage of subtexts based on Novalis' *Heinrich von Ofterdingen* (1802), Theodor Fontane's *Effi Briest* (1894/95) and Robert Musil's *Der Mann ohne Eigenschaften* (The Man without Attributes, 1930, 1933, 1943). Beck, however, does not consider the fact that *Der Fall Franza* was written much earlier than *Malina*. Beck, 310. Beck further cites Hermann Broch's *Die Schlafwandler* (The Sleepwalkers, 1931/32) trilogy as an additional subtext of Bachmann's *Todesarten* trilogy, and one that possibly inspired her to write the trilogy in a chronological and historical order. Beck, 311. The order of Bachmann's novels in *Todesarten* which Beck refers to is incorrect, as I mentioned earlier. Beck bases his chronology on the published *Todesarten*-trilogy from 1978. In this edition the chronology of the novels was based on the status of their completion, rather than on the date that Bachmann began working on her novels.

[111] Beck, 318.

[112] Bartsch, 232.

[113] Bartsch, 223.

[114] Luckwig Tieck's *Liebesgeschichte der schönen Magelone und des Grafen Peter von Provence* (1796), Novalis' *Hyazinth und Rosenblütchen* in *Die Lehrlinge zu Sais* (1798/99), E.T.A. Hoffmann's *Johannes Kreislers Lehrbrief* from *Kreisleriana* (1816) and Karoline von Günderode's

Timur (1802/04) for example. Kohn-Waechter, 49, 60-62.

[115] Gerhart Hoffmeister of the University of California at Santa Barbara pointed out to me in 1996 that strangers sometimes lead Heinrich *away* from poetry, as in *Lehrlinge zu Sais*, in which the stranger represents the Enlightenment.

[116] Novalis' *Heinrich von Ofterdingen*, as cited in Kohn-Waechter, 60.

[117] "Die Schreibart des Romans muß kein Continuum–es muß etwas abgeschnittenes–begränztes ein eignes Ganzes seyn [sic]." Novalis, *Dichter über ihre Dichtungen*, 164.

[118] "Der ächte Märchendichter ist ein Seher der Zukunft [sic]." Mähl, 171.

[119] Kohn-Waechter, 70.

[120] According to Tieck's essay on Novalis' plans for sequels to *Heinrich von Ofterdingen*, Heinrich was to discover that the blue flower is a reference to his bride Mathilde [Novalis 187]. Sophie and Mathilde play the same role in this novel in that they represent "the mother of all things. The floating face in the blue flower in Heinrich's first dream becomes linked to Heinrich's bride Mathilde as well as to the priestess Sophie. The female characters represent a possible fulfillment of longing for the poet as well as a synthesis of the earthly and the ephemeral. However, as Kohn-Waechter points out about Novalis' novel, it is precisely the deaths of the women characters that enable Heinrich to become a poet. In other words, the sacrifice of a woman is necessary for the male poet to succeed. The sacrifice of the woman as necessary for the male artist to succeed as portrayed in past literature has been discussed by many feminist scholars, such as Sigrid Weigel, who stated that "progress is always made through the exclusion of the feminine." Weigel, *Die Stimme der Medusa*, 11.

[121] *Heinrich von Ofterdingen* can be read as a cyclical work in that Heinrich's prophetic dream at the start of the novel is fulfilled at the close. Although the female narrator's utopian dream of salvation is not fulfilled at the conclusion of *Malina* because she is relegated to a crack in the wall, the novel can nonetheless be read as cyclical because it is the female narrator who tells the story from the start. Neva Slibar reads *Malina* as a cyclical novel: the female narrator tells her story in which the ending of *Malina* propels the reader repeatedly to the beginning of the novel, thus emphasizing the multiple layers of meaning and interpretive possibilities within the novel. *Sonderdruck, Ingeborg Buchmann - Neue Beiträge zu*

ihrem Werk, Internationales Symposion Münster 1991, eds. Dirk Göttsche and Hubert Ohl (Würzburg: Königshausen & Neumann), 167-185, 183.

[122] Graziella Hlawaty, *Die Stadt der Lieder* (Vienna: Paul Zsolnay, 1995), 7.

[123] Ilse Aichinger, *Die größere Hoffnung* (Frankfurt a. M.: Fischer, 1991), 26.

[124] Aichinger "Nach der weißen Rose," *Kleist, Moos, Fasane* (Frankfurt a. M.: Fischer, 1987), 28.

[125] In 1930 Bloch wrote that "the fairy tale tells of wish fulfillment that is not only bound to its time and costume of its contents." Ernst Bloch, *Literarische Aufsätze* (Frankfurt a. M., 1965), 196-199.

[126] Hans Höller views the female narrator's wish to write "the beautiful book" as her yearning to unite "life, work, and love." Höller, *Habilitation*, 373.

[127] Sigrid Weigel points out that Bachmann was afraid of criticism concerning her trilogy *Todesarten*, of which she had completed two chapters in 1966. At a reading she said that she was "afraid for her book." Her fears were realized when the public criticized her novel *Malina* as "female sensitivity" and "sick subjectivity." Sigrid Weigel, *Topographien der Geschlechter: Schreibweisen in der Gegenwartsliteratur von Frauen* (Reinbek bei Hamburg: Rowohlt, 1990), 254-255.

[128] The *Todesarten* book which Ivan criticizes is discussed in Bachmann's *Malina*, 53-54, 82.

[129] Letters, and the problems that are associated with writing and answering them, can be found throughout the novel (Bachmann, *Malina*, 50-53, 70-72, 79-80, 106-109, 141-144, 147, 327, 333, 336).

[130] Many of the authors I discuss have or have had academic careers. Bachmann, for instance, was employed by the University of Frankfurt in Germany from 1959 to 1960. The authors Ruth Klüger, Ursula Hegi, and Elizabeth Welt Trahan are professors (emerita) at universities in the United States.

[131] Ursula Hegi, *Stones from the River* (New York: Simon & Schuster, 1994), 450.

[132] Klüger, *weiter leben Eine Jugend*, 283.

[133] The narrators discuss their sometimes ambivalent reactions to events of the war, their fears and apprehensions, instead of emphasizing heroic acts. Theirs is not an "other" voice, but certainly a different and individual voice of experience.

[134] Weigel shows that, in an attempt to secure their own position in

the literary world, women have all too often striven to be identified as the "other." Some women writers have thereby fallen into the trap of emphasizing the polarity of the sexes, in which women are viewed as the "other sex." Weigel maintains further that when women have attempted to create a feminine discourse or to establish images of femininity, they have just repeated images present in the dominant discourse, or created speculative matriarchal myths from a past cultural history. Weigel, *Topographien der Geschlechter*, 260-261. During the 1970s, French women authors and scholars such as Hélène Cixous, Luce Irigaray, and Julia Kristeva discussed the possibility of a specifically female language and voice, independent and different from men's language. However, because men and women have access to the same language it is impossible for there to be a specifically female voice belonging exclusively to women. Instead, the female voice is one that is able to describe experiences specific to women, or each individual woman.

Chapter Two

[135] Grimm, "Der Räuberbräutigam," *Kinder- und Hausmärchen*, ed. Heinz Rölleke, vol. 1 (Stuttgart: Reclam, 1980), 220.

[136] Benigni, Roberto, "Ein Clown in Auschwitz: Interview with Bert Rebhandl," *Format* Oct. 1998 Nr. 2/12: 180-181.

[137] Generally speaking there are four perspectives used in interpreting folk- and fairy tale: the Freudian reading focusing on sexual maturation, the Jungian reading with its exploration of universal motifs, the socio-historical Marxist reading, and the feminist reading, which emphasizes women's roles and gender relations.

[138] The folk tale scholars Antti Aaarne and Stith Thompson address the distinctions between the German and French Bluebeard traditions in their index *Types of the Folktale*. The authors classify types 311 and 312 as Bluebeard tales in which "three sisters [are] rescued from the power of an ogre." Tale type 311 entitled "Rescue by the Sister" addresses the German-language tradition of Bluebeard where the third and youngest sister rescues her elder sisters from a murderer. The rescue by the heroine distinguishes this tale type from type 312, "The Giant-killer and his Dog (Bluebeard)," in which the passive sister is saved by her brother(s), as in the Perrault tale. Even though the female figures in *Todesarten* are not rescued by a sister *or* brother, they expose the destructive and murderous

characteristics of the Bluebeard-like father figure as does the sister in the German-speaking tradition of tale type 311. Antti Aarne and Stith Thompson, *The Types of the Folktale* (Helsinki: Suomalainen Tiedeakatemia, 1961), 100-103.

[139] Georg Trakl, "Blaubart: Ein Puppenspiel," (Fragment) *Dichtungen und Briefe*, eds. Walther Killy and Hans Szklenar, 2nd ed. (1969. Salzburg: Otto Müller Verlag, 1987).

[140] Emil Heckmann, *Blaubart. Ein Beitrag zur vergleichenden Märchenforschung*. Dissertation (Mannheim-Rheinau, 1930).

[141] Ulrike Blaschek, ed., *Märchen vom Blaubart* (Frankfurt a. M.: Fischer, 1989), 15. The Bluebeard tale has been traced as far back as the "Legende von den heiligen Gildas" by Père Albert Le Grand. Elisabeth Frenzel, *Stoffe der Weltliteratur. Ein Lexikon dichtungsgeschichtlicher Längschnitte* (Stuttgart: Alfred Kröner Verlag, 1983), 102.

[142] Hartwig Suhrbier, ed., *Blaubarts Geheimnis* (Köln: Eugen Diederichs Verlag, 1984), 12.

[143] Numerous editions of the Grimm's *Kinder- und Hausmärchen* were published. In 1810, the Grimms submitted a manuscript, containing 53 stories, some only fragments and notes, to Clemens Brentano and Achim von Arnim for inclusion in a collection of folktales and folk songs entitled *Des Knaben Wunderhorn* (The Boy's Magic Horn). The Grimms' manuscript was never returned and was first published by Heinz Rölleke in 1977 as *Märchen aus dem Nachlaß der Brüder Grimm* (Fairy Tales From the Posthumous Papers of the Brothers Grimm, Bonn: Bouvier Verlag, 1977). The Grimms, who had not lost their desire to collect and edit folk and fairy tales, went on with their plans to publish a collection of tales. In 1812 they published their first edition of *Kinder- und Hausmärchen* (Nursery and Household Tales), followed by editions in 1814, 1819, 1822, 1837, 1840, 1843, 1850, and finally 1857. The final 1957 version, with its 200 fairy tales and 10 legends, is most commonly referred to.

[144] John Ellis writes: "Since the entire program of the Grimm collection was to include only German tales passed on from one generation to the next – and any inclusion of a French tale contradictory to the purpose of their publication – tales similar to the French 'Barbe bleue' were left out of later *KHM* editions." John Ellis, *One Fairy Story Too Many: The Brothers Grimm and Their Tales*. (Chicago: The University of Chicago Press, 1983), 47.

[145] Grimm, *Kinder- und Hausmärchen. (1812/1815)*. Ed. Walter

Killy. (Frankfurt a. M.: Fischer Verlag, 1962), 175.

[146] Grimm, "Der Räuberbräutigam," *Kinder- und Hausmärchen*, Band 1 (1980, Stuttgart: Reclam, 1993), 219.

[147] Hans-Jörg Uther, "Der Frauenmörder Blaubart und seine Artverwandten," *Schweizerisches Archiv für Volkskunde, Vierteljahrschrift*, ed. Ueli Gyr Heft 1-2 (Basel, 1988) : 42.

[148] Uther, 44.

[149] Béla Bartók's opera *Duke Bluebeard's Castle* (1911) made Bluebeard a world-famous operatic villain. Movies such as Jane Campion's *The Piano* (1993), Zhang Yimou's *Raise the Red Lantern* (1991), Helma Sanders-Brahms' *Germany, Pale Mother* (1979) are recent films that are based on variants of the Bluebeard tale and deal with the plight of the female protagonists. Maria Tatar refers to earlier films that recall Bluebeard, such as Hitchcock's *Rebecca* (1940), Robert Stevenson's *Jane Eyre* (1944), George Cukor's *Gaslight* (1944), and Fritz Lang's *Secret Beyond the Door*. ("Introduction: Bluebeard," Maria Tatar, ed. *The Classic Fairy Tales: Texts. Criticism* (New York: W. W. Norton & Company, 1999), 140-141.) The Swiss author Max Frisch's *Blaubart* (Bluebeard, 1982), for instance, explores male-female relationships and questions of victimization and guilt, themes that recall Bachmann's references to Bluebeard in her prose. *Blaubart* tells the story of the fifty-four-year-old Dr. Felix Schaad, married seven times and accused of murdering one of his ex-wives. After a trial where he is pronounced innocent because of lack of evidence, Schaad's own personal trial begins, in which he is obsessively seeking the truth about his guilt. Through a series of conversations and confrontations with sixty-one "witnesses," including all of his ex-wives, Schaad must confront his psychologically twisted feelings towards women. After discovering that there is no one "joint memory," Schaad attempts to commit suicide, only to end up maimed in a hospital, the real murderer having been found, and his seventh wife having left him. Readers familiar with Bachmann's prose speculate about whether or not Frisch wrote *Blaubart* in response to Bachmann's portrayal of the Bluebeard character Jordan in *Der Fall Franza*. The recurring structures of male-dominated relationships, multiple murdered wives, as well as motifs such as the bloody chamber in Frisch's and Bachmann's work, emphasize the influence of the Bluebeard tradition within German-language literature.

[150] Charles Perrault, "Bluebeard," *The Classic Fairy Tales*, ed. Maria Tatar, 148.

[151.] Bruno Bettelheim, *The Uses of Enchantment: The Meaning and Importance of Fairy Tales* (New York: Random House, 1977), 302-303.

[152.] Tatar, *The Hard Facts of the Grimms' Fairy-tales*, 158.

[153.] Tatar, *The Hard Facts of the Grimms' Fairy-tales*, 168.

[154.] Ruth Bottigheimer, *Grimms' Bad Girls and Bold Boys* (New Haven and London: Yale University Press, 1987), 87.

[155.] Bottigheimer, 94.

[156.] Bottigheimer, 94.

[157.] Bottigheimer, 92-94.

[158.] Grimm, "Fichters Vogel," *Kinder- und Hausmärchen*, ed. Heinz Rölleke, vol. 1 (Stuttgart: Reclam, 1980), 237.

[159.] J. Cooper, *Fairy-tales. Allegories of the Inner Life* (Great Britain: Aquarian Press, 1983), 73.

[160.] Cooper, 73.

[161.] Marcia Lieberman in Zipes, ed., 187.

[162.] Lieberman in Zipes, ed., 199.

[163.] Rowe in Zipes, ed., 211.

[164.] Rowe in Zipes, ed., 210.

[165.] Angela Carter, *The Bloody Chamber* (New York: Harper & Row, 1981), 1.

[166.] Carter, 37.

[167.] The pool of blood in the secret room might be read as a portrayal of the risks of sexuality for women associated with marriage in the seventeenth through the nineteenth century, as reflected in the Grimms' tales: defloration and child bearing.

[168.] Grimm, "Fitchers Vogel," *Kinder- und Hausmärchen*, vol. 1, 237.

[169.] Grimm, "Breiselbart verführt alle Mädchen," *Märchen aus dem Nachlaß der Brüder Grimm*, ed. Heinz Rölleke (Bonn: Bouvier, 1977), 18. In this fragment, which recalls the Bluebeard tale, the youngest of three sisters, Salome, is able to trick Bluebeard into marriage. After sleeping with Salome's two older sisters and impregnating them, Breiselbart attempts the same with Salome. However, she cleverly puts a doll filled with honey and blood in her bed and hides underneath. After Breiselbart "sheds blood" by "stabbing her in the body" with his sword, Breiselbart realizes his love for her when he tastes the sweet honey that squirted on his lips. After he proclaimes his love for her, Salome crawls out from under the bed, makes her demands, and becomes his wife.

[170.] Grimm, *Kinder- und Hausmärchen. (1812/1815).* Ed. Walter Killy, ed., 175.

[171] Grimm, "Fitchers Vogel," *Kinder- und Hausmärchen*, vol. 1, 236.
[172] Cooper, 73.

Chapter Three

[173] Bachmann, posthumous work, 144 Beilage, Blatt 1582: rot: 9 K-Zahl 6345-6366, Bachmann's *Handschriftensammlung*, Austrian National Library, Vienna, Austria.

[174] As I mentioned earlier, Bachmann worked on the concept of the Bluebeard figure in her short story "Ein Schritt nach Gomorrha" as early as 1961, most likely around the time she began conceptualizing *Der Fall Franza.*

[175] Bachmann's terms "Amnadostrieb" and "Amnadosehe" have baffled even the most curious and enthusiastic Bachmann scholars. Professor Benjamin Dunlap of Wofford College in South Carolina discovered the term "Amnados" in an on-line dictionary of the "Elet Anta" (Language of the Anta), reportedly an ancient language of the British Isles. "Amnados" is noted as a noun meaning "a bore, a boring person, a dull person." *Dictionary*, ed. John Fischer, 25 August 1999 <http://www.drummond.demon.co.uk/anta/vocab/dic1.htm>. The legitimacy of this site could not be verified.

[176] In 1919, the serial killer Henri Landru (1869-1922) was charged with raping and murdering a young boy and ten women in Paris. He was guillotined in 1922. See "Landru," *Le Petit Robert: Dictionnaire Universel des Noms Propres,* 1991 ed. Another serial killer, Gilles de Rais (1404-1440) of Brittany, France, was executed in 1440 and is said to be the original Bluebeard of the *Tales of Mother Goose*. See Thomas Wilson, *Blue-Beard: A Contribution to History and Folk-Lore* (New York: G. P. Putnam's Sons, 1899) title page; and Elisabeth Frenzel, *Stoffe der Weltliteratur* (Stuttgart: Alfred Kröner Verlag, 1983), 103.

[177] Bachmann informed Toni Kienlechner that for over a decade she had been inspired and motivated to write her fiction, especially her novel cycle *Todesarten*, after reading this statement by Hölderlin. Toni Kienlechner, "Wörter und Worte*,*" *du–die Zeitschrift für Kultur*, 65.

[178] Similarly, the Austrian-Jewish author Ruth Klüger recalls lying in bed with a throat infection in March, 1938, in Vienna and hearing the soldiers' shouts outside on the streets. Ruth Klüger, *weiter leben Eine Jugend*, 23.

[179] Höller writes that Bachmann was not in Klagenfurt on March 12, but that the "screaming, singing and marching" she describes continued for weeks afterwards (HIB 18). Höller also points out that Bachmann's father had joined the NSDAP along with the majority of Carinthian teachers as early as 1932 (HIB 25).

[180] See Gerhard Botz, "Historische Brüche und Kontinuitäten als Herausforderungen: Ingeborg Bachmann und post-katastrophische Ge-schichtsmentalitäten in Österreich," *Ingeborg Bachmann-Neue Beiträge zu ihrem Werk. Internationales Symposium Münster, 1991*, eds. Dirk Göttsche and Hubert Ohl (Würzburg: Königshausen & Neumann, 1993), 201. Peter Beicken also cites the "Klagenfurter Zeitung" of March 15, 1938 which called this march into Austria "Austria's homecoming to the motherland." Peter Beicken, *Ingeborg Bachmann* (Munich: Verlag C.H. Beck,1988), 29.

[181] Leni Riefenstahl's 1935 cinematic documentary of the 1934 Nuremberg Party Congress *Triumph des Willens* (*Triumph of the Will*) captures this mass-chanting in adoration of the "Führer." Thomas Bernhard's fictional character Frau Professor Schuster in *Heldenplatz* slowly loses her mind as she constantly recalls the masses crying out "Sieg Heil" in unison below her apartment on the Viennese Heldenplatz after German troops march into Vienna in 1938. Thomas Bernhard, *Heldenplatz* (1988. Frankfurt a. M.: Suhrkamp Verlag, 1992), 159-165.

[182] In May, 1952, Hans Werner Richter invited Bachmann to read at the *Group 47* in Niendorf an der Ostsee. The following year in Mainz, Bachmann won a prize for her work.

[183] The following is taken from Judith Ryan, *The Uncompleted Past. Postwar German Novels and the Third Reich* (Detroit: Wayne State University Press, 1983).

[184] See Ruth Andreas-Friedrich's *Der Schattenmann* (1947/1986), Ruth Klüger's *weiter leben Eine Jugend in Wien.* (1992), and Ruth Dinesen's *Nelly Sachs* (1991).

[185] White, *The Content of the Form: Narrative Discourse and Historical Representation*, 4.

[186] White, 35.

[187] White, 45.

[188] White, 44.

[189] White, 47.

[190] Poland was the country in which the most Jews were murdered during National Socialism, as well as the location of six death camps in

which European Jews were executed systematically. Peter Longerich, ed., *Die Ermordung der europäischen Juden. Eine umfassende Dokumentation des Holocaust 1941-1945* (Munich: Piper, 1989), 188.

[191] Simon Wiesenthal, ed. *Verjährung? 200 Persönlichkeiten des öffentlichen Lebens sagen nein* (Frankfurt a. M.: Europäische Verlagsanstalt, 1965), 16.

[192] Simon Wiesenthal, *Justice Not Vengeance*, trans. Ewald Osers (New York: Grove Weidenfeld, 1989), 161.

[193] HIB 131. (Höller cites Heinrich Böll, "Ich denke an Sie wie an ein Mädchen," *Der Spiegel*, 22. Oktober, 1973. Zit. N. Michael Matthias Schardt, ed. *Über Ingeborg Bachmann*, 473).

[194] Bachmann, "Wahrlich," *Ingeborg Bachmann Werke*. Vol. I, 166.

[195] Thomas Bernhard, *Auslöschung* (Frankfurt a. M.: Suhrkamp, 1986), 215. The novel *Auslöschung* represents Bernhard's tribute to his friend Bachmann. References to Bachmann in the protagonist Maria are unmistakable. Bernhard writes that Maria/Bachmann came "from the small southeastern, ridiculous provincial city in which Musil was born" (232), that she had translated the Ungaretti poems (228), that her dream had always been to write prose (230), that she had managed to "break away" to Germany, then Paris, and finally Rome (234), and had always said "that she wanted to die in Rome" (235). Passages from Bernhard's novel are included in Andrea Stoll's edition *Ingeborg Bachmann's >Malina<* (Frankfurt a. M.: Suhrkamp, 1992), 29-43.

[196] Thomas Bernhard, *Auslöschung*, 237.

[197] Bachmann's close friends commented on her severe addiction to prescribed sedatives that year, taken for her depression. Caduft, "Chronik von Leben und Werk," *du-die Zeitschrift für Kultur*, 84.

[198] See Weigel *Ingeborg Bachmann* regarding Bachmann's friendship with the scholars Gerschom Scholem (5-15), Paul Celan (411-453), Hannah Arendt (462-464), Wolfgang Hildesheimer (467-472), Theodor Adorno (472-474), and Nelly Sachs (476-477).

[199] Corinna Coduff calls Bachmann and Celan's relationship a "love story" which began when Celan came to live in Vienna for a year after the war in 1947. "Chronik von Leben und Werk," *du-die Zeitschrift für Kultur*, 77.

[200] Paul Celan, "Corona," *Gedichte,* vol. 1 of 2 (Frankfurt a. M.: Suhrkamp, 1975), 37; Bachmann, "Dunkles zu sagen," *Werke I,* 32, and Bachmann, *Malina,* 68.

[201] Milo Dor, cited in Gudrun Kohn-Waechter, *Das Verschwinden in*

der Wand, 50.

[202] Höller cites Celan's volume at the German Literature Archive in Marbach, Germany.

[203] Günter Grass, *Schreiben nach Auschwitz: Frankfurt Poetik-Vorlesung* (Frankfurt a. M.: Luchterhand, 1990), 30.

[204] Barbara Wiedermann, ed. *Paul Celan–Nelly Sachs Briefwechsel* (Frankfurt a. M.: Suhrkamp Verlag, 1993), 109.

[205] Jean Améry, "Am Grabe einer unbekannten Freundin [1973]," *Kein Objektives Urteil–Nur ein Lebendiges, eds. Koschel and von Weidenbaum* (Munich: Piper,1989), 201.

[206] Heidelberger-Leonard states that "Drei Wege zum See" was written for Améry, in lieu of the letter the character Elisabeth never writes to Amery. Bachmann writes in *Three Paths to the Lake*: "She [Elisabeth] never got to write the letter" (SEE 421).

[207] Irene Heidelberger-Leonard, "Zur Differenz zwischen der Ästhetisierung des Leidens und der Authentizität traumatischer Erfahrungen," *Ingeborg Bachmann: Neue Beiträge zu ihrem Werk Internationales Symposium, Münster, 1991*, eds. Dirk Göttsche and Hubert Ohl (Würzburg:Köngishausen & Neumann, 1993), 191.

[208] Jean Améry, "Die Tortur," *Jenseits von Schuld und Sühne. Bewältigungsversuche eines Überwältigten* (Stuttgart: Klett- Cotta, 1977), 57. Perhaps Bachmann, who owned a copy of Améry's *Jenseits von Schuld und Sühne* (Deutsches Taschenbuch Verlag, 1970) in her personal library (Robert Pichl, "Katalog der Privatbibliothek Ingeborg Bachmanns," *Ungedrucktes Manuskript*), felt a certain kinship with Améry, as both had experienced the existential shock of being physically struck by another human being. Améry wrote: "With the first blow of the police fist however ... a part of our life comes to an end and can never be brought back," 57.

[209] Améry, *Jenseits von Schuld und Sühne*, 16.

[210] Grass, 42.

[211] Anton Kaes, *Hitler to Heimat: The Return of History as Film* (Cambridge, Mass.: Harvard University Press, 1989), 13.

[212] Bachmann, "Exil," *Werke* Vol. 1, 153

[213] Kurt Bartsch and Dietmar Goltschnigg discuss this "Geschichtslüge" (historical lie) in their article "Österreichische Nachkriegsliteratur. Sozialgeschichtliche Voraussetzungen und Literaturbetrieb," *Modern Austrian Literature* 17.3-4 (1984) : 195.

[214] Hugo von Hofmannsthal illustrates a similar dilemma in his

famous fictional letter to Lord Chandos, when he writes in a very poetic and eloquent manner of his inability to create any more poetic literature.

[215] Information for this paragraph was taken from Jacqueline Vansant, *Against the Horizon. Feminism and Postwar Austrian Women Writers* (Westport, Ct.: Greenwood Press, 1988).

[216] Brigitte Bailer, "1938: NS-Herrschaft in Österreich," eds. Brigitte Bailer, Elisabeth Klamper, Wolfgang Neugebauer. Vienna, 1998: Bundesministerium für Inneres, Dokumentationsarchiv des österreichischen Widerstandes, 21-22.

[217] Jacqueline Vansant observes that Bachmann's fictional women are isolated within society and are constantly being confronted with male projections and definitions of womanhood.Vansant 50. Both Jordan and Martin, for instance, define Franza as "wahnsinnig" in *Der Fall Franza*.

[218] Robert Pichl, "Katalog der Privatbibliothek Ingeborg Bachmanns," *Ungedrucktes Manuskript*.

[219] Sylvia Plath, *The Bell Jar* (New York: Harper & Row, 1971), 40.

[220] Plath, "Daddy," *Ariel* (1961. New York: Harper & Row, 1966).

[221] Steven Axelrod, *Sylvia Plath: The Wound and the Cure of Words* (Baltimore: Johns Hopkins University Press, 1990), 6.

[222] Bachmann,"Das Tremendum - Sylvia Plath: >Die Glasglocke.< *Entwurf, Werke IV*, 359-40.

[223] Sander Gilman, *Jewish Self-Hatred: Anti-Semitism and the Hidden Language of the Jews* (Baltimore: Johns Hopkins University Press, 1986), 243. Bachmann also owned a copy of Rudolph Loewenstein's *Psychoanalyse des Antisemitismus*, trans. Lothar Baier (Frankfurt a. M.: Suhrkamp, 1968).

[224] Otto Weininger, *Geschlecht und Charakter*, 406. Weininger's predecessor Walter Rathenau had stressed the feminine nature of the Jew in an 1897 essay, as discussed in Gilman, *Jewish Self-Hatred*, 243.

[225] Weininger, 404.

[226] Weininger, 93.

[227] Weininger, 411,412,417,414, and 431.

[228] Weininger, 429.

[229] Weininger, 407.

[230] Weininger, 626.

[231] Weininger, 417.

[232] Gilman, *Jewish Self-Hatred*, 244. Furthermore the history of Jewish self-hatred up until the Holocaust is grounded in the history of responses to the double bind of German identity formations. Gilman,

Jewish Self-Hatred, 391.

233. Otto Rank, *Beyond Psychology* (1941. New York: Dover Publications, 1958), 275.

234. Rank, 287-288.

235. Rank, 287.

236. Rank, 288.

237. Many authors besides Otto Rank have discussed the connection between patriarchy and fascism. Compare Christa Wolf, *Kindheitsmuster* (A Model Childhood, 1976), Klaus Theweleit, *Männerphantasien (Male Fantasies,* 1977), and Sylvia Plath,*The Bell Jar,* for instance.

238. Young, *Writing and Rewriting Narrative and the Consequences of Interpretation,* 132.

239. Later Adorno would add: "Den Satz, nach Auschwitz noch Lyrik zu schreiben, sei barbarisch, möchte ich nicht mildern" ("I do not want to soften the phrase that it is barbaric to write poetry after Auschwitz") Theodor Adorno, "Engagement," *Noten zur Literatur III, Gesammelte Schriften,* ed. Rolf Tiedemann (Frankfurt a. M.: Suhrkamp, 1974) 2: 422; "Perennial suffering," Adorno would later state in modifying his much discussed quote, "has as much right to say that after Auschwitz you could no longer write poems." Adorno, *Negative Dialectics,* trans. E. B. Ashton (New York: Continuum, 1973), 362.

240. Berel Lang, ed. "Introduction," *Writing and the Holocaust* (New York: Holmes & Meier, 1988), 2.

241. Grass, 9.

242. Grass, 42 and 43.

243. Lang, ed., "Introduction," *Writing and the Holocaust,* 2.

244. James Young, *Writing and Rewriting the Holocaust: Narrative and the Consequences of Interpretation* (Bloomington: Indiana University Press, 1990), 3.

245. Young, *Writing and Rewriting the Holocaust,* 4.

246. Lawrence L. Langer, "Introduction," *Preempting the Holocaust* (New Haven: Yale University Press, 1998), xix, xvii.

247. Langer, "Preempting the Holocaust," *Preempting the Holocaust,* 22.

248. Young, "Holocaust Documentary Fiction: The Novelist as Eyewitness," Lang, ed. *Writing and the Holocaust,* 201.

249. Young, *Writing and Rewriting the Holocaust,* 1.

250. Irving Howe, "Writing and the Holocaust" and Young, "Holocaust Documentary Fiction: The Novelist as Eyewitness." Lang, ed. *Writing*

and the Holocaust, 182.

[251] Saul Friedländer, "Historical Writing and the Memory of the Holocaust," Lang, ed. *Writing and the Holocaust*, 66-80.

[252] James Young recognizes a continuation of fascistic structures in our western industrialized society in his theoretical writings, much in the way Bachmann does in her fictional works, as he explains. "The interpretation and structural organization of historical events as they occurred may ultimately have determined the horrific course they eventually took." Young, *Writing and Rewriting the Holocaust*, 5.

[253] This passage has been read differently by Hans-Ulrich Thamer who identifies the characters Bertoni, Haderer, Hutter, and Ranitzky as symbols of potential fascism and describes the other characters as "the three potential victims" whose "Jewishness" can be read as a metaphor for their victimization during the war. Hans-Ulrich Thamer, "National-sozialismus und Nachkriegsgesellschaft. Geschichtliche Erfahrung bei Ingeborg Bachmann und der öffentliche Umgang mit der NS-Zeit in Deutschland," *Ingeborg Bachmann-Neue Beiträge zu ihrem Werk. Internationales Symposium Münster, 1991*, eds. Dirk Göttsche and Hubert Ohl (Würzburg: Königshausen & Neumann, 1993), 222.

[254] Majer O'Sickey, "Rereading Ingeborg Bachmann's Malina: Toward a Transformative Feminist Reading Praxis," *Modern Austrian Literature*, 28.1 (1995) : 55-73, 59.

[255] In Charlotte Perkins Gilman's short story "The Yellow Wallpaper" (1892), the female narrator is locked into her room by her husband—a supposedly well-meaning physician—in order to cure her of nervousness and depression. The narrator chronicles her mental unraveling during her imprisonment and reflects that her husband might have been the one who made her ill: "John is a physician, and *perhaps*—(I would not say it to a living soul, of course, but this is dead paper and a great relief to my mind)—*perhaps* that is one reason I do not get well faster." Charlotte Perkins Gilman, *The Yellow Wallpaper and Other Writings* (New York: Bantam Books, 1989), 1-2.

[256] Bachmann owned the work *Medizin ohne Menschlichkeit. Dokumente des Nürnberger Ärzteprozesses*, ed. A. Mitscherlich and F. Mielke (Frankfurt a. M.: Fischer, 1960). In: Robert Pichl, "Katalog der Privatbibliothek Ingeborg Bachmanns," *Ungedrucktes Manuskript*.

[257] A. Mitscherlich and F. Mielke, *The Death Doctors*. trans. James Cleugh (1949. London: Elek Books, 1962), 256.

[258] Mitscherlich and Mielke, *The Death Doctors*, 253.

[259] Mitscherlich and Mielke, *The Death Doctors,* 255.

[260] Mitscherlich and Mielke, *The Death Doctors,* 275.

[261] Mitscherlich and Mielke, *The Death Doctors,* 278-279.

[262] *Der Standard* on-line article from February 8, 2000, "Mutmaß-licher NS-Arzt Heinrich Gross ab 21. März vor Wiener Gericht," documents that psychiatrist Dr. Heinrich Gross, now eighty-four years old, was put on trial on March 21 in Vienna for the murder of nine children under National Socialist euthanasia laws while he was a doctor at the "Am Spiegelgrund" hospital in Vienna in the 1930s and 1940s. A subsequent *Salzburger Nachrichten* on-line article from April 6, 2000 reported that the Viennese Judicial Court ruled that, according to a psychiatric evaluation, Gross was unfit to testify. The public prosecutor demanded an additional report. No further information about this case was available at the time of publication of this book.

[263] Wiesenthal, *Justice Not Vengeance,* 81-82.

[264] Wiesenthal, *Justice Not Vengeance,* 82.

[265] Wiesenthal, *Justice Not Vengeance,* 82-83.

[266] Wiesenthal, *Justice Not Vengeance,* 117.

[267] Helga Embacher, "Außenseiterinnen: bürgerlich, jüdisch, intellek-tuell - links," *L'Homme,* 2. Jg., Heft 2, 1991 and Edith Prost, "Emigration und Exil österreichischer Wissenschaftlerinnen," ed. Friedrich Stadler, *Vertriebene Vernunft I. Emigration und Exil österreichischer Wissenschaft 1930-1940,* Vienna - Munich, 1987. As quoted in *Frauenleben 1945 - Kriegsende in Wien, 205. Sonderausstellung des Historischen Museums der Stadt Wien, 21. September - 19. November, 1995* (Vienna: Eigenverlag der Museen der Stadt Wien, 1995), 101. See also Helga Embacher "Middle Class, Liberal, Intellectual, Female, and Jewish: The Expulsion of 'Female Rationality' from Austria" in Günter Bischof, Anton Pelinka and Erika Thurner, eds. *Women in Austria* (New Brunswick, N.J.: Transaction Publishers, 1998), 5-14. Embacher documents the fate of female intellectuals in Austria and traces the lives of women intellectuals (whom she defines as scientists, artists, physicians and women in politics) born in Austria between 1900 and 1925, many of whom were Jewish and thus forced into exile or murdered.

[268] Erich Fried, *"Die Vertreibung des Geistigen aus Österreich," Nicht verdrängen nicht gewöhnen. Texte zum Thema Österreich,* ed. Michael Lewin (Vienna: Europaverlag, 1987), 76-97.

[269] Fried, 81.

[270] Mitscherlich and Mielke, *The Death Doctors,* 251.

[271] Charlotte Perkins Gilman's "The Yellow Wallpaper" similarly demonstrates how a woman writer is deemed insane by her husband and her society and therefore destroyed.

[272] Gisela Bock, *Zwangssterilisation im Nationalsozialismus* (Opladen: Westdeutscher Verlag, 1986), 25.

[273] Bock, 159.

[274] Bock, 311.

[275] Although Franza is attacked and raped, she bashes her head into a wall to kill herself.

[276] Carolyn Heilbrun has made the same point in her book *Writing a Woman's Life*. In her introduction, which addresses the difficulties a woman has expressing her experiences and finding her voice in fiction, she states: "If one is not permitted to express anger or even to recognize it within oneself, one is, by simple extension, refused both power and control. ... Forbidden anger, women could find no voice in which publicly to complain; they took refuge in depression or madness." Carolyn Heilbrun, *Writing a Woman's Life* (New York: Ballantine Books, 1988), 15.

Chapter Four

[277] Virginia Woolf, *Orlando: A Biography* (1928. San Diego: Harcourt Brace & Company, 1956), 138.

[278] Dinah Dodds' essay emphasizes the "positive view of lesbianism" and "lesbian love" in Bachmann's work. Dodds, however, realizes that Bachmann – whether or not the issue of lesbianism is relevant – brings up a crucial question: "Is it possible for women-loving women to escape the patriarchal modes and forms within which they were raised, and create truly new ones?" Dodds summarizes her essay: "Changing the sex of one partner does not necessarily alter the resulting relationship," Bachmann was likely more interested in examining the issue of sex and gender, rather than that of a "lesbian" relationship. Dinah Dodd, "The Lesbian Relationship in Bachmann's 'Ein Schritt nach Gomorrah,' *Monatshefte für deutschen Unterricht, deutsche Sprache und Literatur*, vol. LXXII, No. 3 (Fall, 1980) : 431-438.

Conclusion

[279] Introductory quote in Jane Yolen's *Briar Rose* (New York: Tom Doherty Associates, 1992).

[280] "Erzähl uns keine Märchen!" Aichinger, *Die größere Hoffnung*, 51.

[281] Cited from the *Todesarten-Projekt*, Bd. IV, 17f.

[282] Novels inspired by Bachmann include Thomas Bernhard's *Auslöschung* (1986) and Karin Struck's *Ingeborg B. Duell mit dem Spiegelbild* (1993). The dance theater in Klagenfurt performed *Malina* in 1993, choreographed by Andreas Staudinger. The theater troupe *Teatro Communale Udine* in Udine, Italy performed *Schatten Rosen Schatten* in 1993. *Ihr glücklichen Augen*, produced by Margareta Heinrich in 1993 and *Malina*, produced by Elfriede Jelinek in 1992 interpret Bachmann's life and work through film.

[283] Allyson Fiddler's anthology *"Other" Austrians. Post-1945 Austrian Women's Writing* from 1996, Günter Bischof, Anton Pelinka and Erika Thurner's anthology *Women in Austria* from 1998, and David Good, Margarete Grandner, and Mary Jo Maynes' edition *Austrian Women in the Nineteenth and Twentieth Centuries* from 1996 are representative of this trend.

[284] Most of Bachmann's correspondence is held at the *Handschriftensammlung* at the Austrian National Library, and will not be available to the public until January 1, 2026.

[285] Brita Steinwendtner, "Ein paar Fragen in Briefen - Gespräch mit Ilse Aichinger," *Ilse Aichinger*, Die Buchreihe über österreichische Autoren. 5, eds. Kurt Bartsch and Gerhard Melzer (Graz: Droschl, 1993) 7-14.

[286] Christine Schmidjell, "Marlen Haushofer:1920-1970. Katalog," *Zirkular* (1990) : 39.

[287] As my introduction illustrated, Barbara Kosta discusses the issue of women "writing themselves free" in her *Recasting Autobiography*, 42. Also see Gättens, 111-112.

[288] Perkins Gilman, "The Yellow Wallpaper," 2.

[289] Perkins Gilman, 16.

[290] Perkins Gilman, 20.

[291] Perkins Gilman, 19.

[292] Bachmann, K-Zahl 7955-8009, 195. Beilage, # 4483, Rot (7), *Handschriftensammlung*, Austrian National Library, Vienna, Austria.

Bibliography

Primary Sources

Bachmann, Ingeborg. *Werke.* Eds. Christine Koschel, Inge von Weidenbaum and Clemens Münster. 4 vols. 1978. Munich and Zurich: Piper, 1993.

—. *Wir müssen wahre Sätze finden: Gespräche und Interviews.* Eds. Christine Koschel and Inge von Weidenbaum. Munich and Zurich: Piper, 1991.

—. *Das Buch Franza: Das "Todesarten" Projekt in Einzelausgaben.* Eds. Monika Albrecht und Dirk Göttsche. 1995. Munich: Piper Verlag, 1998.

—. "Nachlaß." Manuscript and typescript pages of Bachmann's works at the *Handschriftensammlung* at the National Library in Vienna, Austria.

Secondary Sources on Ingeborg Bachmann

Achberger, Karen. "Beyond Patriarchy. Ingeborg Bachmann and Fairy-tales." *Modern Austrian Literature* 18.3-4 (1985): 211-222.

—. *Understanding Ingeborg Bachmann.* Columbia, S. C.: University of South Carolina Press, 1995.

Albrecht, Monika and Jutta Kallhof. "Vorstellungen auf einer Gedankenbühne: Zu Ingeborg Bachmanns 'Todesarten.'" *Modern Austrian Literature* 18.3-4 (1985) : 91-104.

Bartsch, Kurt. "Affinität und Distanz: Ingeborg Bachmann und die Romantik." *Romantik: Eine lebenskräftige Krankheit: Ihre literarischen Nachwirkungen in der Moderne.* Amsterdamer Beiträge zur neueren Germanistik. Band 34 -1991. Ed. Erika Tunner. Amsterdam: Rodopi, 1991 : 209-234.

—. "Ein Ort für Zufälle: Bachmanns Büchnerpreisrede, als poetischer Text gelesen." *Modern Austrian Literature* 18.3-4

(1985) : 135-145.

—. "'Es war Mord': Anmerkungen zur Mann-Frau-Beziehung in Bachmanns Roman *Malina*." *Acta Neophilologica. Sonderband: Ingeborg Bachmann XVII* Ljubljana (1984) : 71-76.

—. *Ingeborg Bachmann.* Stuttgart: Metzlersche Verlagsbuchhandlung, 1988.

Beck, Hans-Joachim. "'MALINA' oder die Romantik: Literarische Rezeption und Komposition in Ingeborg Bachmanns Romantrilogie 'Todesarten.'" *Germanisch-Romanische Monatsschrift–neue Folge.* Band 38 (1988) : 304-324.

Beicken, Peter. *Ingeborg Bachmann.* Munich: Verlag C. H. Beck, 1988.

Borhau, Heidi. *Ingeborg Bachmanns "Malina"- Eine Provokation? Rezeptions- und Wirkungsästhetische Untersuchungen.* Würzburg: Königshausen & Neumann, 1994.

Böschenstein, Bernhard and Sigrid Weigel, eds. *Ingeborg Bachmann und Paul Celan: Poetische Korrespondenzen. Vierzehn Beiträge.* Frankfurt a. M.: Suhrkamp, 1997.

Brinkemper, Peter. "Ingeborg Bachmanns *Der Fall Franza* als Paradigma weiblicher Ästhetik." *Modern Austrian Literature* 18.3-4 (1985) : 147-182.

Brokoph-Mauch, Gudrun. *Thunder Rumbling at My Heels. Tracing Ingeborg Bachmann.* Riverside, California: Ariadne Press, 1998.

Caduft, Corina. "Chronik von Leben und Werk." *Ingeborg Bachmann. Das Lächeln der Sphinx.* Spec. issue of *du-die Zeitschrift für Kultur* Sept. 1994 : 76-87.

Delphendahl, Renate. "Alienation and Self-Discovery in Ingeborg Bachmann's 'Undine Geht.'" *Modern Austrian Literature* 18.3-4 (1985) : 195-265.

Dickinger-Neuwirth, Monika. "Psychoanalytische Aspekte der Interpretation Ingeborg Bachmanns Roman 'Malina.'" Diplomarbeit. Paris-Lodron-Universität Salzburg, 1993.

Dodds, Dinah. "The Lesbian Relationship in Bachmann's 'Ein Schritt nach Gomorrha.'" *Monatshefte für deutschen Unterricht, deutsche Sprache und Literatur.* LXXII.3 (1980) : 431-438.

Erickson, Nancy. "Margins and Madness: Re-Centering the Pages When Writing Women's Lives–In the Works of Ingeborg Bachmann, Elfriede Jelinek and Christa Wolf." Unpublished essay, 1994.

Fischerova, Viola. "Ingeborg Bachmann: 'Der gute Gott von Manhattan'–ein Mythos?" *Literatur und Kritik* 115 (1977) : 279-290.

Göttsche, Dirk and Hubert Ohl, eds. *Ingeborg Bachmann: Neue Beiträge zu ihrem Werk.* Internationales Symposium, Münster. Würzburg: Königshausen & Neumann, 1993.

Grimkowski, Sabine. *Das zerstörte Ich: Erzählstruktur und Identität in Ingeborg Bachmanns "Der Fall Franza" und "Malina."* Würzburg: Königshausen & Neumann, 1992.

Gürtler, Christa. "Schreiben Frauen anders? Untersuchungen zu Ingeborg Bachmann und Barbara Frischmuth." Diss., Universität Salzburg, 1982.

Harris, Judith May. "Modes of Domination: The Social Dimension in Ingeborg Bachmann's Fiction." Diss., University of California, Berkeley, 1983.

Heidelberger-Leonard, Irene. "Zur Differenz zwischen der Ästhetisierung des Leidens und der Authentizität traumatischer Erfahrungen." *Ingeborg Bachmann: Neue Beiträge zu ihrem Werk.* Internationales Symposium, Münster, 1991. Eds. Dirk Göttsche and Hubert Ohl. Würzburg: Köngishausen & Neumann, 1993.

—. *"Text-Tollhaus Für Bachmann-Süchtige?"* Wiesbaden: Westdeutscher Verlag, 1998.

Höller, Hans. "Krieg und Frieden in den poetologischen Überlegungen von Ingeborg Bachmann." *Jahrbuch der Grillparzer Gesellschaft.* 3rd. ser. 14. Vienna: Bergland, 1980.

—. *Der dunkle Schatten dem ich schon seit Anfang folge: Ingeborg Bachmann.* Vienna: Locker, 1982.

—. *Geschichtserfahrung: Das Werk Ingeborg Bachmanns von den frühen Gedichten bis zum Todesarten-Zyklus.* Habilitation. Universität Salzburg, 1984.

—. *Ingeborg Bachmann: Das Werk: Von den frühesten Gedichten bis zum "Todesarten"-Zyklus.* Frankfurt a. M.: Athenäum, 1987.

—. *Ingeborg Bachmann.* Monographie 50545. Reinbek bei Hamburg: Rowohlt Taschenbuch Verlag, 1999.

—. "Krieg und Frieden in den poetologischen Überlegungen von Ingeborg Bachmann." *Acta Neophilologica. Sonderband: Ingeborg Bachmann XVII.* Ljubljana (1984) : 61-70.

—, ed. *Ingeborg Bachmann. Letzte, unveröffentlichte Gedichte, Entwürfe und Fassungen: Edition und Kommentar von Hans Höller.* Frankfurt a. M.: Suhrkamp Verlag, 1998.

Kaiser, Joachim. "Liebe und Tod einer Prinzessin." *Süddeutsche Zeitung.* March 25 1971.

Kann-Coomann, Dagmar. *"...eine geheime langsame Feier...": Zeit und ästhetische Erfahrung im Werk Ingeborg Bachmanns.* Frankfurt a. M.: Peter Lang, 1988.

Kienlechner, Toni. "Wörter und Worte." *Ingeborg Bachmann. Das Lächeln der Sphinx.* Spec. issue of *du-die Zeitschrift für Kultur* Sept. 1994 : 64-65.

Krizman, Mirko. "Ingeborg Bachmann in einem Vergleich mit der österreichischen dichterischen Tradition." *Acta Neophilologica. Sonderband: Ingeborg Bachmann XVII* Ljubljana (1984) : 11-19.

Kohn-Waechter, Gudrun. *Das Verschwinden in der Wand: Destruktive Moderne und Widerspruch eines weiblichen Ich in Ingeborg Bachmanns "Malina."* Stuttgart: J.B. Metzlersche Verlagsbuchhandlung, 1992.

Koschel, Christine, and Inge von Weidenbau, eds. *Kein objektives Urteil–nur ein lebendiges: Texte zum Werk von Ingeborg Bachmann.* Munich: Piper, 1989.

Kunze, Barbara. "Ein Geheimnis der Prinzessin von Kagran: Die ungewöhnliche Quelle zu der 'Legende' in Ingeborg Bachmanns *Malina.*" *Modern Austrian Literature* 18.3-4 (1985) : 105-119.

Lennox, Sara. "Christa Wolf and Ingeborg Bachmann: Difficulties of Writing the Truth." *Responses to Christa Wolf: Critical Essays.* Ed. Marilyn Sibley-Fries. Detroit: Wayne State University Press, 1989. 128-148.

Mahrdt, Helgard. "Ingeborg Bachmann.– Es geht ein Riß durch die Welt: Zu Ingeborg Bachmanns Geschlechter- und Öffentlichkeitskritik." *Rapial* 1 (1991) : 8-10.

Majer O'Sickey, Ingeborg. *Fascistic Discourse in the Narrative of Ingeborg Bachmann and Marguerite Yourcenar*. Diss., The University of Texas at Austin, 1988. Ann Arbor: UMI, 1988.

Neumann, Gerhard. "Christa Wolf: *Selbstversuch*. Ingeborg Bachmann: *Ein Schritt nach Gomorrha*: Beiträge weiblichen Schreibens zur Kurzgeschichte des 20. Jahrhunderts." *Von der Novelle zur Kurzgeschichte: Beiträge zur Geschichte der deutschen Erzählliteratur*. Eds. Dominique Iehl and Horst Hombourg. Frankfurt a. M.: Peter Lang, 1990. 81-99.

Pichl, Robert. "Das Wien Ingeborg Bachmanns: Gedanken zur späten Prosa." *Modern Austrian Literature* 18.3-4 (1985) : 183-193.

—. "Katalog der Privatbibliothek Ingeborg Bachmanns." Ungedrucktes Typoskript.

—. "Voraussetzungen und Problemhorizont der gegenwärtigen Ingeborg-Bachmann-Forschung." *Jahrbuch der Grillparzer Gesellschaft*. 3rd. ser. 14. Vienna: Bergland, 1980.

—. "Zum literarischen Nachlass Ingeborg Bachmanns: Ergebnisse einer ersten Übersicht." *Acta Neophilologica Sonderband: Ingeborg Bachmann XVII*. Ljubljana (1984) : 5-9.

Punte, Maria-Luisa. "Die Bedeutung des Weiblichen im Werk von Ingeborg Bachmann." *Begegnung mit dem Fremden* 10 (1992) : 275-281.

Rauch, Angelika. "Sprache, Weiblichkeit und Utopie bei Ingeborg Bachmann." *Modern Austrian Literature* 18.3-4 (1985) : 21-38.

Remmler, Karen. *Waking the Dead: Correspondences Between Walter Benjamin's Concept of Remembrance and Ingeborg Bachmann's Ways of Dying*. Riverside, California: Ariadne Press, 1996.

Riedel, Ingrid. "Traum und Legende in Ingeborg Bachmanns 'Malina.'" *Psychoanalytische literarische Interpretation* (1982) : 178-207.

Röhnelt, Inge. *Hysterie und Mimesis in 'Malina.'* Frankfurt a. M.: Peter Lang, 1990.

Sauthoff, Stephan. *Die Transformation (auto)biographischer Elemente im Prosawerk Ingeborg Bachmanns.* Frankfurt a. M.: Peter Lang, 1992.

Schiffner, Andrea. "Legende einer Frau, die es nie gegeben hat." *Deutsche Post.* June 5 1972.

Schmid-Bortenschlager, Sigrid. "Spiegelszenen bei Bachmann: Ansätze einer psychoanalytischen Interpretation." *Modern Austrian Literature.* 18.3-4 (1985) : 39-52.

Spiel, Hilde. "Ingeborg Bachmann: Keine Kerze für Florian," *Kleine Schritte: Berichte und Geschichten.* Munich: Edition Spangenberg, Ellermann Verlag, 1976: 158-163.

Stoll, Andrea. *Erinnerung als ästhetische Kategorie des Widerstandes im Werk Ingeborg Bachmanns.* Frankfurt a. M.: Peter Lang, 1991.

—, ed. *Ingeborg Bachmanns "Malina."* Frankfurt a. M.: Suhrkamp Taschenbuch Verlag, 1992.

Thau, Bärbel. *Gesellschaftsbild und Utopie im Spätwerk Ingeborg Bachmanns: Untersuchungen zum "Todesarten"-Zyklus und zu "Simultan."* Frankfurt a. M.: Peter Lang, 1986.

Weigel, Sigrid. *Ingeborg Bachmann. Hinterlassenschaften unter Wahrung des Briefgeheimnisses.* Vienna: Paul Zsolnay Verlag, 1999.

Zahorsky-Suchodolski, A. M. "Anti-Mythos in der österreichischen Literatur: Ingeborg Bachmann." *Literatur und Kritik* 99 (1975) : 523-528.

General Secondary Sources

Aarne, Antti. *The Types of the Folktale: A Classification and Bibliography.* Translated and enlarged by Stith Thompson. Second Revision. Helsinki: Academia Scientiarum Fennica, 1961.

Adorno, Theodor. "Engagement." *Noten zur Literatur III. Gesam-*

melte Schriften, Ed. Rolf Tiedemann. Frankfurt a. M.: Suhrkamp, 1974, 2:422

——. *Negative Dialectics*. Trans. E. B. Ashton. New York: Continuum, 1973.

Aichinger, Ilse. *Die größere Hoffnung*. 1948. Frankfurt a. M.: Fischer Taschenbuch Verlag, 1991.

——. *Eliza Eliza Erzählungen (1958-1968)*. Frankfurt a. M.: Fischer Taschenbuch Verlag, 1991.

——. *Kleist, Moos, Fasane*. Frankfurt a. M.: Fischer Taschenbuch Verlag, 1987.

——. *Meine Sprache und Ich: Erzählungen*. Frankfurt a. M.: Fischer Taschenbuch Verlag, 1987.

Apel, Friedmar. *Die Zaubergärten der Phantasie: Zur Theorie und Geschichte des Kunstmärchens*. Heidelberg: Carl Winter, 1978.

Axelrod, Steven. *Sylvia Plath: The Wound and the Cure of Words*. Baltimore: Johns Hopkins University Press, 1990.

Bailer, Brigitte, Elisabeth Klamper, and Wolfgang Neugebauer, eds. *1938. NS-Herrschaft in Österreich: Texte und Bilder aus der gleichnamigen Ausstellung*. Vienna: Bundesministerium für Inneres, Dokumentationsarchiv des österreichischen Widerstandes, 1998.

Bartsch, Kurt and Dietmar Goltschnigg. "Nachkriegsliteratur-Sozialgeschichtliche Voraussetzungen und Literaturbetrieb." *Modern Austrian Literature* 17.3-4 (1984) : 193-214.

——, and Gerhard Melzer, eds. *Ilse Aichinger*. Die Buchreihe über österreichische Autoren. 5. Graz: Droschl, 1993.

Benesch, Kurt. *Sagen aus Österreich: Oberösterreich. Steiermark. Kärnten*. Vienna: Verlag Kremayr & Scheriau, 1985.

Bernhard, Thomas. *Heldenplatz*. 1988. Frankfurt a. M.: Suhrkamp Verlag, 1992.

——. *Auslöschung*. Frankfurt a. M.: Suhrkamp Verlag, 1988.

Bettelheim, Bruno. *Surviving and Other Essays*. 1952. New York: Alfred Knopf, 1979.

——. *The Uses of Enchantment: The Meaning and Importance of Fairy-tales*. New York: Random House, 1977.

Bienek, Horst. "Noch gibt es Lieder zu singen: Zum Tode von Ingeborg Bachmann." *Frankfurter Allgemeine Zeitung*. 18 Oct. 1973.

Bischof, Günter, Anton Pelinka, and Erika Thurner, eds. *Women in Austria*. New Brunswick, N.J.: Transaction Publishers, 1998.

Bittner, Günther. "Über die Symbolik weiblicher Reifung im Volksmärchen." *Praxis der Kinderpsychologie und Kinderpsychiatrie* 12 (1963) : 210-213.

Blackwell, Jeannine. "Fractured Fairy-tales: German Women Authors and the Grimm Tradition." *The Germanic Review* 62 (1987) : 162-174.

Blaschek, Ulrike, ed. *Märchen vom Blaubart*. Frankfurt a. M.: Fischer Taschenbuch Verlag, 1989.

Bloch, Ernst. *Literarische Aufsätze: Gesamtausgabe*. Band 9. Frankfurt a. M.: Suhrkamp, 1965.

Bock, Gisela. *Zwangssterilisation im Nationalsozialismus: Studien zur Rassenpolitik und Frauenpolitik*. Opladen: Westdeutscher Verlag, 1986.

Bolte, Johannes, and George Políkva. *Anmerkungen zu den Kinder- und den Hausmärchen der Brüder Grimm*. Leipzig: Dieterich, 1913.

Bottigheimer, Ruth B., ed. *Fairy-tales and Society: Illusion, Allusion and Paradigm*. Philadephia: University of Pennsylvania Press, 1986.

—. "Fairy-tale Illustrations: Children's Drawings and the Male Imagination." *Societé Internationale d'Ethnologie et de Folklore* (1990) : 55-62.

—. *Grimms' Bad Girls and Bold Boys: The Moral and Social Vision of the Tales*. New Haven and London: Yale University Press, 1987.

Brennan, Theresa. Introduction. *Between Feminism and Psychoanalysis*. By Brennan. London: Routledge, 1989. 1-23.

Brügman, Margret. "Weiblichkeit im Spiel der Sprache: Über das Verhältnis von Psychoanalyse und *écriture feminine*." *Frauen Literatur Geschichte: Schreibende Frauen vom Mittelalter bis zur Gegenwart.* Eds. Hiltrud Gnüg and Renate Morhmann. Stuttgart: Metzler, 1985. 395-415.

Butler, Judith. *Gender Trouble: Feminism and the Subversion of Identity.* New York: Routledge, 1990.

Carter, Angela. *The Bloody Chamber.* New York: Harper & Row, 1981.

Castein, Hanne. "Arbeiten mit der Romantik heute: zur Romantikerrezeption der DDR, unter besonderer Berücksichtigung des Märchens." *Deutsche Romantik und das 20. Jahrhundert.* Londoner Symposium 1985. Eds. Hanne Castein and Alexander Stillmark. Stuttgart: Akademischer Verlag, 1986. 5-23.

—. "Grass and the Appropriation of the Fairy-tale in the 70s." *Günter Grass' Der Butt: Sexual Politics and the Male Myth of History.* Ed. Philip Brady. Oxford: Clarendon Press, 1990.

Caviola, Hugo. "Behind the Transparent Wall: Marlen Haushofer's Novel *Die Wand.*" *Modern Austrian Literature* 24.1 (1991) : 101-112.

Celan, Paul. *Gedichte.* vol. 1 of 2. Frankfurt a. M.: Suhrkamp, 1975.

Cirlot, J. E. *A Dictionary of Symbols.* New York: Philosophical Library, 1962.

Code, Lorraine. *What Can She Know? Feminist Theory and the Construction of Knowledge.* Ithaca: Cornell University Press, 1991.

Colin, Amy. *Paul Celan: Holograms of Darkness.* Bloomington: Indiana Unversity Press, 1991.

Cooper, J. C. *Fairy-tales. Allegories of the Inner Life: Archetypal Patterns and Symbols in Classic Fairy Stories.* Wellingborough, Northamptonshire: Aquarian Press, 1983.

Dinesen, Ruth. *Nelly Sachs: Eine Biographie.* Trans. Gabriele Gerecke. Frankfurt a. M.: Suhrkamp, 1994.

Doderer, Klaus. "The World of Beautiful Dreams: Fairy-tales in a Modern Society." *German Studies in India* 4.2 (1980) : 81- 87.

Durzak, Manfred. *Der deutsche Roman der Gegenwart.* Stuttgart: Verlag Kohlhammer, 1971.

Eliot, T.S. *The Complete Poems and Plays 1909-1950.* New York:

Harcourt, Brace & World, 1971.

Eller, Rose. *Das Märchen: Ursprung-Symbolik-Sinngehalt*. Vienna: Österreichische Landsmannschaft, 1985.

Ellis, John. *One Fairy Story Too Many: The Brothers Grimm and Their Tales*. Chicago: The University of Chicago Press, 1983.

——. "What Really is the Value of the 'New' Grimm Discovery?" *German Quarterly* 58 (1985) : 87-90.

Epstein, Leslie. "Writing about the Holocaust." *Writing and the Holocaust*. Ed. Berel Lang. New York: Holmes & Meier, 1988.

Fehn, Ann, Ingeborg Hoesterey, and Maria Tatar, eds. *Neverending Stories: Toward a Critical Narratology*. Princeton: Princeton University Press, 1992.

Fetscher, Iring. *Wer hat Dornröschen wachgeküßt? Das Märchenverwirrbuch*. Frankfurt a. M.: Fischer Verlag, 1988.

Fiddler, Allyson, ed. *'Other' Austrians. Post-1945 Austrian Women's Writing: Proceedings of the Conference Held at the University of Nottingham from 18-29 April 1996*. Bern: Peter Lang, 1998.

Filz, Walter. *Es war einmal? Elemente des Märchens in der deutschen Literatur der siebziger Jahre*. Kölner Studien zur Literaturwissenschaft. Frankfurt a. M.: Peter Lang, 1989.

Fraungruber, Hans. *Österreichisches Sagenkränzlein*. Vienna, Stuttgart, Leipzig: Loewe Verlag Ferdinand Carl, 1911.

Freud, Sigmund. *Die Traumdeutung*. Frankfurt a. M.: Fischer, 1991.

——. "Erinnern, Wiederholen und Durcharbeiten." *Elemente der Psychoanalyse*. Band 1. Ed. Anna Freud and Ilse Gubrich-Simitus. Frankfurt a. M.: Fischer, 1978. 518-525.

——. "Märchenstoffe in Träumen." *Gesammelte Werke. 10 Band. Werke aus den Jahren 1913-1917*. London: Imago, 1946/1949.

Friedländer, Saul. "Historical Writing and the Memory of the Holocaust." *Writing and the Holocaust*. Ed. Berel Lang. New York: Holmes & Meier, 1988.

——. *The Origins of Nazi Genocide: From Euthanasia to the Final Solution*. Chapel Hill: The University of North Carolina Press,

1995.

Frisch, Max. *Stiller.* 1954. Frankfurt a. M.: Suhrkamp Verlag, 1992.

Gättens, Marie-Luise. "Die Rekonstruktion der Geschichte: Der Nationalsozialismus in drei Romanen der siebziger Jahre." *Frauen-Fragen in der deutschsprachigen Literatur nach 1945, Amsterdamer Beiträge zur neueren Germanistik.* Eds. Mona Knapp and Gerd Labroisse. Band 29. Amsterdam: Rodopi, 1989. 111-130.

Gilman, Sander L. *Jewish Self-Hatred: Anti-Semitism and the Hidden Language of the Jews.* Baltimore: The Johns Hopkins University Press, 1986.

Gnüg, Hiltrud and Renate Möhrmann. *Frauen Literatur Geschichte: Schreibende Frauen vom Mittelalter bis zur Gegenwart.* Stuttgart: J. B. Metzlersche Verlagsbuchhandlung, 1985.

Good, David F., Margarete Grandner, and Mary Jo Maynes, eds. *Austrian Women in the Nineteenth and Twentieth Centuries: Cross-Disciplinary Perspectives.* Providence: Berghahn Books, 1996.

Graber, Georg, ed. *Sagen aus Kärnten.* Graz: Leykam Verlag, 1944.

Grass, Günter. *Schreiben nach Auschwitz: Frankfurter Poetik-Vorlesung.* Frankfurt a. M.: Luchterhand, 1990.

Greuner, Suzanne. *Schmerzton. Musik in der Schreibweise von Ingeborg Bachmann und Anne Duden. Literatur im historischen Prozeß.* New series 24. Hamburg: Argument-Verlag, 1990.

Grimm, Brüder. *Kinder- und Hausmärchen.* Ausgabe Letzter Hand mit den Originalanmerkungen der Brüder Grimm. Ed. Heinz Rölleke. 3 vols. Stuttgart: Philipp Reclam Jun., 1980.

—. *Kinder- und Hausmärchen. Gesammelt durch die Brüder Grimm.* Band 1. Berlin: Realschulbuchhandlung, 1812. Eds. Heinz Rölleke und Ulrike Marquardt. Göttingen: Vandenhoeck & Ruprecht, 1986.

—. *Kinder- und Hausmärchen. (1812/1815).* Ed. Walter Killy.

Frankfurt a. M.: Fischer Verlag, 1962.

Gugitz, Gustav. *Die Sagen und Legenden der Stadt Wien.* "Österreichische Heimat." Eds. Richard Hollinek and Leopold J. Wetzel. Band 17. Vienna: Verlag Brüder Hollinek, 1952.

Haase, Donald. "Verzauberung der Seele: Das Märchen und die Exilanten der NS Zeit." *Akten des VIII Internationalen Germanisten-Kongresses.* Band 8. Tokyo, 1990. 44-51.

Haase, Horst, and Antal Mádl, eds. *Österreichische Literatur des 20. Jahrhunderts.* Berlin: Volk & Wissen Verlag, 1988.

Haiding, Karl. *Österreichs Märchenschatz.* Vienna: Pro Domo, 1953.

Haslinger, Adolf. "Romantik in der österreichischen Gegenwartsliteratur: Rezeptionsprobleme und Rezeptionsbeispiele." *Deutsche Romantik und das 20. Jahrhundert.* Londoner Symposium 1985. Eds. Hanne Castein and Alexander Stillmark. Stuttgart: Akademischer Verlag, 1986. 157-171.

Haushofer, Marlen. *Die Wand.* 1968. Munich: Deutscher Taschenbuch Verlag, 1991.

Heckmann, Emil. *Blaubart: Ein Beitrag zur vergleichenden Märchenforschung.* Inaugural-Diss. Mannheim-Rheinau, 1930.

Hegi, Ursula. *Stones from the River.* New York: Simon & Schuster, 1994.

Heilbrun, Carolyn G. *Writing a Woman's Life.* New York: Ballantine Books, 1988.

Heinemann, Marlene Eve. *Gender and Destiny: Women Writers and the Holocaust.* New York: Greenwood Press, 1986.

—. "Women Prose Writers of the Nazi Holocaust." Diss. Indiana University, 1981.

Hiller, Helmut. *Lexikon des Aberglaubens.* Munich: Süddeutscher Verlag, 1986.

Hlawaty, Graziella. *Die Stadt der Lieder.* Vienna: Paul Zsolnay Verlag, 1995.

Hollinek, Richard, and Leopold Wetzel, eds. *Die Sagen und Legenden der Stadt Wien.* "Österreichische Heimat." Band 17. Vienna: Verlag Brüder Hollinek, 1952.

Holmqvist, Bengt, ed. *Das Buch der Nelly Sachs.* Frankfurt a. M.:

Suhrkamp Verlag, 1968.

Horn, Katalin. "Grimmsche Märchen als Quellen für Metaphern und Vergleiche in der Sprache der Werbung, des Journalismus und der Literatur." *Muttersprache* XCI (1981) : 106-115.

Howe, Irving. "Writing and the Holocaust." Ed. Berel Lang. *Writing and the Holocaust.* New York: Holmes & Meier, 1988.

Ingrisch, Doris. "Vertriebene und Verbliebene: Zur Geschichte intellektueller Frauen in Österreich." *Antisemitismus und Zionismus Zeitgeschichte 1/2* (Jänner/Feb. 1997) : 30-48.

Jacoby, Mario, Verena Kast, and Ingrid Riedel, eds. *Witches, Ogres, and the Devil's Daughter: Encounters with Evil in Fairy-tales.* Trans. Michael Kohn. Boston: Shambala, 1992.

Kaes, Anton. *Hitler to Heimat: The Return of History as Film.* Cambridge. Mass.: Harvard University Press, 1989.

Kawai, Hayao. "The 'Forbidden Chamber' Motif in a Japanese Fairy-tale." *The Empire of Signs: Semiotic Essays on Japanese Culture.* Ed. Yoshihiko Ikegami. Amsterdam: John Benjamin Publishing, 1991. 157-180.

Kirchner, Klaus. *Flugblatt-Propaganda im 2. Weltkrieg.* Erlangen: Verlag für zeitgeschichtliche Dokumente und Curiosa, 1979.

Kleist, Jürgen. *Zur Kunst- und Künstlerproblematik in der deutsch-sprachigen Prosa nach 1945.* Berkeley and Los Angeles: University of California Press, 1985.

Klinger, Kurt. "Die österreichische Nachkriegsliteratur." *Literatur und Kritik* 61 (1972) : 145-157.

Klotz, Volker. *Das europäische Kunstmärchen.* Stuttgart: Metzlersche Verlagsbuchhandlung, 1985.

Klüger, Ruth. *weiter leben: eine Jugend.* 1992. Göttingen: Wallenstein Verlag, 1994.

Kovács, Agnes, ed. *Ungarische Volksmärchen.* Köln and Düsseldorf: Eugen Diederichs Verlag, 1982.

Krainz, Johann. *Mythen und Sagen aus dem steirischen Hochlande.* 1880. Vaduz, Liechtenstein: Sändig Reprint Verlag, 1985.

Kuhn, Hans. "Die Kinder- und Hausmärchen: Zwischen

Nationalität und Universal, zwischen Literatur und Volks-kunde." *Akten 7. Internationales Germanisten Kongress* 11 (1986) : 228-235.

Lang, Berel. Introduction. *Writing and the Holocaust*. Ed. Berel Lang. New York and London: Holmes & Meier, 1988.

Langer, Lawrence L. *Preempting the Holocaust*. New Haven: Yale University Press, 1998.

Levi, Primo. *Die Atempause*. Trans. Barbara and Robert Picht. Munich: Deutscher Taschenbuch Verlag, 1994. Trans. of *La tregua*. 1963.

Liang, Yea-Jen. "Kennen Chinesen die Märchen der Brüder Grimm?" *Brüder Grimm Gedenken*. Ed. Ludwig Denecke. Band 5. Marburg: N.G. Elwert Verlag, 1985. 176-191.

Lindemann, Gisela. *Ilse Aichinger*. Munich: Beck, 1988.

Longerich, Peter, ed. *Die Ermordung der europäischen Juden: Eine Umfassende Dokumentation des Holocaust 1941-1945*. Munich and Zurich: Piper, 1989.

Lopate, Phillip. "Resistance to the Holocaust." *Tikkun* 4.3. (1989) : 55-65.

Lorenz, Dagmar C. G. "Autobiographie und Fiktion bei Aichinger und Fried." *Modern Austrian Literature* 24.3-4 (1991) : 43-53.

—. *Keepers of the Motherland: German Texts by Jewish Women Authors*. Lincoln: University of Nebraska Press, 1997.

Lukács, Georg. "Die Romantik als Wendung in der deutschen Literatur." *Romantikforschung seit 1945*. Ed. Klaus Peter. Königstein: Verlagsgruppe Athenäum, 1980. 40-52.

Lundell, Torborg. *Fairy-tale Mothers*. Frankfurt a. M.: Peter Lang, 1990.

—. "Gender-Related Biases in the Type and Motif Indexes of Aarne and Thompson." *Fairy-tales and Society: Illusion, Allusion, and Paradigm*. Ed. Ruth B. Bottigheimer. Phila-delphia: University of Pennsylvania Press, 1986. 149-163.

Lüthi, Max. *Das europäische Volksmärchen*. Munich: Francke, 1981.

Lützeler, Paul Michael, ed. *Deutsche Romane des 20. Jahr-hunderts*. Königstein: Athenäum, 1983.

Lyotard, Jean-François. *Instructions païennes*. Paris: Galilee, 1977.

Margetts, John. "Hope Unfulfilled: Observations on the Impact of Ilse Aichinger's Novel *Die Größere Hoffnung*." *Neophilologus* 74 (1990) : 408-425.

Martin, Elaine, ed, *Gender Patriarchy and Fascism in the Third Reich: The Response of Women Writers*. Detroit: Wayne State University Press, 1993.

McGlathery, James M. *Fairy-tale Romance: The Grimms, Basile and Perrault*. Urbana and Chicago: University of Illinois Press, 1990.

McVeigh, Joseph. *Kontinuität und Vergangenheitsbewältigung in der österreichischen Literatur nach 1945*. Vienna: Braumüller, 1988.

Mechtenberg, Theo. *Utopie als ästhetische Kategorie*. Stuttgart: Heinz, 1978.

Mitscherlich, Alexander and Margarete. *Die Unfähigkeit zu trauern*. Munich: Piper, 1967.

Mitscherlich, A. and F. Mielke. *The Death Doctors*. Trans. James Cleugh. 1949. London: Elek Books, 1962.

Mitterruzzner, Christa and Gerhard Ungar, Eds. *Widerstand und Verfolgung in Salzburg 1934–1945. Eine Dokumentation. Band 2*. Vienna: Österreichischer Bundesverlag, 1991.

Morford, Mark and Robert Lenardon. *Classical Mythology*. New York: Longman, 1985.

Musil, Robert. "Isis und Osiris." *Gesammelte Werke: Prosa und Stücke*. vol. 6. Reinbek bei Hamburg: Rowohlt, 1978.

N.a. *Sagen aus Österreich*. Vienna: Verlag Carl Ueberreuter, 1948/1949.

Neugebauer, Wolfgang. "Zur Psychiatrie in Österreich 1938–1945: "Euthanasie" und Sterilisierung Symposium." *Schutz der Persönlichkeitsrechte am Beispiel der Behandlung von Geisteskranken, 1780-1982*. 22 and 23 Oct., 1982. Vienna: Bundesministerium für Justiz, 1983.

Novalis. *Dichter über ihre Dichtungen*. vol. 15. Ed. Hans-Joachim Mähl. Passau: Heimeran Verlag: 1976.

Oberfeld, Charlotte. "Märchen und Utopie." *Das Selbstver-*

ständliche Wunder: Beiträge Germanistischer Märchenforschung. Eds. Wilhelm Solms and Charlotte Oberfeld. Marburg: Hitzeroth, 1986.

Perkins Gilman, Charlotte. *The Yellow Wallpaper and Other Writings.* New York: Bantam Books, 1989.

Perrault, Charles. *Contes, Textes établis et présentés par Marc Soriano.* Paris: Flammarion, 1989.

Petersdorf, Bodo von. *Märchen der Völker: Österreich.* Essen: Magnus Verlag, n.d.

Petzoldt, Leander, ed. *Märchen aus Österreich.* Munich: Eugen Diederichs Verlag, 1991.

—, ed. *Sagen aus der Steiermark.* Munich: Eugen Diederichs Verlag, 1993.

Pischinger, Alois. *Sagen aus Österreich.* Vienna: Verlag Carl Ueberreuter, 1961.

Plath, Sylvia. *Ariel* 1961. New York: Harper & Row, 1966.

—. *Die Glasglocke.* Frankfurt a. M.: Suhrkamp Verlag, 1968.

—. *The Bell Jar.* New York: Harper & Row, 1971.

Radin, Paul. *The Trickster: A Study in American Indian Mythology.* New York: Philosophical Library, 1956.

Rank, Otto. *Beyond Psychology.* 1941. New York: Dover Publications, 1958.

Reichart, Elisabeth. *Februarschatten.* 1984. Frankfurt a. M.: Fischer, 1989.

Reichensperger, Richard. *Die Bergung der Opfer in der Sprache: Über Ilse Aichinger–Leben und Werk.* Frankfurt a. M.: Fischer, 1991.

Reiffenstein, Ingo, ed. *Österreichische Märchen.* Cologne: Eugen Diederichs Verlag, 1979.

Röhrich, Lutz. "Das Bild der Frau im Märchen und im Volkslied." *Jacob und Wilhelm Grimm zu Ehren.* Eds. Hans-Bernd Harder and Dieter Hennig. Marburg: Hitzeroth, 1989. 35-61.

Rölleke, Heinz, ed. *Die älteste Märchensammlung der Brüder Grimm: Synopse der handschriftlichen Urfassung von 1810 und der Erstdrucke von 1812.* Cologne-Genève: Fondation Martin Bodmer, 1975.

—. "Die Frau in den Märchen der Brüder Grimm." *Die Frau im Märchen*. Eds. Sigrid Früh and Rainer Wehse. Kassel: Erich Röth Verlag, 1985. 72-88.

—. "Die 'Kinder- und Hausmärchen' der Brüder Grimm." *Märchen in unserer Zeit: Zu Erscheinungsformen eines populären Erzählgenres*. Ed. Hans-Jörg Uther. Munich: Eugen Diederichs Verlag, 1990. 92-101.

—. *Die Märchen der Brüder Grimm: Eine Einführung von Heinz Rölleke*. Munich and Zurich: Artemis Verlag, 1985.

—. ed. *Märchen aus dem Nachlaß der Brüder Grimm*. 2. verbesserte Auflage. Bonn: Bouvier Verlag Herbert Grundmann, 1979.

—. ed. *Unbekannte Märchen von Wilhelm und Jacob Grimm*. Köln: Eugen Diederichs Verlag, 1987.

Rosenfeld, Hellmut. *Legende*. Stuttgart: J. B. Metzlersche Verlagsbuchhandlung, 1982.

Ruthmaner, Friedrich, ed. *Österreichische Volkssagen*. Straubing: Attenkofersche Verlagsbuchhandlung, 1914.

Ryan, Judith. *The Uncompleted Past: Postwar German Novels and the Third Reich*. Detroit: Wayne State University Press, 1983.

Saur, Pamela S. "A Feminist Reading of Barbara Frischmuth's Trilogy." *Modern Austrian Literature* 23.3-4 (1990) : 167-178.

Scherf, Walter. *Die Herausforderung des Dämons: Form und Funktion grausiger Kindermärchen*. Munich: K.G. Saur, 1987.

—. *Lexikon der Zaubermärchen*. Stuttgart: Alfred Kröner Verlag, 1982.

Schmidjell, Christine, ed. "Marlen Haushofer: 1920-1970: Katalog." *Zirkular* Sondernummer 22 (1990) : 39.

Schuster-Fields, Hanna. *Mythologie und Dialektik in Ilse Aichinger's "Die größere Hoffnung."* Diss. University of Texas at Austin, 1991. Ann Arbor: UMI, 1991.

Sonderausstellung des Historischen Museums der Stadt Wien. *Frauenleben 1945–Kriegsende in Wien. 21. September–19. November 1995*. Vienna: Eigenverlag der Museen der Stadt Wien, 1995.

Stalzer, Alfred, ed. *Jewish Vienna: Heritage and Mission*. Vienna:

Vienna Tourist Board, 1995.

Stephan, Inge, Regula Venske, and Sigrid Weigel, eds. *Frauen-literatur ohne Tradition? Neun Autorinnenporträts.* Frankfurt a. M.: Fischer Taschenbuch Verlag, 1987.

Stebich, Max. *Donausagen.* Vienna: Julius Breitschopf jun., 1958.

Tatar, Maria. *Off with Their Heads! Fairy-tales and the Culture of Childhood.* Princeton: Princeton University Press, 1992.

—. *The Hard Facts of the Grimm's Fairy-tales.* Princeton: Princeton University Press, 1987.

—, ed. *The Classic Fairy Tales: Texts. Criticism.* New York: W. W. Norton & Company, 1999.

Thau, Bärbel. *Gesellschaftsbild und Utopie im Spätwerk Ingeborg Bachmanns: Untersuchungen zum "Todesarten"-Zyklus und zu "Simultan."* Frankfurt a. M.: Peter Lang, 1986.

Theweleit, Klaus. *Männerphantasien.* Reinbek bei Hamburg: Rowohlt, 1977.

Tismar, Jens. *Kunstmärchen.* Stuttgart: Metzler Verlag, 1977.

—. "Volksmärchen und Kunstmärchen." *Deutsche Literatur: Eine Sozialgeschichte* 5 (1985) : 196-215.

Trahan, Elisabeth. *Geisterbeschwörung: Eine jüdische Jugend im Wien der Kriegsjahre.* (Vienna: Picus, 1996)

Trakl, Georg. "Blaubart: Ein Puppenspiel. Fragment." *Dichtungen und Briefe.* Ed. Walther Killy and Hans Szklenar. 2nd ed. 1969. Salzburg: Otto Müller Verlag, 1987.

Uther, Hans-Jörg. "Der Frauenmörder Blaubart und seine Artver-wandten." *Schweizerisches Archiv für Volkskunde* 84 (1988) : 35-54.

Vansant, Jacqueline, *Against the Horizon: Feminism and Postwar Austrian Women Writers.* New York: Greenwood Press, 1988.

Venske, Regula. "'Dieses eine Ziel werde ich erreichen...' Tod und Utopie bei Marlen Haushofer." *Weiblichkeit und Tod in der Literatur.* Eds. Renate Berger and Inge Stephan. Köln: Böhlau Verlag, 1987.

Verband Deutscher Vereine für Volkskunde, ed. *Handwörter-bücher zur Deutschen Volkskunde.*1930. Berlin: Walter de Gruyter Verlag, 1933.

Vries, Ad de. *Dictionary of Symbols and Imagery*. Amsterdam/ London: n.p., 1974.

Wakefield, H. Russel. *Landru: The French Bluebeard*. London: Duckworth, 1936.

Weigel, Hans. "Es begann mit Ilse Aichinger." *Protokolle* (1966) : 3-8.

Weigel, Sigrid. *Die Stimme der Medusa: Schreibweisen in der Gegenwartsliteratur von Frauen*. Reinbek bei Hamburg: Rowohlt, 1989.

—. *Topographien der Geschlechter: Kulturgeschichtliche Studien zur Literatur*. Reinbek bei Hamburg: Rowohlt, 1990.

Weininger, Otto. *Geschlecht und Charakter*. 1903. Munich: Matthes & Seitz Verlag, 1980.

Weiss, Walter, and Sigrid Schmid, eds. *Zwischenbilanz: Eine Anthologie österreichischer Gegenwartsliteratur*. Salzburg: Residenz Verlag, 1976.

Welsh, Renate. *Das Lufthaus*. Graz: Styria, 1994.

White, Hayden. *The Content of the Form: Narrative Discourse and Historical Representation*. Baltimore: The Johns Hopkins University Press, 1987.

Wiedemann, Barbara, ed. *Paul Celan–Nelly Sachs Briefwechsel*. Frankfurt a. M.: Suhrkamp Verlag, 1993.

Wiesenthal, Simon. *Justice Not Vengeance*. Trans. Ewald Osers. New York: Grove Weidenfeld, 1989.

Woolf, Virginia. *Orlando*. 1928. San Diego: Harcourt Brace & Company, 1956.

Wührl, Paul-Wolfgang. *Das deutsche Kunstmärchen: Geschichte, Botschaft und Erzählstrukturen*. Heidelberg: Quelle & Meyer, 1984.

Young, James, E. "Holocaust Documentary Fiction: The Novelist as Eyewitness." *Writing and the Holocaust*. Ed. Berel Lang. New York and London: Holmes & Meier, 1988.

Zaunert, Paul, ed. *Deutsche Märchen aus dem Donauland*. Düsseldorf and Cologne: Eugen Diederichs Verlag, 1958.

Ziegelhauser, Leopold. *Schattenbilder der Vorzeit. Ein Kranz von Geschichten, Sagen, Legenden, Mährchen, Skizzen und*

Heldenmahlen. Vienna: Michael Lechner, 1844.

Zipes, Jack. *Breaking the Magic Spell: Radical Theories of Folk & Fairy-tales.* Austin: University of Texas Press, 1979.

—. "Der Prinz wird nicht kommen: Feministische Märchen und Kulturkritik in den USA und in England." *Die Frau im Märchen.* Eds. Sigrid Früh und Rainer Wehse. Kassel: Erich Röth Verlag, 1985. 174-192.

—. *Don't Bet on the Prince: Contemporary Feminist Fairy-tales in North America and England.* New York: Gower, 1986.

—. *Fairy-tales and Fables from the Weimar Days.* Hanover and London: University Press of New England, 1989.

—. *Fairy-tales and the Art of Subversion: The Classical Genre for Children and the Process of Civilization.* New York: Wildman Press, 1983.

—. "The Grimms and the German Obsession with Fairy-tales." *Fairy-tales and Society: Illusion, Allusion, and Paradigm.* Ed. Ruth B. Bottigheimer. Philadelphia: University of Pennsylvania Press, 1986. 271-285.

—. *The Brothers Grimm: From Enchanted Forests to the Modern World.* New York: Routledge, 1988.

General Index

Author-Title Index

Ariadne Press
Studies

Major Figures of
Modern Austrian Literature
Edited by Donald G. Daviau

Major Figures of Austrian Literature
The Interwar Years 1918-1938
Edited by Donald G. Daviau

Major Figures of Turn-of-the-Century
Austrian Literature
Edited by Donald G. Daviau

Austrian Writers and the Anschluss
Understanding the Past –
Overcoming the Past
Edited by Donald G. Daviau

Austria in the Thirties
Culture and Politics
Edited by K. Segar and J. Warren

Jura Soyfer and His Time
Edited by Donald G. Daviau

Austria in Literature
Edited by Donald G. Daviau

Stefan Zweig
An International Bibliography
By Randolph A. Klawiter

Franz Karka
A Writer's Life
By Joachim Unseld

Kafka and Language: In the
Stream of Thoughts and Life
By G. von Natzmer Cooper

Of Reason and Love
The Life and Works of Marie
von Ebner-Eschenbach
By Carl Steiner

Marie von Ebner-Eschenbach
The Victory of a Tenacious Will
By Doris M. Klostermaier

"What People Call Pessimism"
Freud, Schnitzler and the 19th-Century
Controversy at the University of
Vienna Medical School
By Mark Luprecht

Arthur Schnitzler and Politics
By Adrian Clive Roberts

Structures of Disintegration
Narrative Strategies in Elias Canetti's
Die Blendung
By David Darby

Blind Reflections
Gender in Canetti's Die Blendung
By Kristie A. Foell

Robert Musil and the Tradition
of the German Novelle
By Kathleen O'Connor

Ariadne Press
Studies

Major Figures of
Nineteenth-Century Austrian
Literature
Edited by Donald G. Daviau

"I Am Too Many People"
Peter Turrini:
Poet, Playwright, Essayist
Edited by Jutta Landa

Out from the Shadows
Essays on Contemporary Austrian
Women Writers and Filmmakers
Edited by M. Lamb-Faffelberger

After Postmodernism
Austrian Literature and Film
in Transition
Edited by Willy Riemer

Modern Austrian Prose
Interpretations and Insights
Edited by Paul F. Dvorak

The Legacy of Kafka in
Contemporary Austrian Literature
By Frank Pilipp

Die Rezeption von
Arthur Schnitzlers Reigen:
Pressespiegel und andere
zeitgenössische Kommentare
Herausgegeben von
Gerd K. Schneider

Felix Mitterer
A Critical Introduction
By Nicholas J. Meyerhofer
and Karl E. Webb

Phantom Empires
The Novels of Alexander
Lernet-Holenia and the Question
of Postimperial Austrian Identity
By Robert Dassanowsky

Thunder Rumbling at My Heels
Tracing Ingeborg Bachmann
Edited by Gudrun Brokoph-Mauch

Rilke's Duino Elegies
Cambridge Readings
Edited by Roger Paulin and
Peter Hutchinson

Barbara Frischmuth
in Contemporary Context
Edited by Renate S. Posthofen

Critical Essays on
Julian Schutting
Edited by Harriet Murphy

"Erst bricht man Fenster.
Dann wird man selbst eines."
Zum 100. Geburtstag von
Heimito von Doderer
Hrsg. von Gerald Sommer und
Wendelin Schmidt-Dengler